Rural Tax Reform in China

This book examines questions of change and inertia in the context of the long-standing grievances over excessive taxation in rural China. How can some changes be sustained, while others cannot? How can a long-standing administrative practice be changed or even terminated, when previous attempts at change have failed?

Using extensive interview data with local and central bureaucrats, Li's findings highlight the role of parallel developments and agency in the change process, as well as the prevalence of contingency and uncertainty. It also elegantly blends the narrative of the rural tax and administrative reforms with theoretical discussions to deepen our understanding of policy process and institutional change in twenty-first century China. Despite the authoritarian political system, the Chinese state-in-action which emerges from this book sees actions stemming from both the central and local levels, mediated by strategic design as well as contingency.

This book will be of interest to students and scholars of Chinese Studies, political science and policy and development studies.

Linda Chelan Li is Professor at the Department of Public and Social Administration, City University of Hong Kong.

Routledge Studies on China in Transition
Series Editor: David S. G. Goodman

Rural Tax Reform in China

Policy process and institutional change

Linda Chelan Li

Routledge
Taylor & Francis Group

LONDON AND NEW YORK

First published 2012
by Routledge
2 Park Square, Milton Park, Abingdon, Oxfordshire OX14 4RN

Simultaneously published in the USA and Canada
by Routledge
711 Third Avenue, New York, NY 10017

First issued in paperback 2015

Routledge is an imprint of the Taylor & Francis Group, an informa business

British Library Cataloging in Publication Data
A catalogue record for this book is available from the British Library

Library of Congress Cataloging in Publication Data
Li, Linda Chelan.
Rural tax reform in China: policy process and institutional change / Linda Chelan Li.
p. cm.—(Routledge studies on China in transition ; 41)
Includes bibliographical references and index.
1. Taxation—China. 2. Peasants—Taxation–China. 3. Rural population—Economic aspects—China. I. Title.
HJ2981.L5247 2011
336.200951′091732-dc23
2011019192

ISBN 13: 978-1-138-93740-6 (pbk)
ISBN 13: 978-0-415-58751-8 (hbk)

Typset in Times New Roman
by Book Now Ltd, London

For Loksee and Lokhan

Contents

Illustrations

Tables

Figures

Preface

This research into the policy and institutional change processes in relation to rural state extraction in China is itself an outcome of an evolving process. I first developed a keen interest in institutional change during an early study of central–local power relations over investment implementation. Central–local conflicts and cooperation have long captured the hearts and minds of political practitioners and observers of China. The longevity of the Chinese state despite the ferocity of many instances of central–local conflicts begs an explanation even today. How should we interpret the mixes of tensions and cooperation that have taken place; and can we possibly anticipate, if not predict, possibilities for the future? The themes of central–local politics continue to permeate the current study of state extraction in the Chinese countryside.

Many individuals and organizations have contributed their agency to this process of inquiry. The Hong Kong Research Grant Council funds the multiple-year research activities, including extensive field research in China, archival research in Hong Kong and a six-month sabbatical leave in University of California, Berkeley, when I immersed in writing as Fulbright Scholar. My peers at the Department of Public and Social Administration, City University of Hong Kong, have supplied generous collegial support and intellectual stimulation during our many seminars and informal discussions. Most ideas in the book have been presented at numerous workshops and conferences, and benefited from comments and suggestions made by colleagues and students, observers as well as practitioners. The Department also funded the final preparation of the book manuscript.

Professors Wu Licai and Wang Jingyao, of Central China Normal University, and Professor Yue Fangmin of Guangdong Administrative College assisted dearly in my research on Anhui, Hubei and Guangdong with their extensive knowledge of the subject matter and detailed understanding of the local situations. Several of our co-authored articles, published in prestigious refereed journals in China, have impacted considerably on academic and policy discussions in China. Li Kin-on and Xu Yamin provided exemplary research assistance from data collation to endless administrative matters, enabling me to carve space for writing. Xu Lanlan, Yang Zhenjie, Yuan Fangcheng and Luo Feng, doctoral students at various times, contributed many constructive comments and ideas to my thoughts in the book in our numerous discussions.

Many people have been talked to, and listened to, in various Chinese cities, towns and villages in the course of this research. Our records of interviews show a total of over 150 interviews with some 105 respondents. But many more discussions took place in informal settings, over telephone conversations, in conferences or across dinner tables that nonetheless entered our intellectual horizon and enriched our contextual understanding of the issues and actors involved. A select portion of these conversations are incorporated in the pages that follow. Cited explicitly or not, the conversations have educated me deeply on the subject, and they underline much of the reflective thinking done in this book. Many of these people are officials; others are academics, policy observers or 'ordinary rural citizens'. Conversations with some of them extended over several years. I am grateful to their trust in telling me *their* story. I hope they will agree, if they happen to read the book, that I have not failed them in the accounts that follow. But this is *not* through saying what my respondents would want me to say. By telling a blend of multiple stories critically and independently, I seek to place each story in a fuller perspective; hopefully a more 'accurate' story emerges as a result.

This book is able to incorporate a major part of our work in this research process, thanks to the support of the editors of the journals (*The China Journal*, *Modern Asian Studies*, *The Pacific Review*, *Public Administration and Development* and *Policy and Society*) where some of the chapters have previously appeared. All chapters have been revised and updated, where appropriate, for the book. I am grateful to Professor David S.G. Goodman who enthusiastically supported the book idea and agreed to include the book in the 'China in Transition' book series. I am grateful to the professionalism and patience of the editors and production team at Routledge, who expertly executed the book's production.

Ultimately, I owe my thanks to my family, and especially to my daughter Lokhan and son Loksee who were just one and six, respectively, when the research project 'officially' started. Fieldwork mandated many days of physical absences from home, which was difficult for a young family. It is to them, their father and other families, for their forbearance, consideration and love, that this book is dedicated.

Linda Chelan Li
City University of Hong Kong
Tat Chee Avenue, Hong Kong
April 2011

Introduction

> Our relations with the peasants matter a great deal: it signals whether the Party gets the support of the people and masses. If we fail in this regard, we risk losing our broadest-based, and the most reliable, ally, shaking the basis of our country and revolution. Thus peasants' burden is not only an economic issue; it is political – it's about the long-term stability and prosperity of our country.
>
> (Jiang Zemin, then State President and Secretary General of CCP, in the countryside of Henan Province, 4 June 1996)

Can entrenched practices be changed, and will the change last? If institutions are defined by their durability, how does institutional change take place? How can we ensure the changes are for the better by what, and whose, criteria? These questions have dominated the policy debates on the Chinese rural tax reform since the late 1990s, when policies were experimented with to change local extraction practices in light of escalating social tensions in the Chinese countryside. At stake was the well-being of some 700,000,000 rural citizens, more than two-thirds of the total population of the most populous nation of the world. Despite the early successes in agricultural reform in the 1980s, heavy state extraction in the 1990s not only eliminated the earning gains but also severely strained any trust that might have existed between residents and grassroots-level officials in earlier decades. By the late 1990s, capping the rural tax burden and rural discontent had become a matter of 'life and death' for the Chinese Communist Party, instrumental to stopping the erosion to the Communist Party's long-cherished base of revolutionary support and legitimacy.[1] When reform was finally implemented across the country in 2002 to shake up the rural tax regime, after almost a decade of local experiments, the pressure to score success was predictably immense. Notwithstanding the local origins of the reform, specific targets to reduce the tax burden were prescribed from the top, which local governments competed hastily to meet. The reform was soon declared, officially, a success, only to subsequently leave more questions. Were the changes brought by the reform genuine, and in what respects? How *could* quick fixes work, given the complexity of the problems? Did the reform measures address only part of the problems? Could changes last, or would the old pattern return after a while?

Understanding the problem of peasants' burden and evaluating the reforms meant to alleviate it hinges upon the welfare of more than one-eighth of the world's population. At the same time, both the collection of research materials and their analysis pose an immense challenge to the research team. While we have successfully gathered a good amount of tax statistics and documentary materials on the reform, their analysis and interpretation demand the command of broader, contextual knowledge of some considerable depth. This has resulted in the special emphasis we place, in this book, on the importance of understanding the *process* of change in order to understand change itself – its objectives, measures and impacts, as per the advice of much of the institutionalism literature (Greenwood *et al.* 2008; Hill and Hupe 2002; Hupe and Hill 2006; Winter 2006; May 2003). The resultant work which is presented here thus also contributes to the more general and theoretical inquiry into the intricacies of change process from policy adoption, implementation to sustainability, as it sheds light on a major reform and policy in China. How does the process of 'deinstitutionalization' work out as we deviate from existing practices? Does change come first from ideas *or* actions, and how do these two link? What does a process of 'reinstitutionalization' (Oliver 1992; Dacin and Dacin 2008) consist of, so that changes will last beyond repetitive actions (Huges 1936)?

Studies on policy implementation and reform in China have blossomed since the pioneering works of the 1980s (Lampton 1987; Lieberthal and Oksenberg 1988). A major focus of these studies is on the roles of specific institutional arrangements in China's evolving reform agenda, for example, market (Mok 2000; Knight and Song 1995; World Bank 1990), decentralization (World Bank 2005a; Martinez-Vazquez *et al.* 2008; Yeo and Pearson 2008), fiscal federalism (Jin *et al.* 2005; Sinha 2005), rule of law (Clarke 2007; Pan 2003; Diamond 2003) and transparency (Feinerman 2007). These works have drawn normative conclusions on what constitutes the 'desirable' institutions or directions of reform: less state and more market, more or less decentralization, a higher level of transparency in government, more public participation in policymaking and so on. Another body of works emphasizes the political dynamics between actors/ stakeholders over a policy or political issue, in order to explain the evolution/ impacts/characteristics of the policy or issue (Tanner and Green 2007; Li 2000; Mah and Hills 2008). A third body stresses the discursive dimension, and asks how actors have socially constructed the issues and their roles in them, how perceptions fed into the contemplation of responses and choice of actions, and how actions of some influenced others' future choices, and *vice versa*, in an interactive 'loop' (Li 2009; Li and Wu 2005, 2008; Pan 2008, 2009; Edwards 2009; Jeffreys 2009). The latter two bodies of studies share an emphasis on policy process and the conduct, or governmentality, of reform and policymaking as part of the interpreted, socially constructed reality resultant from actors' interactions, rather than assessing policies or reforms 'as they are' as in the first body of works. Focusing on the processes of change and employing alternative accounts to assess the process and impacts of reform, this book joins this growing litera-ture on governmentality. The central question is: if excessive tax extractions have been (as is often *posited*) an enduring practice in rural China, what kind of actions, and processes, *can* possibly bring about their discontinuance, and how long may such discontinuance last?

Defining and measuring peasants' burden

Despite a rocketing rate of urbanization since the 1980s, two-thirds of China's population as of the late 1990s still lived in the rural part of the country and earned, on average, 40 per cent of the average urban income on a per capita basis.[2] Rural residents, who are often described as 'peasants' (*nongmin*) in Chinese offi-cial terminology and day-to-day discourse, were taxed more heavily than the aver-age urbanites, while rural public goods were only a fraction of those available in cities. Corruption and maladministration were prevalent, causing waves of public protests and criticisms from the international community. Critical to the rural tax reform is the notion of peasants' burden. Simple as the notion may initially appear, its varied definitions and boundaries have a direct implication for the deli-mitation of the scope of measures targeted towards its alleviation, which in turn impacts upon the evaluation of reform. This section will discuss the nuances around the definitions of what was considered to constitute 'peasants' burden', before we outline the reform measures in the next section.

We start with the concept of the 'peasant'. Two meanings are given in *Merriam Webster's Collegiate Dictionary*, Tenth Edition: (1) a member of a class of persons who till the soil as small landowner or labourer; (2) an uneducated per-son with low social status. The first meaning, similar to the definition given in *Encyclopedia Britannica*, denotes 'peasant' in the economic sense, referring to the type of productive activities the peasant engages in or the nature of production relations he is embedded within. The concept is also traced to the 'small-scale agriculturalists' in Europe in historic times. The second, and sociological, defini-tion focuses on the cultural attributes of the peasant relative to other dominant social classes. Major dictionaries published in China have adopted an economic definition, seeing *nongmin* as 'labourers directly engaging in agricultural produc-tion',[3] though the term has had more varied usages in China in practice. During the 1950s, the peasant soil tiller was officially differentiated into the rich peasant, the middle peasant, the middle and lower peasant, and the poor peasant, accord-ing to the amount of land owned by the soil tiller and the degree of his direct involvement in the tilling of the soil, with a direct impact on the apportionment of political rights and socio-economic resources. The concept soon underwent another metamorphosis as collectivization in the mid-1950s deprived every pea-sant of effective ownership of his land. 'Peasant' came to mean simply a member of the rural communes, and for a time even its use as a term was eclipsed by the new notion of 'commune member' (*sheyuan*), only to come back as communes disintegrated in the early 1980s and collectively owned land contracted to individ-ual households under the 'household responsibility' system.

Further to these, in the actual day-to-day usage of the term in contemporary China, the 'peasant' is far more than a description of a trade or the economic activity one conducts for a livelihood, but refers to one's rural residence status (*hukou*) irrespective of occupation (Shi 2008: 206–14). As the term *nongmingong* (literally 'peasant worker') denotes, a person who works in a city unit whether it be a factory or a restaurant, if s/he holds a rural residence status in the government's household registration system, is described as peasant worker, meaning essentially a peasant who takes up the job of a (urban-based) worker. The 'peasant' becomes no more than another description of a 'holder of rural household registration status' (Ai 2005: 8), while the type of economic activities (agriculture, industry, transport or teaching) or the *actual* physical residence (urban or rural) are merely contingent occurrences.

The complexity, and ambiguity, of the peasant concept has aroused sufficient controversy to contribute to the abortion of the legislation of the proposed *Law on the Protection of Peasants' Rights and Interests* in 2008, which previously had had a decade of discussion, drafting and consultation. The need to enact a law to better protect peasants' rights and interests had gained currency among the national policy circle at about the same time as the onset of the rural tax reform process in the late 1990s. Serious discussions started at meetings of the Ninth National People's Congress in 1998–99 and the proposed law was included in the legislative plan of the Tenth National People's Congress in 2003.[4] However, as more details of the draft bill came to light, doubts emerged as to its feasibility and desirability. The law might ironically serve to codify – and thus strengthen – the problematic dimensions in the loosely conceived concept of the peasant, some sceptics argued, and reinforce the dualistic urban-*versus*-rural social structure. The relationship between the proposed law and other existing laws with provisions on matters in relation to peasants, such as land and education, was also unclear. Worries were that, short of a clear definition to demarcate the boundaries of *who* is and is not a peasant, or *what* makes one a peasant (but a clear definition was argued to be counterproductive), it would be impossible to delimit the boundary of the scope of protection the law is to extend, hence reducing the proposed law to a general statement of political intent with little practical impact.[5] Questions were asked whether yet another law – especially a law of such generality – was the best way or even helpful to improve the lot of the peasants, as this might unintentionally (or intentionally?) distract policy attention from pursuing reforms – and actions, as opposed to pledges and promises – in specific policy arenas.[6]

What follows from the above is that the peasants' burden includes extraction not only from agriculture and related industries but more broadly from all rural dwellers and migrants in cities holding the rural registration status. Mirroring the varied meanings of the peasant are the diverse contents and ambiguous boundaries of the peasants' burden, as displayed in Table 0.1.

Table 0.1 disaggregates the peasants' burden into its components. It shows the varying magnitudes of the various definitions of the burden, calculated by different scopes, across a decade of reform. These different scopes of peasants' burden are commensurate to three concentric circles (Figure 0.1). The innermost circle

Table 0.1 Peasants' burden: disaggregating its components (billion yuan)

	National agricultural taxes						Legal local fees									
	1 Agriculture and husbandry tax	2 Tax on special agriculture	3 Slaughter tax	4 Contract tax	5 Tax on use of arable land	6 Tobacco leaf tax	7 Village and township levies: 'san ti wu tong'	8 Forced labour contributions	9 Administrative fees, and other payments	10 Surcharges on (1) & (2)	11 Official peasants' burden (1–3, 7–10)	12 Illegal levies, fines and funds: 'san luan'	13 Commodity turnover taxes paid by peasants	14 Accountable peasants' burden (11, 4–6, 12–13)	15 Contingent township–village liabilities (cumulative)	16 Price scissors (per year)
1996	18.20	13.10	2.06	2.52	3.12	N/A	60.61	8.73	13.10	n.a.	112.8	n.a.	n.a.	n.a.	177–326	Scissors 1
1997	18.23	15.00	2.40	3.23	3.25	N/A	64.63	8.10	24.04	n.a.	128.1	n.a.	n.a.	n.a.		20–30 price differentials:
1998	17.86	12.78	1.91	5.90	3.33	N/A	65.06	9.70	27.77	n.a.	136.0	n.a.	n.a.	n.a.		industrial and
1999	16.30	13.14	2.09	9.56	3.30	N/A	60.08	6.41	27.50	n.a.	125.5	~35.0	236.29	~410	600~1000	agricultural
2000	16.81	13.07	2.34	13.10	3.53	N/A	~108.3	n.a.	n.a.	2.78	~140.0	~36.1	255.78	~450		products
2001	16.43	12.19	2.47	15.70	3.83	N/A	Reform implemented in 20 provinces: items 7–9 abolished			3.10	n.a.	n.a.	283.39	n.a.		Scissors 2
2002	32.14	9.99	0.985	23.90	5.73	N/A				7.35	n.a.	n.a.	321.60	n.a.		350–400 suppressed
2003	33.42	8.96	0.23	35.80	3.99	N/A	Reform implemented nationwide items 7–9 abolished			7.82	50.4	n.a.	368.18	~460		wage levels of rural
2004	19.87	4.32	0.003	54.00	12.0	N/A	N/A	N/A	N/A	3.74	28.0	n.a.	412.38	~500		migrant workers
2005	1.28	4.66	0.00016	73.51	14.18	N/A	N/A	N/A	N/A	0.34	6.3	n.a.	475.01	~570	n.a.	Scissors 3
2006	0.013	0.35	N/A	86.76	17.11	4.16	N/A	N/A	N/A	N/A	0	n.a.	547.71	~650		220–350 suppressed
2007	N/A	N/A	N/A	120.6	18.5	4.78	N/A	N/A	N/A	N/A	0	n.a.	656.56	~800		compensation
																payments for rural
																lands in developments

Sources: Items 1, 2, 4–6 figures are extracted from *China Fiscal Yearbook* 1997: 446, 2001: 130, 2002: 116, 2003: 127, 2004: 128, 2009: 481.

Item 3 is extracted from Xue (2006: 26–7). Items 4–6 are *excluded* from the official scope of peasants' burden, as deduced from the calculation of the official burden in a report by the Rural Tax-for-fee Reform Working Group of the State Council (Office of the State Council Rural Tax-for-fee Reform Working Group 2004). Items 7–9: 1999 figures are constructed from information in Office of the State Council Rural Tax-for-fee Reform Working Group (2004: 2); 2000 figures constructed from China Tax-for-fee Reform Research Group (2003: 3–10). Item 10 figures are extracted from *China Fiscal Yearbook*, various years. No data are available before the year of 1999.

Item 11 presents the official scope of total peasants' burden, which consists of items 1–3, and 7–10. The delineation of the scope conforms with the calculation of burdens and specification of burden reduction reform measures in Office of the State Council Rural Tax-for-fee Reform Working Group (2004) and Central Document (2000) No. 7, 24 June, 2000, respectively. Item 12: 1999 figure comes from Chen (2009); 2000 figure from Rural Tax-for-fee Reform Research Group (2003). No data for other years. Item 13 figures are constructed from information on total commodity turnover tax revenues and the proportions of rural–urban consumption, available in *China Statistical Yearbook* 2008: 55 and *China Fiscal Yearbook* 2008: 402–4.

Item 14 'Accountable Peasant Burden' refers to the total fiscal revenue that different levels of governments extracted from peasants, and is the sum of legal extractions (items 4–6, 13), illegal local levies (item 12) and official burden (item 11).

Items 15 and 16 are two 'border' components of peasants' burden whose exact magnitudes are difficult to ascertain. Item 15 figures are extracted from Ministry of Finance, Fiscal Research Institute (2004: 1–8) and Rural Tax-for-fee Reform Research Group (2003). Item 16 figures are from Kong and He (2009), Yan et al. (1990), T. Wen (2000), Wan (2003) and Zhou (2007).

Notes: N/A Not applicable; n.a. Not available.

Figure 0.1 Peasants' burden: differential scopes.

denotes the narrowest scope of the official burden. The second circle represents the 'accountable' burden and the third, outermost, circle denotes the widest scope of the burden which includes contingent township–village liabilities and various types of 'price scissors'.

A few observations may be highlighted here. First, the plurality of scopes of peasants' burden demands some elaboration of their constitution. The definition of the official burden (item 11, Table 0.1) can be traced back to the Regulation on Peasants' Burden and Labour Services (Nongmin Chengdan Feiyong he Laowu Guanli Tiaoli), promulgated by the State Council in 1991. Outlining the national reform package, Central Document No. 7 (2000) contains no new definition of peasants' burden and has basically adopted the framework of the 1991 Regulation – the constituent categories of peasants' burden – in delineating reform measures. These comprise three different agricultural taxes (items 1, 2, 3) and their respective local surtaxes (item 10), village and township levies (item 7), forced labour contributions (item 8) and administrative fees and other payments (item 9). The official burden peaks at about 140 billion yuan in 2000 and is reduced to virtually 'zero' since 2006, according to government statistics.

The second of the three concentric circles – the 'accountable burden' – casts a wider net to include *all* revenues that various government levels extract from the peasants, irrespective of legal status, that can be reasonably traced and accounted for. This will include, on top of what is counted in the official burden, three other agriculture-related national taxes (item 4: Contract tax; item 5: Tax on use of arable land; and item 6: Tobacco leaf tax), commodity turnover taxes (item 13) and illegal local levies (item 12). It is worth noting that the concept of 'accountable burden' is a value-neutral one that we have specifically constructed to denote the total scope of *direct* state fiscal extraction from the rural community irrespective of occupation or industry. At a minimum of 450 billion yuan, the accountable burden is at least three times as much as the official burden in 2000. Moreover, while official burden was basically eliminated by 2006, the accountable burden continued to hover up to 650 billion yuan and to 800 billion yuan in 2007, due to large increases in overall contract, land and turnover tax revenues as the rural economy picked up since 2003.

The outermost circle in Figure 0.1 adds contingent extractions and forgone incomes (items 15 and 16) to the accountable burden. These items are placed outside the scope of the accountable burden since they refer to *possible* additional extractions to repay local government or collective debts (item 15), or incomes peasants should have earned but were deprived of historically (item 16) – as opposed to direct state fiscal extraction in the case of the accountable burden depicted in the second circle. The magnitude of items 15–16 is also highly difficult if not impossible to ascertain and has been everyone's guesses, thus the use of a broken line in Figure 0.1 to indicate the uncertain whereabouts of the outermost circle.[7] However, the inclusion of these items in a full definition of peasants' burden has been argued by many analysts, including some in the national policy circle, as necessary for a proper understanding of the problems of peasants' burden and local finance (Kong and He 2009; Yan *et al.* 1990; T. Wen 2000; Zhou 2007; Chen 2007; Chen and Duan 2010).

Indeed in the popular discourse on rural issues, the official definition of peasants' burden has been confronted with alternative articulations from the very beginning. The often-cited folklore – the 'first (-layer) burden' is light; the 'second (-layer)' is heavy; while the 'third (-layer) burden' is (like) a bottomless pit' (*tou shui qing, er shui zhong, san shui shi ge wu di dong*) – testifies that peasants have shouldered far more than what official documents prescribed, as only the first and second layers fall within the official scope of peasants' burden (Figure 0.2). Interestingly, this three-layer notion of peasants' burden was also widely adopted in official discussions, oral or written, of peasants' burden and related issues (e.g. Ministry of Agriculture, Office of the Rural Reform Experimental Zones 1995: 391; author's interviews in Beijing, Hubei, Anhui and Guangdong), despite its deviation from the official definition. On the one hand, this may be explained by the awareness of officials of the existence of the third layer, despite its illegitimate status, and thus underlining the need for reform in order to eradicate it. On the other hand, references to the third-layer burden in the reform documents have been conspicuously general and vague. Most reform measures dealt

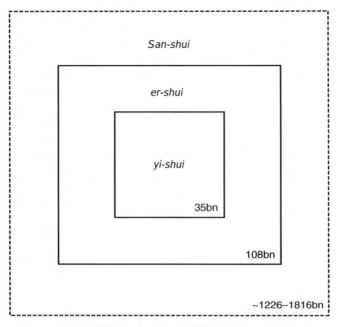

2000 Burden levels (billion yuan)

Figure 0.2 Popular conception of peasants' burden: first, second and third (layered) 'taxes'.

explicitly with the first- and second-layer burden only, for instance, the adjustment to the Agricultural Taxes (first layer), phasing out of forced labour services and contributions and abolition of township and village levies (second layer), which we shall note further in the next section. The obvious question is: if the issue of peasants' burden lies in the proliferation of illegitimate charges, should these illegitimate charges not be the primary target of reform actions rather than only the legitimate ones? The continuing ambiguities and the lack of a clear definition of peasants' burden, even after the launch of the rural tax reform, point to both the complexity of the issues and the limits to the reform.

A close reading of the various components of peasants' burden in Table 0.1 also confirms the popular conception in China on what constitutes the lion's share of the burden: the 'third (-layer) burden' is (like) a bottomless pit' (He and Wang 2003). Items 1–3 and 10 constitute the first layer and items 7–9 the second layer; both account for 23 per cent and 77 per cent of the official burden, respectively. The third layer comprises a host of problematic levies and charges charged by local governments (item 12), the contingent township–village liabilities (item 15) and various 'price scissors' (item 16). Notice is drawn to the fact that items 4–6 and 13, which are legal national taxes collected from peasants, are not usually included in any of these three 'layers' of burden in either popular or policy discourse, even though they together accounted for 60 per cent of the 'accountable burden' of the peasants in 2000. The third, bottomless, layer of burden in Figure 0.2 is thus a combination of some components in the second circle of Figure 0.1 (item 12: Illegal local levies) and the outermost circle (items 15 and 16). In 2000, this amounts to 1226 billion yuan at the lower end estimate to 1816 billion yuan at the higher end. This compares to 35 billion yuan for the first-layer burden and 108 billion yuan for the second layer in 2000.

Reform objectives and measures

Any sketch of a complex and evolving reform programme carries a risk of misrepresentation while seeking to facilitate understanding. With this statement of caution Figure 0.3 outlines the identified problems, reform objectives and major measures of the rural tax reform by its four phases: local experimental, national reform design, evolving-through-implementation, and institutional interaction and consolidation.

A number of features stand out from Figure 0.3. First is the continuous evolution, and changes, in all three columns – problems, objectives and reform measures – which are organized into the four identified phases. The notions of 'evolution', 'change' and 'phase' implies a chronological dimension, so that each of the four phases occurred at different junctures temporally. At the same time, there is considerable 'overlap' between the 'phases'. National agenda setting and reform design overlaps partially with the local experimental phase; the implementation phase almost runs parallel to institutional interactions and consolidation. To better capture this temporal coexistence of the 'phases', we have adopted the notion of '*process*' to depict the full dynamics of the reform development trajectory. Thus the rural tax reform is the consequence and summation of four different processes which *sometimes* coexist in the same time period and interact. Subsequent chapters in this book will elaborate the characteristics of these processes and how they impact on one another across various times.

Second, on the substantive problems and objectives, while the reduction of peasants' burden remains the most persistent concern across various times and processes, the issues of concern and the scope of reform objectives have broadened as the reform develops. In addition to burden reduction and local fiscal security, which dominated the earlier processes, later processes have become more preoccupied with cost and sustainability of reform, rural basic goods provision and the role of township government in the national administrative and fiscal systems.

Third, on the reform measures, the early reform measures focused largely on the official burden, which is the innermost circle in Figure 0.1 and the first- and second-layer 'squares' depicted in Figure 0.2, although the third-layer burden was the main subject of concern underlining the reform. The only reference to weeding out the unauthorized local fees in the national reform package of 2000 is

Phase-process	Identified problems	Reform objectives	Reform measures and activities
Local experimental (~1988–1998)	1. Heavy peasants' burden 2. Difficulties in collecting rural taxes and fees from peasants at township–village levels	1. Reduce peasants' burden 2. Rationalize rural tax-fee regime and its collection 3. Guarantee a stable level of fiscal revenues for rural local governments	1. Lobbying by key local proponents (e.g. He Kaiyin of Anhui Province) at local, provincial and national levels 2. Minor variations around these measures in Anhui, Hebei and Jiangsu provinces: (i) taxation-in-kind combines various taxes and fees and replaces contractual produce procurement; (ii) tax (in kind) rate stabilized over 3–5 years (iii) collecting authority translate in-kind tax to fiscal revenues for state coffers and township/village authorities (iv) all other *unauthorized* fees are prohibited
National agenda setting and reform design (~1995–2000)	1. Heavy peasants' burden 2. Increasing rural unrests 3. Reform design options 4. Local implementation gap and agency control	1. Reduce peasants' burden 2. Regularize and rationalize the rural tax-fee regime and collection mechanism 3. Heavy burden seen as a local implementation problem; local governments to pay up most costs of reform	1. Attention of central leaders drawn to the local reforms; central documents endorsing local reforms (1995–96) 2. Twists and turns; policy option learning (1997–98) 3. National task force established to work on detailed reform design (1998–2000): (i) Agriculture Tax rate raised from 3% to up to 7% (ii) All township and village levies abolished; township and village finance to be supported by 20% local surtax of the Agriculture Tax (i.e. effective maximal tax rate of Agriculture Tax at 8.4%) (iii) Abolition of Slaughter Tax and banning of all other fees (iv) Forced labour contributions to phase out in 3 years (v) Provincial governments to screen rural administrative fees and weed out *unauthorized* items as a *complementary* reform measure

Figure 0.3 Reform objectives and measures: four phase-processes.

in a six-line paragraph of the seven-page long Central Document No. 7 (2000), in a subsidiary section on 'complementary reforms'. It requires localities to 'clean-up' their various fees that contributed to the peasants' burden, and announces that local governments and sectoral ministries could no longer authorize new administrative fees and fund-raising projects that could add to peasants' burden. Which level of 'local' governments is to take responsibility in this important clean-up exercise was however not specified, nor was monitoring arrangement mentioned to ensure proper execution.

Mirroring the gradual broadening of reform objectives as the reform evolved, reform measures in the later years were increasingly in the diverse areas of 'complementary' reform rather than targeting the rural tax-fee regime. For the latter, the emphasis also saw a dramatic shift from rationalization and regulation to outright elimination. Indeed the shift in reform focus from narrowly fiscal to the more broadly administrative presents a certain difficulty in the discussion and analysis of the reform. The rural tax reform seems to have reached an end in 2006 when Agriculture Taxes were wiped out nationwide. At the same time, there are indications that the original concerns over peasants' burden and consequent rural unrests have not disappeared entirely. The accountable burden in Table 0.1 shows that peasants have been facing a *heavier* burden since 2000, and especially so since 2006. There are also *new* concerns over the difficulty to raise *incomes* of peasants quickly in order to genuinely improve the well-being of the peasants, as against the earlier sole focus on extractions. The emphasis laid on the agricultural taxes as the prime focus of reform, *versus* the neglect over the wide array of unauthorized fees, means that a reform *has to* end although its identified problems have, still, largely remained.

Alternative accounts

At the core of controversies in the rural tax reform is the deceptively simple question: who was responsible for the suffering of the peasantry, and hence what served as remedy. Essentially, central government blamed local officials, who in turn complained of their bosses' failure to understand local needs. During definitive policy deliberations, the onus was however almost without exception squarely placed on local officials. Documents from the Party Central Committee and State Council in the 1990s routinely include paragraphs criticizing officials at township and village levels for causing excessive extraction and often end with calling for a tighter scrutiny over local administration. The following is an example:

> Why has it been so difficult to contain the level of peasants' burden, and why does burden, even once placed under control, keep rebounding? There are many reasons, but the major ones are: some localities have sought economic development beyond their fiscal capacity, with the peasants pressured to pay up the debts; some departments have demanded excessively high standards and overlooked local conditions and affordability in implementing

policy; some township and village cadres are crude and violent in dealing with local communities, insensitive to popular moods, and even act against the law; many townships are overstaffed with too many bureaus and departments; payroll and running costs are too high relative to the capacity of most local economies, and are paid for almost entirely by fees collected from the peasants.

(Decision of Party Central Committee and State Council on Alleviating Peasants' Burden, 1996)

A decade later in 2006, another central document on the peasants' burden – now warning against rebounding of the burden levels after local extraction came under initial control – exhibits a strikingly similar tone with respect to where responsibility lies,

Some local cadres have lately been over-optimistic and lax in monitoring the burden level; some localities started to impose new fee categories and penalty charges; … many localities are half-hearted in implementing the central policies on supporting rural developments; the interests and rights of peasants are still often compromised in many local development projects.

(Document of General Office of National State Council on Alleviating Peasants' Burden, 2006)

These official accounts depict a 'split' state: peasants were pushed to the brink of rebellion as a result of excessive local extraction to feed the greed of local officials and pay for controversial expenses which the central government did not approve.[8] Given this definition of problem as, basically, a local issue, the prescribed remedy was, accordingly, tighter oversight over the local cadres, who should not be allowed to tax the peasants and recruit staff without due approval from upper levels. Any 'excess' staff should be removed from the ranks of government. Little attention is paid, in these accounts, to the role of national policies and institutions in the predatory behaviour of local governments.

This 'centrist' version of the peasant problem has been disputed by many county and township-level officials who stressed that local extraction had stayed high due to unfunded mandates by the upper levels (He and Wang 2002; Luo 2007; Tao *et al.* 2004). 'Problems surface at the grassroots levels of townships and villages, but the roots [to the problems] lie at the upper levels, from the county all the way up to the central level' (J. Zhang 2002; He and Wang 2003). Local governance problems were largely a consequence of upper-level governments' failures in fulfilling their fair share of responsibility to provide sufficient resources to local governments to do their job (Wong 1997; World Bank 2002). Governments at the bottom levels of the administrative hierarchy have been responsible for delivering most public services. With no lower levels to pass on their responsibilities, many have resorted to meeting the revenue gap through additional charges from the peasants. Upper levels have tolerated such a practice 'normally', only to scapegoat local cadres when peasants' grievances go high.

That said, this second picture of the burden issue, seeing it as largely a central problem, will not absolve local officials entirely of responsibility. County and township officials at the frontlines of government bear responsibility for the sufferings of peasants *as policy executors*, not to say that some, if not many, local officials do 'free ride' on national policies for their private gain. As other studies on the subject have noted, a combination of the centrist and localist stories is probably closer to the actual situation than either of them (Bernstein and Lü 2003; Yep 2004; Chen and Chun 2004; Göbel 2010). On the one hand, gaps in national policies and institutional designs (such as the lack of sound zoning of spending responsibilities and inadequacies in revenue sharing arrangements across government levels, and efficiency-accountability problems in the treasury management system) have given rise to a proliferation of 'informal' local extraction and a culture of neglect in public services. At the same time, these outcomes have facilitated, reinforced and even encouraged abuses by local officials, exacerbating the plight of the peasants. The embedded nature of the rural governance issues is well known in the Chinese policy circle (Chen *et al.* 2005; Cui 2004; Yao and Dong 2006). What is curious is how this knowledge was, apparently, ignored at the time of policymaking, so that a simplistic account ascribing almost sole responsibility to local officials could have dominated national policy deliberations.

Our approach: tracing the process

The approach adopted in this book draws upon the insights from the Actor-Network Theory (ANT), which revitalizes the old historical method – tracing the steps of actors through going back along the timeline – to attempts of understanding contentious topics with messy boundaries.[9] In Latour's words, if the objective is to explain and make sense of a scientific product (or policy, decision, a 'problem'),

> we will not try to analyse the final products; ... instead we will follow scientists and engineers [relevant actors] at the time and at the places where they plan a nuclear plant, undo a cosmological theory, modify the structure of a hormone for contraception, or disaggregate figures used in a new model of the economy. We go from final products to production ... Instead of black boxing the technical aspects of science and *then* looking for social influences and biases, we realized ... how much simpler it was to be there *before* the box closes and becomes black.
>
> (Latour 1987: 21; emphasis original)

It is, obviously, not as simple as just 'to be there', since the time before the black box closes, at the time when the researcher seeks to understand what the inside of the box is like, is already *past*. Thus what is actually suggested is that researchers, rather than focus on the finished product (the black box) and ponder its various features from outside (colour, texture, weight, functions, etc.), had better find means to 'travel back along the timeline' (*via* interviews, reading documents, imaginative mapping, etc.) so as to reconstruct the process of the *product-in-the-making* as much as possible.

But why do we need to 'go back along the timeline', given the imperfections of such artificial travels as, after all, the perfect 'time machine' has yet to be invented? Why cannot we just focus on and study the finished product as it stands, taking hints from its 'characteristics' and 'broader contexts'? The answer is this will not work for complex situations – where 'innovations proliferate, where group boundaries are uncertain, [and] when the range of entities to be taken into account fluctuates' (Latour 2005: 11). In these cases, static analysis of the product, no matter how thorough, will not help much to illuminate under-standing as to how the product comes about, how it is likely to evolve further and indeed what the product is exactly and what functions it performs. For com-plex situations with abundant contingencies, analysis that focuses on the finished product often results in oversimplification, like taking 'a still photograph of the current of the river' (Scott 1998: 46). Description of how things happen *along the way* – through interaction of heterogeneous actors – even if it is incomplete, offers the best feasible option to researchers to get hold of the variability of the changing situations. Indeed James Scott points out that a whole range of human activities, like teaching, navigation, driving and cooking, is beyond capture of words and documented knowledge. Codification in these cases brings simplifica-tion and distortion. Instead, these activities are best learnt through *practice*, and the knowledge attained is inherently local and practical, which he described as 'mētis':

> Mētis is most applicable to broadly similar but never precisely identical situations requiring a quick and practiced adaptation that becomes almost second nature to the practitioner. The skills of mêtis may well involve rules of thumb, but such rules are largely acquired through practice ... and a developed feel or knack for strategy. Mêtis resists simplification into deduc-tive principles which can successfully be transmitted through book learning, because the environments in which it is exercised are so complex and non-repeatable that formal procedures of rational decision making are impossible to apply. In a sense, mêtis lies in that large space between the realm of gen-ius, to which no formula can apply, and the realm of codified knowledge, which can be learned by rote.
>
> (Scott 1998: 315–16)

To understand a complex phenomenon, the clue is to 'take a walk' around the multiple dimensions as well as go 'back along the timeline' to see how actors have made moves around the dimensions that contributed to a critical event.

> If you can have many points of views on a statue, it's because the statue itself is in three-dimensions and allows you, yes, allows you to *move around*

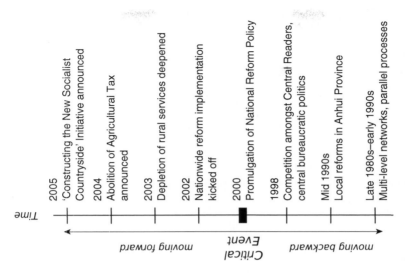

Figure 0.4 Moving back and forth along the timeline.

> it. If something supports many viewpoints, it's just that it's highly complex,
> intricately folded, nicely organized, and beautiful …
>
> (Latour 2005: 145–6; emphasis added)

From where, and at which point of time, should we start the walk around the various dimensions? Start from the critical event that you would like to explain and know more about. From that particular juncture, which is at a point backward from the time-point where the researcher is now, we may need to travel further backward, or forward, along the timeline depending on our interest. In this case of Chinese rural extraction and tax reform, the main interest lies in explaining the possibilities of change, given the intricate complexities and historical embeddedness of the peasants' burden problem. To look for an explanation, we start our analysis from the critical event of the adoption of national rural tax reform that signals a major effort for change, and then trace the steps of actors *back, and then forth*, along the timeline from that juncture in order to discover the moves, concerns and hesitation of each of the actors, as well as their interactions (Figure 0.4).

Going backward from the point of national reform promulgation in 2000 unearths the various processes wherein national reform, bit by bit, emerged. We see the twists and turns of the policy-in-formation and the shades of anticipation, excitement, hesitation and worries of the diverse players (government actors at various township, county, city, provincial and central levels, and peasants) as various forms of reform initiatives were tried out, abandoned and extended in localities in Anhui Province and others. In other words, we shall observe the interactions between the local experimental process and the national agenda-setting process

(Figure 0.3). Following the events alerts us to the contingent nature of reform: that those local experiments of the early-1990s which laid the ground for national reform a few years later *might* have *not* taken place at all. Even if experiments of a related kind might still emerge at some point, whether these could make a national impact was highly uncertain, as were the eventual contents of national reform – in terms of reform design – that might transpire.

Apart from the contingency of the policymaking process, tracing events backward enables us to see in full the differential definitions of the rural extraction problem upheld by different actors. With diverse views as to what the problem is, and who/what causes it, there come differential prescriptions of what remedy needs to be done and by whom. Whether it is defining the problem or prescribing remedy, the assignment of responsibility is present throughout. As noted earlier, the central government saw excessive extraction as primarily a local implementation problem, while local officials bitterly complained of being made the scapegoat of inadequacies in national policies and institutions.

It thus follows that tracing actors in either the 'backward' or 'forward' direction is *not* two unrelated, distinct tasks. The observations obtained from tracing from one end become instrumental to our understanding of events unfolding in the other direction, an analytical method described as 'within case analysis' (Bennett and Elman 2006). We know, through tracing backward from the time of national reform promulgation, for instance, that the reform package announced in 2000 was in fact highly contested, its design considered by many local officials charged with its implementation as problematic and impractical. This enables us to *anticipate* the reactions of local officials during the implementation process, when we trace the events *forward* further down the timeline, and facilitates meaningful interpretations of empirical phenomena which, in isolation, might appear muddled and confusing. An interesting observation of this study is that as many township officials eventually gave up their resistance in resignation, as top-down pressures in an authoritarian system were applied to their full, the reduced local agency ironically induced the central government to take up a *larger* role in rural governance, a responsibility it had previously sought to shirk.

Outline of the book

What follows are six essays each addressing a critical dimension of the multifarious change processes. Chapter 1 ('Path creation?') discusses the early processes of 'path creation', critical to the 'local experimental' process in Figure 0.3. The analysis highlights the critical importance of networks, parallel processes and agency not only in attaining policy objectives but also in fostering resilience and a capacity to tolerate setbacks and frustrations. It asks and answers a key question on institutional change and policymaking: why do local, and subordinate, officials bother about initiating local experiments *despite* the absence of firm hierarchical support for their efforts? The chapter covers local developments of the reform in the 1990s and ends its story with central acceptance of the need for national rural tax reform around 1998–2000.

Chapter 2 ('Differentiated actors') examines the politics in policy formulation during the early phase of the national reform (around 2000–03) – the 'national agenda setting and reform design' process in Figure 0.3. Through a careful content analysis of the national reform design, and drawing from fieldwork observations on local implementation of the early policy and documentary research, this chapter illustrates the spectre of 'excessive decentralization' for effective policy: decisions and responsibilities which should have been made at the central level were left to provincial and local actors without proper monitoring. The chapter argues for a more vigorous differentiation of the roles and responsibilities of government across levels during the reform design process in order to improve reform implementation.

As reform policy was formulated, implemented and adjusted, the next question that emerged was how sustainable the reform, and its initial results, could be. How can a reform – a programme of action seeking change – survive institutional inertia and active resistance by stakeholders whose interests will be threatened? Chapter 3 ('Embedded institutionalization') discusses reform sustainability and the transition from deinstitutionalization to reinstitutionalization through an analysis of policy change across institutional fields. The impact of an innovative measure in cadre management for rural tax burdens in this respect was examined, drawing from discussions on institutional logics. The subject of discussion here spans the two processes of 'evolving-design-through-implementation' and 'institutional interactions and consolidation' in Figure 0.3.

Local administrative reform and rural public service provision are part and parcel of the rural tax reform process, if only because peasants' burden was defined (in the centrist version) as a consequence of an oversized local government offering inadequate services. However, despite their salience as the crux of problems, reform ideas seldom went beyond the traditional calls for downsizing. Chapter 4 ('State and market') examines a local innovation in this respect, which aims at improving rural service provision through adjusting the mix of state and the market. This discussion, similarly on the dual processes of 'implementation' and 'institutional interactions' as the last chapter, reveals the challenge and opportunities of policy innovation, which emerges through a dialectical process of interactions between reformers and resisters.

Chapter 5 ('Path dependence') continues the discussion on local administrative reform but shifts the focus to the logics of national policymaking *after* local experimentation. The central questions asked here are: how do policymakers make up their minds? What goes into their calculations when deciding whether a proposed policy or reform measure should or should not be adopted? It is thus about how the implementation process *interacts* with the national agenda setting and reform process. The chapter observes that policymakers are inclined to focus on costs and neglect possible benefits due to past reform trajectory, as most previous township reforms have failed. Policymakers are predisposed to perceive most stakeholders as 'resisters' of change or passive beneficiaries. This chapter contemplates the possibility of improving national decision-making capacity by recognizing, and fostering, the agency role of 'reform targets'.

Again on the interaction of the national policy and local implementation processes, Chapter 6 ('Working for the peasants') returns to the theme of multi-level politics and argues that, contrary to official rhetoric, the burden-reduction reform since 2000 has *not* been part of a concerted and coordinated programme of the central government to improve the lot of the peasants. Drawing from both the central and local ends of the reform process, the chapter details how the strategic interactions of central and local state actors have led to burden reduction, and the shouldering of more responsibilities in rural governance by the central and provincial governments, as *unintended* outcomes.

1 Path creation? Processes and networks

How the Chinese rural tax reform began*

How can we possibly deviate from trodden paths and accustomed practices, given the weight of institutional inertia and resistance against change, as so often asserted? On a day-to-day basis, innovations are regarded as unusual and celebrated events, no matter whether in technology, organization forms or policy.[1] Analysts in various intellectual streams and 'networks' have sought, with varying degrees of success, to demystify innovations and explain how change *could* happen despite immense resistance. Institutionalists of various strands have grappled, for example, with the tension between the 'definitive' feature of institutions – stability and resilience to disruption, and the prevalence of change *over time* empirically.[2] The path dependence and creation literature places a premium on the impact of history on the present, *and* potentialities for deviations from existing paths through a possibility to 'disembed' from the historically embedded (Garud and Karnoe 2001a). New ideas emerge when individuals mindfully deviate from an existing path and envision something different, out of a *reconsideration* of past, and current, situations. Innovating entrepreneurs are said to be 'embedded agents' and are often as preoccupied with the dominant concerns of their time as their contemporaries (Garud and Karnoe 2001b: 9).[3]

Against these attempts to grapple with change, the radical Actor-Network Theory (ANT) literature turns the subject on its head.[4] For ANT scholars, the problem is stability and durability of a relation, not the change of it, as change *is* with us everyday.[5] Through using a process approach and disaggregating the 'Actor' into a network of interacting, heterogeneous elements, including people and non-human 'objects', the ANT embraces change as building blocks in its explanatory framework to understand how a certain state of things (a new order, or continuation of a pre-existing, 'old' order) emerges *as a result*.[6] The approach is inherently dynamic – change is the implied *default* state, and the researcher's job is to trace the steps of such changes in all their diversities undertaken by heterogeneous actors (Latour 2005: 11). Unlike the other more 'mainstream' approaches problematizing change *vis-à-vis* stability, the critical question ANT poses, in relation to change, is why change is of *this* magnitude along *that* direction.

Seen with an ANT perspective, both the institutionalist and path dependence–creation scholarships have, to an extent, self-inflicted difficulties in their approach to change. Both start their inquiry from some presupposed, a priori chosen analytical categories. Institutionalists start with the central role of institution, which is *defined* to exhibit features of durability, stability and resilience to change. Change is hence explained away, or at least marginalized, from the very beginning, making it immensely difficult for institutionalists to account for change. In the case of path-dependence literature, the concept of 'the path' is heavily loaded with 'connectedness' both across time and domains.

While path-dependence writers emphasize the possibility of path deviation, it is difficult to conceive clearly how dependence and creation coexist. How, for instance, does one stop from being 'dependent' on a pre-existing path and start transgressing onto a new path? How does this 'leap' from one path to another, and the creation of the new one, happen? Are we talking about a choice among different paths, while currently embedded in one of them, or are we talking about *creating* entirely new ones from an existing path? What do we *exactly* mean when we say an 'embedded agent' does nevertheless 'disembed'? Is the very act of 'disembedding' still embedded in the pre-existing path? If yes, to what extent is this act a 'disembedding' move rather than an elaboration of the existing path? If not, that the disembedding act itself is not embedded in the pre-existing path, can we still say the agent is an embedded agent? And since when, and how, does an embedded agent become 'disembedded', to be 'set free' from the influence of history to start a new path? What exactly does 'embeddedness', and its reverse, 'disembedding', mean? The questions thus turn full circle. Lying at the core of the puzzles is an ambiguous theory of agency wavering between dependence and creativity: the classic problem between structure and agency remains unresolved.

In comparison, an explanation based on ANT suppositions is more straightforward. It squarely points to the beauty of following the process of events, and listening to actors' accounts in charting the story of change. Instead of having researchers formulate complex concepts and theories of action, and then qualify and complicate them even more when the reality does not fit into the concepts, ANT suggests we drop, as much as possible, our 'intellectual baggage' and 'travel light' to observe and listen to actors on the ground (Latour 2005: 11, 25). We can then collect a lot more information as we see and hear things, with minimal presuppositions.[7] Out of the accounts from actors – through our observation of their actions and their own discursive accounts, we build up a theory of how, and what, *changes* take place. As Law (1992) acknowledges, the processes of change are 'always contingent, local and variable', and can only be fully understood in the specific context of an empirical innovation. Theory is constituted, therefore, *in* accounts of empirical processes, not the reverse.

Drawing upon these insights, this chapter looks into the emergence of the Chinese rural tax-for-fee reform in the 1990s. Discussions on the Chinese rural tax-for-fee reform,[8] within and without China, have so far focused mostly on complexities over implementation and worries with sustainability – what the reform has precisely brought about and whether it could last.[9] The magnitude of the peasant burden problem was so obviously large that the necessity for tax reform, and thus its adoption, tended to be taken for granted, especially once the reform got off the ground. In this chapter, I shift the focus of attention 'back the timeline' to the emergence of change[10] – when ideas are first translated into practice. By illuminating how things happened during an earlier time period – who and what were involved, how and why – I seek to enable a better assessment of the extent that there *have been* changes and what these were exactly. An implicit message is that an answer to the sustainability question in fact hinges upon, to a considerable extent, an in-depth understanding of how change could have possibly emerged in the first place.

The chapter will proceed as follows. The next section outlines how a critical agent of change – an 'entrepreneur' – came into being in the arena of rural tax reform in China: what his ideas were and how contingencies have come into the processes of agency formation. Innovative ideas are the starting point of change, and yet change also needs to acquire a sufficiently large magnitude in order to have any practical meaning. For this to happen, multiple networks need to come into existence and operate in a way that, in terms of effect, resistance to change is minimized or 'bracketed', and support put to maximal, even dramatic, use in favour of the desired change.[11] The following is an account of how these have happened.

Ideas and entrepreneurs

As we look back in time to trace the early trajectory of the rural tax reform – back to the emergence of the reform ideas – a critical development was the events surrounding the writing of an essay in late 1988 in response to a national essay contest. The contest was organized by the Central Rural Policy Research Office with eight other units to commemorate a full decade of rural reform, which started with the *dabaogan* movement (rural decollectivization, resulting in family-based farming units) in 1978.[12] This essay, entitled 'On deepening further rural reform' written by He Kaiyin, a 53-year-old modest styled agrarian technician-turned-rural policy researcher in Anhui Province, gives a scathing analysis of the problems emerging in agriculture and rural development subsequent to and despite the overwhelming increase in agricultural productivity in the early 1980s. To sustain early improvements to rural life and to solve emerging problems,[13] He argued for further, more fundamental and broader, reforms, and set out to outline in considerable detail what were needed. He's essay won the 'excellent chapter' award, together with 134 other essays, out of a total of more than 2400 submissions from central and provincial officials, scholars and researchers. The award-winning articles were compiled into a book,[14] and some of them, including He's, were also extracted and published in central 'internal intelligence' bulletins and journals circulated among senior central leaders and party–government officials.[15]

Despite the lacklustre performance in total output since 1985, agriculture was, at the time of 1988–9, regarded within the central policy circles as generally 'healthy', having 'won the battle' by and large. The notion of 'continuous rural reform' entered official policy as early as 1985,[16] but there was little sense of urgency, the focus of policy attention being shifted, since 1984, to the urban sector and industries in particular.[17] 'Peasants are getting rich now and remaining problems can wait', was the going mood among the policy elites at the national capital.[18] It is therefore plausible that the intended purpose of the essay contest was largely to *celebrate* the tenth anniversary of rural reform through a review of past achievements. Indeed, the opening statement of the 'preface' to He and Wang (1990) so states,

> Rural reform in China since 1978 has won wide acclaim internationally of its immense achievements. At a time when rural reform is to enter its second decade, it will be necessary and valuable for us to review the reform practice of the first decade, and to anticipate what next needs to be resolved and achieved.

As part of the review, new suggestions would be put forward, but the tone was expected to be positive and the scale of further work marginal, at least at this stage.[19] Still, one can easily find a fair amount of critical analysis from among the 135 published essays. In his essay, He Kaiyin dwelled on the limitations of previous reform and pounced on the urgency of more liberalizing *rural* reforms, including a switch to permanent land tenure system, developing a land tenure rights market and ending state controls over the distribution and sale of agricultural products. Radical as these ideas were, when compared to then existing policy (and those on land tenure remain controversial as of today), He was *not* alone in raising them. Indeed, a quick browse through the essays reveals that the idea of developing a land tenure market, based upon a permanent or semi-permanent land tenure system, was well-shared within rural policy circles at central and provincial levels.[20] The significance of He's essay in the eventual emergence of rural tax reform in the 1990s thus does not lie in the novelty of the ideas contained therein but in its effect in *motivating or reinforcing He* in furthering his inquisitive activities into rural reform issues. In other words, it is about *how* He continued his agency, and *what* made him do so, in the matter of rural reform.

To appreciate the effect of this essay for *future* events, we need to place it in the context of He's *previous* life experience and trajectory. For instance, how did He come to his view – that decollectivization was insufficient and more radical change could not wait?[21] Or since others had held similar ideas, some of them were more privileged placed in the state-party hierarchy than He himself, why should subsequent developments unfold as they did – that He (and not, say, a rural expert in State Council) became the pioneer in rural tax reform which in 2000 became national policy?

To make sense of history, it is perhaps best to go further back into history itself. Through going back further in time, we may likely discover the considerations of the actors, and the contingencies at that earlier point of time that had led to what subsequently happened. Branded as a 'rightist' and 'counter-revolutionary' during his last year of university education, He spent his prime years from 1958 to 1974 on a state farm in Heilongjiang Province in Northeast China working as a peasant.

When returning to his home province of Anhui after 16 years, he was assigned to conduct agricultural technical research in the Provincial Agricultural Institute. Long years on state farms and life as a peasant had ingrained in He a strong sense of commitment towards rural well-being, as well as cultivating an in-depth understanding of the problems in the countryside. Thus when decollectivization reform was fermenting in Anhui from the bottom-up, He quickly teamed up with local reform elites, through former ties, in the earliest waves of contagion of the *dabaogan* initiative in 1978.[22] The eventual national success of grassroots experiments in Anhui further fed his motivation, during later years, in pursuing further rural development from where he was. As a result of his participation in the early reforms, He was promoted along with other pioneering cadres. In 1983, He was drafted to the Provincial Government General Office by the newly promoted provincial governor and former reform 'comrade' Wang Yuzhao.[23] The net effect was that he acquired a status and the command of resources – time, materials and access to information – which facilitated his continual inquiry into rural issues. Wang was subsequently further promoted to the central government, and as the vice-director of the Central Rural Policy Research Office, Wang sent He the notice of the March 1989 national essay contest, knowing that his old-time colleague and friend would have something to say.[24]

Agency in change process is thus often the combined effect of diverse developments, as well as being a process under change and formation itself. A history of close partnership with reform elites, and the extended experience of rural life, brought to He not only knowledge about the peasantry and agriculture but also a value orientation that fed into motivations and a capacity to withstand frustrations. The promotion to the provincial general office, which itself was largely a result of close partnership with 1978 reform elites, made available an enhanced space to imagine and advocate. Then the dynamics of in-group interactions, whereby political actors reciprocated favours and assistance so as to maximize one's future capacity to perform, provided an opening – in the 1989 national essay contest – through which the idea of fundamental rural reform from an obscure provincial official was circulated among the central policy circle. While a single essay by itself may indeed be insignificant in the charting of *new* policy paths, the very participation in the essay contest itself, as well as its immediate results (winning an award and the chapter being extracted in internal circulations) were motivators *propelling further actions*, from He himself if not yet from others.

Networking the actors

From the central to the provincial

Rural reform remained sidelined in the aftermath of the discussions during the essay contest. Partly this was to be expected. After all central leaders and their policy elites had then been primarily concerned with urban issues, and the year 1988 had witnessed a series of major moves on the urban front.[25] It would thus have raised even more eyebrows had a few papers caused *any* substantive action. In any event, the 'climate' for radical reform, urban or rural, was further dampened in the aftermath of political crisis in spring 1989.

At this juncture, He Kaiyin did not simply set aside his ideas, as he could have easily done, but rather kept probing for an appropriate route to get his message across more effectively. Seeing the 'conservative turn' in political climate, he wrote another piece in the Fall of 1989 to rebuff the emerging scepticism towards decollectivization and the market, and to further elaborate his ideas on permanent land tenure and associated reforms. He had planned to send the paper to the Central Rural Policy Research Office, where his old friend Wang Yuzhao was vice-director. To his surprise, when he called Wang on the phone to alert him of the paper, Wang told him that the Research Office had been scrapped shortly after events in June 1989, and its function subsumed under the Ministry of Agriculture. Wang also warned He of criticisms against him in Beijing, in light of his earlier liberalizing ideas (Chen and Chun 2004: 250–7). While taken aback by such news, He remained resilient. Instead of giving up at this point, and seeking refuge from political criticisms, He chose, albeit not before considerable pondering, to press on and this time he aimed at appealing to central leaders directly. When asked why he was so 'unrepentant', he told a story going back in time: 'Well I had done this before … and I just couldn't help it'.[26] During the years in the Heilongjiang state farm, he had sent a 'petition' to the then Provincial Party Secretary requesting him to forward it to Premier Zhou Enlai. In the letter, he suggested an alternative incentive system to improve agricultural productivity in the province, based on his observation on how peasants worked in the farm. Such an act – offering unsolicited advice of a controversial nature to high levels – was highly dangerous at the time, and friendly advice from fellow peasants all urged him to drop the idea. He insisted on speaking his mind. It turned out to be not as bad as many would have thought. He was soon summoned to the Provincial Government General Office where he was told that the Party Secretary was warmly surprised by his bold move. However, the Secretary was not prepared to forward his letter to Premier Zhou, as this would imply the provincial leadership's backing for He's suggestion. Despite this soft 'no' to his request, He was nonetheless greatly encouraged by the friendliness of the response. After all, as he knew through his own and others' experience, much worse could have happened (Chen and Chun 2004: 258).

He thus pondered that the risk could not have been larger in 1990 than back then, in the midst of Cultural Revolution. Past experience has an impact on future actions. Still, he took a couple of precautions. The paper was retitled from the original 'A Proposal on Permanent Rural Land Tenure to Peasants' to the more tentative 'Some Thoughts on Deepening Rural Reform' (Chen and Chun 2004: 251, 259), to 'camouflage' its radicalism and reduce the probability of its being censored at first instance. Then the paper was sent to an Anhui-based Xinhua (New China News Agency) journalist, instead of directly to the central government. The media had long had a dual role in the Party, namely reporting news publicly and collecting 'intelligence' for the reference of senior officials.

Given He's position in the Provincial Government General Office, his sending a paper to a locally based reporter would appear commonplace and routine. This strategy apparently worked. He's paper was promptly reported, in February 1990, in Xinhua's 'internal reference reports' and the 'internal supplement' of the *People's Daily*. The State Council's reference bulletin, *Juece Chankou*, also summarized its major arguments. Within Anhui, the paper was included in a provincial internal bulletin by He's senior in the Provincial Government General Office. As a result, He's ideas on rural reform not only caught the eyes of some central officials and leaders, as in 1988, but also provincial leaders. A few provincial leaders including the Party Secretary indicated interest in the proposals and instructed the Provincial Agriculture Bureau to undertake further investigation (Chen and Chun 2004: 260; Author's interviews 2004).

However in 1990, China was entering economic recession in addition to the conservative turn in politics and policy. He's calls for further radical reforms were out of step with the spirit of the time.[27] A meeting of Anhui's rural policy officials to deliberate on He's proposals 'naturally' adopted a pedantic approach, focusing more on their legality as compared to current policies and regulations, than on their appropriateness or desirability as reform proposals. With a 'no' recommendation from sympathetic experts, provincial leaders played safe and stayed silent. He's proposals were hence 'shelved' for the record (Chen and Chun 2004: 261; Author's interviews 2004).

On the other hand, it turned out that, the unfavourable larger context notwithstanding, He had won some sympathetic ears among the central leadership. During a trip to Beijing in January 1991, He was unexpectedly summoned to a meeting with the State Council Research Office, where he was told that Premier Li Peng had read earlier reports on his reform ideas with interest. The State Council official then conveyed to He the views of the Premier:

> Now the job is to operationalize the reform ideas into feasible, concrete reform measures that can work in practice ... Given the current macroeconomic situation – we are still in the period of retrenchment – big moves are inappropriate, not to say there are still substantial differences amongst people's views on these reform ideas.

The official continued,

> In this circumstance, I suggest you proceed with further investigations and work out a feasible reform plan, then ask for support from the Provincial Party Committee and Government to launch pilots within Anhui ... We hope Anhui will again take a lead in rural reform this round.
>
> (He and Sun 2000: 8; Chen and Chun 2004: 262)

Greatly encouraged, He was however denied any written confirmation of central support. 'No, the central government could not issue any document', was the reply when He asked for a written note to confirm the message just conveyed to him.

In other words, in order to reduce risks nationally, He was asked to take initiatives *on his own* – including the formulation of detailed reform measures as well as acquiring provincial support to execute them, on a trial basis. What makes this otherwise incredible *privatized* approach more plausible – a potentially major reform affecting 70 per cent of the national population was at stake – is that there was indeed *no* central support in an organizational sense at that time. The matter had not been discussed formally within the central government, and that there were still, as the State Council official revealed, 'substantial differences in views'. After all the focus of central policy attention at that time was on the accumulating 'chains of debts' between state-owned banks and enterprises.

It is worth asking why Premier Li Peng had picked He to convey such a message. As mentioned previously, He Kaiyin was only one among others – in central government and in other provinces – who had proposed similar 'radical' reforms. A hint of an answer may be found in the reference to *Anhui taking a lead again* in the second stage of rural reform, as it had done so in the decollectivization movement which swept the country during the early 1980s. Past developments, or history, do shape expectations and influence actions. Indeed, He himself was immensely motivated by the wish to see Anhui take a similar lead again, and had expressed a deep sense of frustration when he contrasted the lacklustre support of rural tax reform from within Anhui to the much stronger support in provinces like Hebei and Henan.[28] In one instance, when asked why he could not simply offer help to whoever was interested in piloting his ideas, whether it was from within Anhui or not, and not bothered with the lack of persistent support within Anhui's provincial leadership, He gave the following response.

> Well, I did give help to people from Hebei and Henan, but what I *most* wanted to do and see was to have the reform implemented in Anhui. I am from Anhui and Anhui *should* take a lead in the reform process.
>
> (Author's interviews 2005, emphasis original)

An informal, un-minuted conversation was, as expected, quickly dismissed by Anhui's provincial leaders to be of sufficient weight, or credibility, to warrant a break with existing policy. Back home, He refined further his reform ideas and identified two areas for priority actions – rural land use and rural taxes and fees – in a report submitted to the provincial leadership. His suggestion was however ignored (Chen and Chun 2004: 264). He kept trying to arouse interest among city and county officials in several localities, but to no avail (Author's interviews 2005).

Then in 1992, the larger political climate seemed to change, as reform and development became 'in fashion' again after the 'Southern Tour' of the paramount leader Deng Xiaoping.[29] At this juncture, He Kaiyin met the heavyweight rural expert and policy advocate Du Rensheng, formerly director of the now disbanded Central Rural Policy Research Office, at a 1992 land meeting in Anhui. He grasped the opportunity to show Du his newly refined reform proposals, and almost immediately won Du's support (Author's interviews 2002). At this time,

Du was invited by the Fuyang Prefecture to visit Fuyang (in Anhui) after the conference, where Du had been party secretary many years earlier. Due partly to its connection to Du, Fuyang had been made the first 'rural reform experimental zone' nationally in 1987 in a new initiative engineered by Du. Unable to make the visit, Du recommended his new friend He to Fuyang's leaders instead. In Fuyang, He's tax-fee reform proposals were enthusiastically received. The prefectural party secretary, and the deputy secretaries, proclaimed their plan to put He's ideas into practice. An overjoyed He was careful still to send a cautionary note – given the lack of explicit provincial and central approval. Party Secretary Wang Zhaoyao replied, 'well, Fuyang Prefecture had been made an experimental zone for rural reform by the central government since 1987, and with this we could, and indeed were expected to, depart from existing policy!' (Chen and Chun 2004: 271). Fuyang's leaders needed to deliver as part of their job in developing a reform experimental zone,[30] and the pressure for actions and change had become more profound given the recent shift in national policy. Supply of reform ideas, therefore, was eventually met with demand.

The prefectural

In Fuyang, He Kaiyin found an 'ally' who was willing and capable to act. Yet the process of putting ideas into practice turned out to be more complex than expected. What Wang did was to take He Kaiyin with him to look for volunteers one level down the administrative hierarchy – from among the counties within Fuyang Prefecture. In the process, he took care to exert the 'right' amount of influence on county leaders, while maintaining a distance from the subject. On the one hand, his very presence with He and his speaking positively on the proposals served to send a message that he himself, and the prefectural leadership, was in favour of the reform. On the other hand, in meetings with county leaders, he explicitly stressed that 'it is entirely for you in the county to decide if you want to do it. We in the prefecture would not impose a decision' (Chen and Chun 2004: 271). To minimize political risk in undertaking an unapproved reform, Wang left ambiguous, somewhat deliberately, the 'official' status of the reform – whether it was a 'personal' project of He's and its adoption or not was entirely up to the county leaders themselves – in that case making it *their* own project; or whether it was a project suggested by He but already adopted by the prefecture for pilot implementation (even though the counties would still have discretion to decide if they wanted to do it now or later). By playing with ambiguity, Wang hoped to sway county leaders into making a decision which he wanted, while at the same time limiting his own political risk by requiring them to *make a decision*.

'Decentralization' thus played an interesting role here by enabling the senior level to limit its risks and share, if not shirk, responsibilities with the lower level.[31] A major contrast in Wang's move was, as compared to the central and provincial leaders, the visibility and public nature of his endorsement, through his physical presence and words, while the sympathetic attitudes of central and provincial leaders remained informal and non-committal, known only to a small circle of their assistants. It could be precisely because the support from the central and provincial had been so weak that it failed to produce initiatives the senior levels would have wished for. It would have been indeed absurd if Anhui's leaders had embarked on radical reforms at a time of retrenchment simply on the basis of what He Kaiyin told them without any independent indications from the central government. Likewise, the absence of positive signals from provincial leaders had a restraining effect on Wang Zhaoyao's enthusiasm – Wang consciously limited his role to one of tacit influence rather than direct leadership.

The logic of risk aversion is plain and clear. If the senior-level leaders find it difficult to commit themselves to innovations, then it could only be even harder for lower-level leaders to bear the responsibility *entirely* on their own. No innovation will be attempted since the lower level will find the risk too large to bear. This had been the response of He Kaiyin too at one juncture, his high level of enthusiasm notwithstanding. During He's meeting with the State Council official in early 1991, He's initial excitement when he first heard of Premier Li Peng's interest in his reform ideas quickly evaporated when he understood what he was being asked to do – essentially make the reform a project of his own:

> He could not help giggle, whilst nodding his head to Yu's (the State Council official) words encouraging him to start up reform … 'How could I a private individual be expected to "represent" the Anhui Province and set out from here to launch reform on my own?'.
>
> (Chen and Chun 2004: 263)

What was new in developments in Fuyang, in comparison, was that its party secretary had come forward into the open and hence shouldered part of the responsibility – should any county eventually volunteer to go ahead with reform in these terms.[32] While Wang's commitment was still ambiguous – it is unclear *what* decision the prefectural leadership had made and what was left to the county's discretion – nonetheless *some* portion of the risk, and responsibility, now clearly resided in the prefecture. This fact was likely to increase the chance of the lower level meeting the challenge – as the risk was now smaller. Despite Wang's lingering hesitation, Fuyang Prefecture rural tax reform finally moved beyond the personal championship of its innovator to a broader network of actors.

From counties to townships

It was far from a straight road from there, however. After the Fuyang meeting, Wang and He went to two counties – trying to 'lobby' them into piloting He's tax-fee reform ideas.[33] While Wang's presence helped – important members of the county leaderships did show interest – scepticism remained strong in some quarters. The major reservation aired at the county meetings was whether the reform was legal. 'The proposed measure', which would combine the agricultural taxes and all fees into one levy, and ban any further fees, 'contravenes existing regulations!', the Director of Yongshang County People's Congress proclaimed. Underlying the legality concern was grumbling over the ban of fees other than the combined levy, thus greatly constraining the power of local officials to extract revenues as and when required. Wang was reluctant to step in, given his position that reform was a *county* decision. The net effect was that the dissenting minority acquired the power of a veto. Given the substantial political risk in undertaking unapproved reforms, sympathetic county leaders were loath to press for action short of a 'united front' among their own ranks.

The power of the dissenters requires further analysis, especially in the cases where the dissenters were the 'weaker' members in the county leadership, namely officials in the local people's congress, while the sympathizers were the party secretaries and county mayors – the core of party-state authority. 'Normally the party secretary's view prevails and the director of the local people's congress always supports decisions of the (local) party', remarked an informed source (Author's interviews 2005). What made the people's congress officials so defiant against their senior partners, and why did the party secretaries give in rather than asserting their superior authority in the county leadership?

> Thus everyone knew, without saying it in open at the time, that the directors of the people's congress must be acting out of a 'script' from somewhere – likely someone from above who did not want reform to be piloted in Anhui …

commented a source. It would be difficult to validate such guesses short of a revelation by the individuals involved. But the fact that such conjectures existed serves to remind us of the vulnerability of bottom-up initiatives in situations of political domination.

Wang Zhaoyao's presence at the county meetings had served to give the *impression* that there *was* support from above to local reform decisions. But whatever effect of support Wang had brought was eliminated when a local leader spoke out in unambiguous terms about the illegality of the reform – and especially since Wang turned silent during those critical junctures. The conjecture that local dissenters may be speaking on behalf of higher authorities also suggests a persistent anxiety to watch out for disapproval from the top. Since the tax-fee reform was formally illegal, conducting it would be relatively safe *only if* there was consensus among one's next-level superiors that the law would *not* be enforced. The absence of such consensus increased enormously the risk of lower levels experimenting on innovations, making bottom-up initiatives unlikely.

'Being unlikely' did not foreclose all likelihood, however. As it turned out, a breakthrough came entirely independent of the processes described above. At Xinxing Town, Woyang County (in Fuyang Prefecture) in late 1992, the town party secretary and director came across a newspaper article by a Hebei official Yang Wenliang outlining ideas of a simplified way to collect revenue through a one-off collection of combined rural taxes and fees.[34] Long troubled by the never-ending tasks of collecting diverse taxes and fees from peasants, which often dragged on during the entire year, and had caused heightened tension in the community, the two Xinxing leaders, Liu and Li, decided to experiment with ideas as outlined in the newspaper article. The ideas Yang wrote can be traced, as we go back in time, to He Kaiyin's. Back in February 1990, the then Hebei Governor Yue Qifeng had read with interest about He's reform ideas in a *People's Daily* internal supplement, and requested further exploration into the subject. Yang, then working in the provincial research office, was assigned the job. However due to subsequent shuffles in provincial leadership, this subject was not picked up again by a new provincial leadership until mid-1993, when Hebei Province also contemplated piloting the rural tax reform (W. Yang 2001). Thus in Anhui and Hebei, we witness a gradual emergence of networks working parallel to one another. When they intersect, the points of co-evolution lead to an acceleration of events.

What evolved in Xinxing Town in late 1992 is worth more elaboration, especially since the developments there exhibit significant discrepancies from, as well as similarities with, what we have noted as the risk-averse culture among political actors. In contrast to hesitation prevalent in the upper levels, in Xinxing town, leaders focused on the potential benefits the new initiative might bring. There was similarly no upper-level support when Party Secretary Liu and Mayor Li contemplated the reform ideas in an obscure newspaper article. No senior leaders and indeed nobody sympathetic to the reform ideas had visited the Town. The drive to find a way out of their current difficulties was strong enough, however, to produce the will to give new ideas a try, even when these had been casually encountered.

> Year after year our people spent the bulk of their time and energy on revenue collection, but still we had a hard time to meet the revenue targets from above! And (with the high level of tax burden) peasants were getting furious with us, making our revenue collection task even more difficult. We had to find a way out of this impossible situation.
>
> (Liu from Chen and Chun 2004: 275)

Liu and Li together worked out a draft plan following the sketches in Yang's article. To test the waters, they had their people present the plan door-by-door to peasants and obtain feedback. With an enthusiastic response from below, Liu then convened a meeting with other town leaders in which a decision was made to go ahead. Only then did they turn their attention to soliciting support from the upper level. At Woyang County, their proposal to undertake rural tax-fee reform was warmly welcomed by the county secretary and mayor, who had responded sympathetically to similar ideas by He Kaiyin when Wang and He visited the county. The trip to the county government alerted Liu of the complexity of the subject, as the earlier opposition of the Director of the County People's Congress became known to him. This did not stop him, however, and only made him more careful of details. To enhance legitimacy, for example, the reform was presented to the Town People's Congress for approval (Chen and Chun 2004: 276–8).

What is worth noting here is that when assessing the feasibility of the draft plan, Liu and Li set out first to ask the peasants, and only later – when the tax-fee reform was deemed desirable within the town – did they seek backing from superiors. The latter was necessary to make a local initiative politically legitimate, but only if the initiative itself was adequate for the purpose it was intended to serve. This simple principle of feasibility studies is however often ignored in many occasions of decision-making in China. Reports abound on planning blunders – either immature proposals were submitted to the upper levels for approval, or upper-level authorities imposed rudimentary and poorly examined ideas as polished policies for implementation at lower levels.[35] In either case, there is a lapse in responsibility. The fact that this commonplace malice did not recur in Xinxing Town in late 1992 is not accidental. After all, the hard constraints of rural life had motivated the positive *actions* of Liu and Li. The overriding objective was to improve the rural situation wherein town party–government leaders were embedded. Only by ending the pre-existing hopelessly vicious cycles of extraction and degradation could there be a better prospect of their delivering a good performance at work, *and thereby winning promotion to higher ranks*. Liu and Li thus had to turn to the villagers for indications if their plan would work or not. Situated at the lowest level of the administrative hierarchy, town leaders did not have any lower levels to shirk responsibility to should things go wrong. Paradoxically, therefore, the weakest-positioned officials in the state became also the best positioned to exercise the most agency in breaking away from paths set by their superiors

Conclusion

These discussions suggest that the emergence of change itself was a highly unstable event. Contingencies and unintended consequences proliferated. Vision and ambiguities coexisted. Rational calculations of risks and potential benefits counted a lot, and so did the 'affective' effects of previous life experiences, and in-group interactions of friends and former colleagues. These diverse processes all played a major role in deciding what and how people – with heterogeneous interests and agendas – have acted and interacted.

In this process, agency plays a prominent role – thus the relevance of the 'entrepreneurship' concept. Agency does not operate in the straightforward, purposive mode as depicted in linear models of decision-making, however. Making change happen requires the toleration of ambiguities as well as their reduction, a capacity to react *post hoc* to contingencies and unintended consequences. The art of agency, or innovation entrepreneurship, rests in a capacity to address values and interests other than the ones championed in the innovation, and to take in the unanticipated as much as to work towards the anticipated.

This chapter employs ethnographic methods of research and a 'back along the timeline' narrative to lay out the processes leading to the translation of reform ideas into initial reform practice in the case of the Chinese rural tax reform.

Theory has been kept to a minimum: to provide a guide to basic questions – change and agency, and to illuminate, through interpreting, a story or observation from the actors themselves. The centre stage is left to the narrative of the actors. In this way, this chapter hopes to go a small step beyond the much-criticized 'theory-lag' in much of the area studies literature, as well as the 'strait-jacketing' of reality in much of literature in the disciplines.

This account also suggests that it is futile to look for parameters defining 'conditions' of sustainability. Eager to anticipate the chance of success (or failure) of ongoing change processes as we may be, we cannot possibly foresee what may happen tomorrow and the day after tomorrow from what has happened today and yesterday. The possibilities of contingencies and the existence of parallel, diverse processes are real and abundant, so that what has taken place – which we as analysts take note of – will only have a *partial* influence on future events. It could be that just round the corner, a process that seems totally irrelevant as of yesterday will 'co-evolve' to a point of relevance – but we could only know that *after* such co-evolution happens, at a later point of time. That does not imply incessant chaos and volatility in our vision of the future, however. To the extent that we cannot predict what will happen tomorrow, we know *by and large* how things will be, and the manner and processes whereby change may happen, or not happen, by taking a closer look at the past. We know there will be contingencies. We know we are all influenced by history. We know we can all make a difference, if we want to. As a result, life has its side of 'stability' and 'certainty', as well as being dotted by 'surprises', nice or bitter. A 'back along the timeline' account reveals all these dependence–stability influences and agency processes in their full manifestation, and thus enables us to ground the eclectic observations that shape the future. The work of social analysis is to reveal in full how ambiguities work, not to explain them away and replace them with self-imposed simplicity.

2 Differentiated actors

Central–local politics in reform evolution*

How are decisions and policies made and implemented? This classical question in political science has attracted a considerable literature amongst observers of *realpolitik* in China, with its continental size, 1.3 billion population and five layers of government.[1] Mirroring the move away from the traditional dualism of 'top-down' versus 'bottom-up' approaches in the general implementation literature,[2] recent literature on Chinese central–local politics emphasizes the co-participation of central and local actors in decision-making and the dialectical interactive relationship between central and local power.[3] Goodman recognizes, for instance, that central and local actors have *differentiated* roles to play in decision-making (Goodman 1989: 425–44). Li makes the case of interactive central–local power, calling for a reconceptualization of central–local relations in a non-zero-sum schema (Li 1998). Recent studies on the 'Open Up the West' national policy augment the claim for 'disaggregating' China, and the relevance of the provincial, regional and local as levels and foci of analysis.[4] Against the traditional emphasis over central predominance versus provincial power, this body of literature, adopting a 'non-dualistic' approach to power, highlights the coexistence of central and local power in a diffuse, complex decision-making process (Holbig 2004: 335–57).

If central and local actors are all players with differentiated roles in decision-making, as the literature has convincingly argued, the next question in line is *what exactly* these roles are. So far these studies have produced a substantial amount of 'thick' description of central–local interactions employing, mostly, the inductive method. There is a need to consolidate previous observations to theorize the *specific* central and local roles as differentiated actors in *generic* terms. Case materials will continue to be useful as the derivation of specific roles will necessarily be informed by the contexts, but the literature needs to go *beyond* the description of single cases and do more theorizing based on the cases.

The concentration so far in descriptive accounts has contributed to the continual relevance of the dualistic approach.[5] New studies in the field continue to pose the central leaders against the local officials in a zero-sum relationship, arguing for a dominant role for the central in some cases, and for the local in others.[6] This is despite the fact that the raison d'être of the dualistic account has been thoroughly criticized by the non-dualistic challenge. In the dualistic framework, the key to effective decision-making and implementation lies in enhanced incentive structures, effective compliance monitoring mechanisms and the development of adequate capacity. Such prescriptions remain daunted, however, by the inability of the dualistic account to explain why these same institutions have not been in place from the beginning. As Li points out, there is a built-in reliance upon *ad hoc*, circumstantial factors exogenous to the central–local relationship for change to happen in the dualistic account, short of which changes are left highly indeterminate.[7]

This chapter seeks to go one small step further in the direction of filling the 'specificity gap'. It discusses the specific roles of central and local actors *qua co-participants* in reform decisions, using observations acquired through archival research and interviews on the shifting designs of China's rural 'tax-for-fee' reform – a national reform to address the intriguing question of excessive state extraction and state–society relations in China's vast countryside. The chapter notes traces of dualistic thinking in the official definition of reform issues and reform designs, but argues that the evolution of reform details is better explained in a non-dualistic framework. Central and local actors are more co-participants in reform decisions than holders of diametrical roles, one as reformer and the other as 'targets' of reform. Bearing in mind the need to go beyond thick description of cases – the current subject of 'tax-for-fee' reform is obviously a case – the chapter will explicitly identify and analyze the differentiated roles of central and local actors, drawing from but not confined to a description of case materials.

Definition of reform issues, objectives and reform design

The plight of peasants has increasingly commanded the attention of China's political leaders after the 1993 riot in Sichuan Province of south-west China.[8] Peasant incomes have deteriorated, the urban–rural gap widened up[9] and violent clashes between local government personnel and rural residents on the rise.[10] A somewhat radical approach was attempted to relieve tension during the 1990s, through the opening up of village-level elections and improving transparency in grassroots administration.[11] These did not bring the desired results, however.[12] By the late 1990s, attention shifted to what were perceived to be the direct causes of rural grievances: the high level of state extraction, and depressed rural incomes – thus the 'tax-for-fee' reform agenda.[13]

The decision to reform the rural tax regime nationwide has its origin, according to official record, in a Party Central Committee Plenum held in 1998, though the decision then contains only a vague reference to the need for some kind of tax reform with few details.[14] A team of three was formed under the State Council to oversee the formulation of a reform programme.[15] After some consultation with provinces, the contours of the national reform package were laid down in 2000 (Wen 2000: 211–12). All these suggest a largely 'bottom-up' process wherein the central government felt its way to respond to societal tensions. The overriding objective was to reduce state extraction and pacify rural agitation. However, as Yep points out, the complex cures of an equitable fiscal system and ending systemic discrimination against peasants were abandoned for a simpler recipe putting the blame mostly at local officials (Yep 2004: 43–70). In the reform design, excessive extraction was defined largely as an implementation issue, disregarding the historical and institutional embeddedness of the current problems of peasants' burden, (Bernstein and Lü 2003).[16] Peasants suffered because there were too many local officials to feed, and many were corrupt and abused their powers. Inefficient local governments therefore needed to downsize to minimize waste, and better monitoring and control from above would provide the cures. Reducing the problems to an agency issue in a dualistic model of central–local politics, the reform measures prescribe adjustments to the carrot-and-stick mix to enhance the control of the principal.

This definition of reform issues as enhancing agency control is evident in the key contours of reform design. First, a minimal reduction rate (20 per cent) of state extraction was prescribed nationally for all localities, failing which the local chiefs would be penalized and their positions endangered.[17] The effect was provincial and local governments competed to exceed the official requirement, producing a tremendously higher reduction rate of up to 74 per cent in the first year of nationwide implementation.[18] Second, given the proliferation of fees and charges, central officials lamented that the central government could not be expected to underwrite local abuses and provide compensation for lost incomes.[19] Local officials were instead told to abolish all fees, except for those properly authorized, and to shed staff and cut expenses in order to make ends meet. The latent message is that local officials were the culprits of the excessive state extraction, through employing too many people and wasteful expenditures, if not sheer corruption. They were thus to clean up their own backyard under tightened rules. County governments were required, as a rule, to reduce their staff by 20 per cent, and the more, the better.[20] Third, despite the reluctance to underwrite *all* local fees, the loss of revenue from *legitimate* local fees abolished in the reform needed compensation, which was done through an upward adjustment of Agriculture Taxes and central transfer payments. Defining the boundary of legitimate fees was, however, highly contentious, given the complex context and trajectories wherein the fees had come into being historically, and problems in the national fiscal and tax system. Central subsidies rose from 1.1 billion yuan to Anhui Province in 2000 to 30 billion yuan nationwide in 2003, and over 50 billion yuan in 2004,[21] reflecting the scale of interest involved and the magnitude of tension between central and local actors on this issue (Figure 2.1).

As the reform was implemented, doubts about its sustainability grew. Despite the remarkable burden of reduction rates, even some official reports have pointed to the re-emergence of fees and charges under disguised forms, the difficulty to downsize local governments and reduce public spending, and the limited

---

Burden reduction

1. Abolition of township and village levies, and other administrative fees/charges
2. Abolition of Slaughter Tax (formerly charged to the slaughter of pigs but widely abused, with a fixed amount imposed indiscriminately on every rural household)
3. Phasing out (within 3 years) of corvée labour services
4. Adjustment to agricultural taxes: effective tax rate to rise from 3% to 8.4%, (including a 1.4% surtax going to the village level) to compensate for the loss of revenue from abolition of the village/township levies
5. Increase of fiscal transfer payments to the townships from county, city, province and central coffers

Rationalization of tax/fiscal system

6. Rationalizing tax collection in villages (Set up Agricultural Taxes Bureau as part of the County Finance Bureau to collect agricultural tax from peasants, rather than relying on township and village officials.)
7. Public finance and budget management reforms: enhancing transparency and external monitoring of revenue and expenditure
8. Township government administrative reforms: downsizing by a minimum of 20%, reducing bureaucracy and adjusting government functions to achieve slim government

Sustainability

9. Adjusting expenditure responsibility between governments: education at village and township levels become the responsibility of county governments or above; township roads to be financed through the budget, making support from higher levels more possible
10. Improving rural governance: strengthening the accountability mechanisms of township governments to the local population

---

Figure 2.1 National reform measures (2000), classified by objectives.

Source: Compiled from Central Document No. 7 (2000), and related documents.

capacity of the central coffers to compensate for lost local revenues from the reform.[22] Namely, if the problem behind the reform is agency control, the impact of the reform measures has been less than conclusive.

In this context, the developments in 2004 reflected a further attempt of the central government to push forward the reform agenda. In a directive sealed in late 2003, the new central leadership under State President Hu Jintao and Premier Wen Jiabao announced plans to phase out the tax on agriculture in 5 years' time.[23] Officially, the decision was part of a larger drive to boost peasants' income, including measures such as 10 billion yuan of direct subsidies annually to grain producers, business tax exemptions to small traders of agricultural produce, more public goods provision in the countryside and stepped up assistance to agricultural production and rural industries.[24] Privately, central officials admitted that the impact on peasants' incomes of the tax adjustment and suspension *per se* was likely to be marginal,[25] and that the move was intended more to deprive local officials of a convenient 'vehicle' to append their 'illegal' extractions.[26]

We understand that abolishing the Agriculture Tax will create new problems in the future, not the least how to find a new tax for the rural economy. In fact research is being conducted on this latter question. But we cannot afford to wait to have everything ready. We need to find some means *now* to contain the (continuing) local practice of imposing abusive fees to peasants. Phasing out Agriculture Tax is one way towards this.

With the abolition of the only nationally endorsed tax on agriculture, it was hoped that any future illegitimate local extractions would become more visible, and thus more susceptible to external monitoring and control. This is a significant departure from the previous focus on reduction and rationalization of rural taxes, and reflects an emerging pessimism regarding the prospect of achieving control despite the reform, in light of the information asymmetry in favour of the locale.[27] However, if agency control is so difficult, how may the new measure possibly achieve its intended objective? I put this question to a Beijing researcher and the response suggests a rather indirect linkage hinging upon, interestingly, peasants' activism.

When Agriculture Tax is eventually phased out in a few years' time, peasants would know that the central government no longer requires them to pay tax. Period! This would improve the transparency of the rural tax regime and enable the peasants to protest more effectively against any illegal fees when imposed, simply because local governments would have no vehicle to free ride.

As in the introduction of village elections in the 1990s, the central government is again counting upon bottom-up monitoring from the peasants themselves to address the agency problem at local levels. Whether peasant activism may work *for* the centre without having the central government's authority also challenged will need more observation, however. Recent studies on rural political agitation may have provided some consolation on this point, pointing out that the higher up the level of government the more trust it enjoyed from the peasants (Li, L. 2004: 228–58; Li and O'Brien 1996: 28–61; O'Brien 2002: 139–54; Bernstein and Lü 2003; Unger 2002: 215). The same literature has, however, also warned of signs of trust on the wane.[28] In any event, there is evident discrepancy between the actual situation and the central formulation as suggested. For instance, the claim that peasants will not be paying any tax once the Agriculture Tax is dropped is plainly misplaced. Peasants have been paying and will continue to pay taxes imposed on transactions of agricultural products. When they engage in non-agricultural economic activities, such as transportation and trade, they will be liable to Value-added Tax and Business Tax. Peasants are also subject to income taxes as everyone else under the Income Tax Law. The No. 1 (2004) Directive offered some tax relief in these respects, including a moratorium of personal income tax for peasants,[29] but the rules are complex and subject to abuse.[30] A provincial fiscal official involved in reform implementation dismissed the exemptions as 'cosmetic', since as a matter of practice no personal income tax had been collected from peasants before, though the tax theoretically also applied to peasants.[31]

Despite the latest developments, exempting the peasants from paying tax permanently was never the intention. Chen Xiwen, Vice-Director of State Council Development Research Center, had said in a press interview he did not agree with the suggestion from some quarters that peasants be totally exempted from tax, and that the challenge was instead to design an adequate tax system for the countryside.[32] Indeed, proposals on alternative tax plans were mooted before the 2004 plan to phase out Agriculture Tax was finalized.[33] A total exemption was apparently regarded inequitable as a matter of principle, since 'everyone should share the responsibility to contribute to the national coffers'.[34]

An agency definition of the problem prescribes solutions in a carrot-and-stick mode. Two kinds of capacity are critical in this regard: (1) the centre's fiscal capacity to provide sufficient cash in transfer payments and (2) the capacity of the local governments to find sufficient alternative employment opportunities for their cadres and population. There has been some limited optimism on the first, which underlines the 2004 plan to phase out Agriculture Tax. It was felt that Agriculture Tax accounted for an only negligible share of the rising total national revenue, so that China could now afford to stop 'taxing agriculture'.[35] The problem of this line of thinking is that Agriculture Tax *per se* has never been the root of excessive rural extraction. It is tenuous to assume that the bulk of problematic fees that previously 'travelled' on the back of Agriculture Tax would disappear together with the phasing out of the Tax, rather than finding other vehicles to free ride on. At the same time, the lack of alternative employment opportunities remains a problem in most parts of China, where a job in the local government still gives a handsome pay and substantial job security, not to say a 'licence' to get rich through malicious use of state power.

A non-dualistic reconceptualization: differentiated roles

Not only is the solution in the dualistic account intractable, it also rests on slippery assumptions of what causes the problem. Local actors play a far more complex role than the conventional image of troublemakers sabotaging reform as assumed in the dualistic account. This section visits a couple of features in the reform package and their development processes to elucidate this observation, and to specify the differentiated roles of central and local actors in the rural tax reform. Through the identification of these specific roles *qua* co-participants, we point to the ways whereby the reform may be improved.

Abolishing all fees? The centre's role of defining parameters

The single most important measure in the 'tax-for-fee' reform, given its primary objective of reducing rural state extraction, is arguably the requirement that *all* rural administrative fees be abolished. Central Document No. 7 of 2000, announcing the launch of national test point in Anhui Province, states that 'all kinds of administrative fees, charges and government funds that targeted specifically peasants' have to go.[36] The situation turned out to be less clear cut, however. In a follow-up directive, the Ministry of Finance added that when announcing to the public their fee-clean-up exercise, provinces needed to specify the administrative fees and charges to be abolished, 'those to be *retained*' (emphasis added), and at what level and scope.[37] The implied message is that provinces could retain some fees after screening, rather than have the fees all removed. Field interviews with a provincial fiscal official also highlight the existence of ambiguities.

> The key concept, 'administrative fees specifically targeting peasants' (*she-nong shoufei*), is poorly defined and its boundary unclear. This has brought some awkward results. On the one hand new rural fees have been tightly controlled since reform: from 2002 the central government has centralized authority to promulgate new fees under this category, and so far has not approved any. At the same time many fees not captured in the official scope of 'peasants' burden' are still collected in the villages. The pretext is that these fees do not 'target' *specifically* at peasants, but are paid likewise by urban dwellers. Examples are education-related fees and charges (school tuition fees, fees for books and stationery, school meal expenses, etc.), road maintenance fees, licence fees for motor bikes, etc.
>
> (Author's interviews, Wuhan, 2004)

A loophole has thus enabled existing fees payable by peasants to continue, and even new fees to be imposed, as long as they can escape central scrutiny, or are defined out of the official scope of control. A handbook of 'rural administrative fees' of a province contains a list of 30 fees collected by at least nine government departments.[38] Some examples are: licence and inspection fees for tractors and agricultural mechanics, various permits and licences for, say, the 'use of waters', fishing boats and 'special' fishing rights, immunization fees for poultry and farm animals, hunting fee, logging permit, residents' identity cards, education fees, school boarding and meal charges, fertility control, fees on outgoing migrant workers, and irrigation and flood control water charges. If the reform objective was to abolish 'unwarranted', or 'illegitimate', fees, rather than *all* administrative fees as originally stated then the critical question was how to draw the line. In this regard, it is telling that this important task – differentiating illegitimate from legitimate fees – was simply left to provincial governments. There was no guideline on how to conduct screening, nor was there requirement to report to central government the screening result.

What followed was much as expected. Facing intense pressure to find monies to pay for expenses, many local governments made cosmetic changes only, collecting the fees still in disguised forms. One disguise was user charges. In theory, these charges were costs of services rendered and purchased in a market situation, and were thus radically different from administrative fees, which had a fiscal nature. In practice, the 'users' often had no free choice as to whether they wanted the service, to the extent that payments might be 'assigned' without any services provided.[39]

Despite repeated warnings of abuse, until 2003, there had been few new substantive measures.[40] In May 2003, provincial governments were, for the first time, asked to report to the State Council the fees they had abolished, and retained, and told the criteria in the screening exercise.[41] All fees that had not been previously approved by the central or provincial governments prior to the reform needed to go. So was the case for fees which had exceeded the originally approved levels.

The requirement to report is a small improvement. At least provinces had to make known the fees they abolished, and those they continued to charge. It was, however, uncertain how effective transparency alone could be in containing abuse. Added to the doubt is the observation that the screening criteria belatedly outlined, upon examination, merely reiterated pre-existing rules governing the approval of fees before 'tax-for-fee' reform. Many provincial governments also simply relayed the central notice to subordinate governments for implementation, without elaborating on details as to how the 'clean-up' exercise should be conducted.[42] The author's field research in Hubei Province, central China, observes that some provincial and local departments have introduced new fees and made changes to existing fee levels without going through the 'proper' channels.[43]

The issue here is not whether or not provincial governments should play a part in screening decisions. China's continental size and diversity necessitate decentralization in policy formulation, a feature which is squarely recognized in the reform documents. Central Document No. 7 (2000) explicitly states, 'Due to diverse local conditions in our large country, the rural "tax-for-fee" reform requires not only a unified national policy, but a mechanism of decentralized decision-making to cater for local conditions'.[44] Nevertheless, what is required is some clear specification regarding boundaries, operative principles and the interface between the local role and that of the central government. In other words, given the need for a local role, *how* the central and local actors share the job of distinguishing legitimate from illegitimate fees needs to be better delineated.

In view of the immense fiscal pressure for local governments to raise revenue, the central government should have prescribed definitively the parameters for the screening exercise, and demand timely reports to monitor compliance. Most pre-existing fees had formerly been endorsed or approved by provincial governments prior to reform, so that a mechanism of external monitoring from outside the province was necessary to make provincial screening not a reiteration of previous *provincial* decisions. Defining the parameters and strengthening external monitoring from the centre will not reduce provinces to passive agents. Provincial authorities would still be required to come up with details of the exercise, day-to-day monitoring of the implementation by sub-provincial authorities, as well as providing feedback to central authorities for future policy adjustments. What is important is that the centre should not, in the name of decentralization, abrogate responsibility which only the centre is capable of fulfilling. By making the necessary hard decisions, the central government will prepare the ground for collaborative local decisions, and better reform results are likely to follow.

Agricultural taxes: provinces as reformers

A reform that seeks to end excessive and arbitrary state extraction demands that an alternative, more reasonable, system be put in place, in addition to slashing the unjustified items. In this regard, the agricultural taxes were designed to perform this role, until the latest twist in 2004 as noted above.[45] Here we focus on one part of the original, pre-2004, plan – the reform of the Agricultural Special Products Tax – to show that provinces were actively involved in the reformulation of the rural tax regime.[46]

Agricultural Special Products Tax was first enacted in 1994 as a special variant of the Agriculture Tax to enable local governments to impose differentiated, and higher, tax rates on more profitable agricultural products such as tea, tobacco, fruit, flowers and aquatic products.[47] The intention was to rationalize the incentive structures of the production of various agricultural products, and to give adequate protection to grain production, as the more lowly priced grain would then be taxed differently (with a lower effective tax rate) from the more pricy 'special products'. The implementation of the tax had caused much controversy, however, with many complaints of abuse and double taxing, the clearing of which formed part of the reform programme. In particular, Central Document No. 7 (2000) conferred on provincial governments a new discretion on *whether* or not the Special Products Tax was to be imposed at all:

> … Regarding taxing agricultural special products …, provincial governments may decide to collect Agricultural Tax or the Agricultural Special Products Tax. The provincial governments may also decide to collect *only* the Special Products Tax in areas where most outputs produced are in fact special products, and collect only the Agriculture Tax in other areas (where there is a mix of 'regular' agricultural products and special products) …
>
> (Clause (5), Section 3)

The meaning of this provision requires some elaboration. First, it is a clear departure from pre-existing regulations on the Agricultural Special Product Tax, which prescribed that in places where Agriculture Tax normally applied (meaning: had historically been collected) but actually grew special products, the products should be taxed on the basis of Agriculture Tax, *plus* the difference between calculated tax returns of the Special Product Tax and that of the Agriculture Tax.[48] The new provision quoted above thus appears to give provincial governments a seemingly free hand to decide *which* of the two kinds of agricultural taxes would be collected from special products, irrespective of the differences in tax returns as a result of their choice one way or the other.

However, this large room for provincial discretion is somehow circumscribed by the second statement in the quote, which states that 'in those areas where most outputs are in fact special products', provincial governments 'may decide to collect the Special Products Tax', and to collect the (regular) Agriculture Tax in 'other areas'. Provinces were hence given advice, if not an instruction, as to how they may exercise their discretion.

The importance of such fine distinction of the boundary of local discretion is made evident when we examine local implementation. In well off southern Guangdong, south China, local officials at Shunde District decided in 2002 that Shunde would only apply the regular Agriculture Tax although Shunde grew only 'special products',[49] so that Shunde's peasants could receive a smaller tax bill.[50] A local official so described the rationale of this decision.

> A few years back we had very high yield in our main produce – eels, which commanded a very good price. Since then the price had come down considerably. However, under the national (tax-for-fee) reform policy, we need to assess current taxable value of output in accordance with the historical average output value of 1993–8. Given the high value achieved then, this places our peasants in a disadvantaged position. If we taxed our products by the higher Special Products Tax, and based our calculation of taxable value on the market situation of the earlier period, our people would pay even more than before the reform, not less. This would not be acceptable to our people and also squarely contradict the spirit of the reform.
>
> (Author's interviews 2003)

In a follow-up interview, it was confirmed that taxing special products with the lower tax rate of the Agriculture Tax was locally initiated.

> Initially we proposed to the provincial government that we should scrap the Special Products Tax altogether. This was rejected since such a move was considered not in line with central policy. Then we came to the current proposition, that when *choosing a specific tax rate* for our agricultural product, we would opt for the one which is lower. This enabled us to follow the spirit of the central policy of relieving peasants' burden, and the provincial government agreed.

What is worth noting is that strictly speaking, Shunde's formulation was not in line with the specific provisions in Central Document No. 7. As noted previously, the central government had attached strings to new freedoms given to provinces regarding the *choice of taxes* (not tax rates) to be applied. The expressed guideline was that 'in areas where most agricultural outputs are in fact special products', provincial governments may 'decide to collect only the Special Products Tax', and 'collect only the Agriculture Tax in other areas'. This means that Shunde should have collected special products tax instead, since most, if not all, agricultural products in Shunde were special products. But certainly Shunde's peasants would become worse off after reform if this provision had been strictly implemented. The central guideline was formulated on the basis of rationalizing the *overlap* of the two kinds of agricultural taxes, the rationality of each of the two taken for granted. To rescue the spirit of the central policy, some subtle twist of policy was made locally to fill in the gap, as in this case.

Guangdong in 2002 moved cautiously to camouflage its local adaptation of central policy. A clear break was left to Anhui Province, which announced in late March 2003 that with immediate effect *all* agricultural products would be taxed by a rate of no higher than 7 per cent, effectively making the Special Products Tax redundant in the province.[51] Four days after Anhui's announcement, Premier Wen Jiabao conferred his *post hoc* endorsement in a national meeting,

> The abolition of the Agricultural Special Products Tax should become the next major move in the rural tax reform. By now most regions have attained the conditions to contemplate the abolition of the tax. For these regions, this tax may now be abolished. For the minority of regions which cannot do it as yet, the objective is to reduce its scope of application, lower its tax rates, so as to pave the way for its eventual abolition.[52]

This endorsement was formalized in a joint notice by the Ministry of Finance and the National Taxation Bureau 2 months later. Provincial governments were explicitly empowered to decide whether to retain or abolish the Agricultural Special Products in their jurisdictions, and the tax rates to be applied to those former 'special products', so long as total tax burden would not go up as a result.[53]

Anhui was, once again, therefore, a pioneer of central policy. One month after the new central regulation, in July 2003, Guangdong Provincial Government followed suit and suspended the Special Products Tax in its new reform plan, which also suspended the 20 per cent surcharge to Agriculture Tax, and lowered the rate of Agriculture Tax to 6 per cent, from the national ceiling of 7 per cent.[54] A new baseline was hence drawn, culminating in the wholesale downward adjustment of the Agriculture Tax and abolition of the Special Products Tax nationally in 2004.

Conclusion

In an attempt to transcend the longstanding debate between the 'top-down' and 'bottom-up' approaches to policymaking and implementation, Richard Matland put forward his 'ambiguity-conflict model' to distinguish circumstances whereby one approach rather than the other applies.[55] In his model, the amount of ambiguity in the policy (goals, means, issues, etc.), and of conflict in the political context is instrumental. The top-down model applies in situations of low ambiguity and low political conflict, and bottom-up model in the case of high ambiguity and high conflict. The key is the identification of specific contexts, since it is quite out of the question that either approach is totally wrong. Likewise, as Margaret Archer argues over the structure–agency question, common sense experience tells us that the Individual account or the Collectivist account cannot be all right, and the other all wrong. Both structure and agency are relevant, and they interpenetrate and interact. The challenge is to specify the details *how* structure and agency interpenetrate and interact without mingling their boundaries, or defining away one or the other.[56] This chapter seeks to meet this challenge somewhat in the context of central–local politics – through delineating the specific differentiated roles of the central and local actors.[57] As co-makers of policy, the roles of central and local officials are not interchangeable but possess clear boundaries.

Discussion in the chapter brings home two messages. The first confirms the basic framework of the non-dualistic account: that the rural 'tax-for-fee' reform was a central–local 'joint-venture'. Local processes in reform implementation went far beyond the 'shirking' behaviour depicted in the principal–agent framework.[58] In the case of agricultural taxes, local actions did not sabotage the central objective of reform, but supplemented, and even led, central policy in its fine print. The fact that local actions sometimes also contravened central directives suggests the obsolete nature of central policy, and the *need* for a local role in the ongoing process of policy formulation. As noted over Agricultural Special Product Tax, local initiatives met almost instant central endorsement and helped make new national policy, vindicating the collaborative status of local actions in the national reform.

A second observation is that the central actors have *not* played a sufficiently active role in the reform process. With the primary reform objective seen as capping local state extraction, and local officials criticized as the culprit, one would expect the central government to keep a tight rein over reform plans and implementation. This chapter finds that this was not the case. In critical junctures of, say, what fees may be retained and how much tax was to be collected, the central government had left key decisions to provincial and local levels. Parameters remained under-defined, and monitoring was, until 2003, weak. Political rhetoric on reform urgency was not complemented by a similar vigilance in the design of detailed mechanisms to ensure effective implementation.

The emergent picture is an image of central and local actors as co-participants in the reform decision and implementation processes, but where each has its obliged roles to fulfil. Two sets of roles are identified in this chapter. The first pair sees the instrumental role of provincial and local actors in refining and redefining national policy, and the parallel enabling role of the central government, which facilitates the active role of the local actors. Upon closer examination, there are two strands in this role of local actor in decision-making. In the first strand, local actions fill in details of policy during reform implementation, as diverse local situations logically dictate. The local adaptations buttress national policy and are very much expected in any account of policymaking. This first genre of local decision-making *qua implementation* may develop into a second strand – local role *qua decision-makers*, when the local content illuminates major weaknesses in the national policy, or when feedback from local experimentation suggests a more desirable, and alternative, direction of change nationally. Parallel to this latter, and more substantive, strand of local role, the central government needs to recognize the legitimacy of pluralities within the general confines of national policy, and be ready to incorporate local contents and experience to improve further national policy itself. While both central and local actors are all active agents, the emphasis here is placed more on the actions of the local, with the central taking up a largely enabling role.

The second set of differentiated roles focuses more on the central government. Central actors have a responsibility in (re)defining the major parameters of behaviour, and specifying the new rules of the game, given the chosen goal and the historical context in which the desired change is being sought. It is insufficient for the central actors to announce the reform objectives, only to leave the specific mechanisms as to how to get there entirely to the provincial and local actors, on the pretext that all details are 'routine' implementation matters. Discussion on China's rural tax reform in this chapter shows that central actors could not assume local officials would 'auto-pilot' and work out the details independently, especially if local officials themselves are part of the problem to be addressed. Given what is noted above on the local role in decision-making, the challenge is, obviously, to figure out how much, and which part, of the details the central needs to decide itself and how much, and what, it may comfortably leave for the local levels to 'fill the gap'. The answer to this critical decision is necessarily context-specific, depending on the substantive issues being pursued, the goal chosen and the historical baseline situation. The important principle is, however, that this decision – of how much and what to decide itself and what and how much to delegate – lies squarely with the central actor. In other words, the central government needs to accept *explicitly* a *responsibility* to make this judgement, applies itself to make the best possible judgement and be ready to revise it whenever necessary.

The central actor is thus obliged to define the goal of action, delineate the ground rules of behaviour and to design means to monitor implementation. It is the duty of the central actor to make sure that the parameters it has laid down are fit, taking into account of, and despite, possible adaptations at the local level. In other words, the national parameters prevailing at any point of time should *enable* as well as *regulate* collaborative local actions, including actions seeking improvements of the parameters themselves. The two sets of roles hence interact and support one another in actual operation, while being analytically distinct with obvious boundaries.[59]

3 Embedded institutionalization
Sustaining reform effects*

The very definitive features of institutions – permanence and path dependence (David 1985, 1986; Arthur 1989) – make institutional change contingent upon the emergence of *alternative* institutionalization processes. Apart from executing changes to a pre-existing, durable pattern, the changed, new order also needs to sustain.[1] Without this new process of institutionalization, the new-found changes would require continuous interventions to sustain and can become unstable, including a possible relapse to a variant of the previous situation.[2] In other words, actions *alone* will not suffice to sustain the changes originally resultant from the actions.

Then what more is required? What constitutes the institutionalization process that serves to sustain change? Making changes last has been a major preoccupation among observers of the Chinese rural tax reforms unfolding since the late 1990s. The reform targeted the heavy extractions imposed on the rural populations and demanded substantial reduction of the range and level of fees and taxes. Many were sceptical of its chance of success, however. One popular theme of discourse maintained that the heavy tax burden was historically and institutionally embedded, that previous attempts to relieve peasants' burden, dating back to the dynastic times, had all failed, and that this latest intervention was, subsequently, unlikely to make any genuine, and sustained, impact (Qin 1997, 2000).[3] Ironically, the reform had in fact made considerable successes, including the 'disappearance' of the Agriculture Tax nationwide in 2006.[4] Such reform achievements worked to *aggravate*, rather than ameliorate, the worry over sustainability. The bigger a difference the reform initiatives produced *initially*, it seemed, the larger was the probability, among the conventional perception, that these actions could cause counteracting responses from within the status quo, to the effect that the initial impacts could be neutralized and outweighed, further actions for change made difficult, and the reform grinding to a halt and eventually backtracked.[5] Such a scenario fits perfectly with path dependence arguments: actions and initiatives – in the form of 'reforms' – are insufficient to change the course of deep-rooted, institutionally entrenched behavioural patterns.

But why is it so? What makes existing practices so resilient and attempted reforms to change them so difficult to sustain? If, according to the theoretical literature, institutional change requires the institutionalization of the new changes to complete, then what makes this institutionalization process possible? In the case of the Chinese rural tax reform, there was the perception that the objective of the reform – reduction of peasants' burden – would undercut the interests of local officials (Wedeman 1997; Bernstein and Lü 2003; Yep 2004).[6] These interests would need to be compensated, so follows the argument, if the reform was to succeed, and peasants' burden not to rebound. The central government had, to this aim, formulated two measures, namely local administrative restructuring and downsizing, and the provision of fiscal subsidies through central transfer payments. The intended objective of downsizing was explicitly to reduce total local government expenditures and thus the need for excessive extractions from peasants, with central fiscal subsidy as an incentive or facilitation device.[7]

This dual approach – injecting more fiscal resources from above into local coffers and making downsizing mandatory for local governments – had obvious limits, however. First, the new monies made available were necessarily limited and thus insufficient relative to the scale of tax burden reduction required.[8] In the words of a central official, 'the appetite in the localities for central transfers is insatiable. Central coffers simply cannot fill up a bottomless pit' (Author's interviews, Beijing, 2002). Central injection of monies would have, therefore, at most a partial effect in terms of compensation. Second, it was questionable whether the sustainability problem could be sufficiently met by reducing the size of local government at the township level. The idea behind downsizing was to eliminate altogether the source of overspending, namely the township officials, or the 'excess' of them. If burdens may rebound because township officials lived on extractions, then downsizing would remove, it was thought, a major source of pressure for burdens to go up. Such logic had, in part, contributed to a heated debate recently in China over the status of townships as an independent level of government.[9] This logic was deceptively simple, however. Past practice has seen governments expand regardless of previous downsizing, and official establishment figures had at best a disjointed relevance with actual strength of staff (Author's interviews, Beijing, 2002; D.L. Yang 2001: 19–45; Brodsgaard 2002). Empirical studies had also raised doubts as to whether downsizing, if achieved, could produce any saving, at least in the short to medium term (Li 2004). As Li (2006a) and others had pointed out, there were inherently structural limits to the degree of local government downsizing in poorer regions.[10]

Chapter 2 observes that the central government's approach to the sustainability issue was embedded in a dualistic framework of analysis, and burden reduction was defined largely as a matter of agency control. Further to this, the current chapter offers an alternative perspective emanating from local experience. In an aggressive programme of cadre reforms in a central China county – Xian-an District in Hubei Province – the chapter sees the potential that rural tax reforms – and its goal of reducing peasants' burden – may be sustained not through cost-saving exclusively but through a variety of avenues. The chapter observes that cadre reform had enabled the county to attract additional fiscal resources from senior government levels. The reform also produced some cost-saving. More importantly, the chapter contends, the cadre reform had had a positive impact on the capacity and propensity of local officials to adjust to the new requirements demanded of governments in the broader context of transitions to market economy. Through transforming the 'structure of interests' of local officials, the cadre reform could subsequently work its way to help sustain the rural tax reform.

Reducing peasants' burden in Xian-an

Xian-an District had a modest economy and a rural household income level of about the national, and provincial, average.[11] Similar to many local governments, it was dependent on net fiscal inflows from upper levels to finance its rising expenditure bills.[12] The county-district commenced the rural tax reform in the second half of 2002, as part of a provincial led development. Here two features are noted of the reform in Xian-an: (1) there was a quite handsome reduction in peasants' burden, attracting praise from provincial authorities; (2) the county secured a high level of compensation in terms of incoming transfer payments.

High burden reduction

The county registered almost instant success in achieving the reform objective in 2002, cutting peasants' burden by 56.7 per cent when compared to 2001, and 66.9 per cent relative to 1999.[13] In 2003, peasants' burden dropped by a further 9 per cent over the 2002 level. Table 3.1 shows the details.

Table 3.1 Peasants' burden in Xian-an (million yuan)

	1999 (pre-reform)	2001 (pre-reform)	2002 (post-reform)	2003 (post-reform)
A Centrally endorsed burden	44.7	37.1	22.9	20.8
B Provincially endorsed add-ons	4.8	0.2	0	0
C Local add-ons (*luan shoufei*)	19.6	15.6	0	0
A + B + C Total peasants' burden (A + B + C)	69.1	52.9	22.9	20.8
Reduction rate (%)	n.a.	n.a.	66.9 (over 1999) 56.7 (over 2001)	70 (over 1999) 60.7 (over 2001) 9 (over 2002)

Source: Author's interviews (2004).

A few explanations of the concept, and coverage, of peasants' burden are in order here. First, the scope of peasants' burden, as used in official statistics, did not cover all revenues collected from peasants. Excluded from Table 3.1 are various taxes, fees and charges that did not 'target specifically the rural population', but imposed on economic activities and public services generally – and thus also paid by peasants both before and after the rural tax reform. Examples were school-related fees (books and stationery, boarding and meals, etc.), road maintenance fee, motor cycle licence fee and value-added taxes. In the case of the last item, for instance, peasants needed to pay value-added taxes, as urban dwellers did, when they bought and sold agricultural and consumer products (State Council No. 92 (1991); Author's interviews, Wuhan, 2004).[14]

Second, the scope of peasants' burden, apart from the exclusions above, constituted three concentric circles – central, provincial and sub-provincial – reflecting the different sources authorizing the extraction.[15] On the first circle, the centrally endorsed peasants' burden, pre-reform, included six categories: (1) Agriculture Taxes and surtaxes, (2) the three village levies, (3) the five township levies, (4) Slaughter Tax, (5) education surcharges and (6) education fund-raising.[16] Before the reform provincial government could also promulgate fees for peasants (e.g. the rural flood-control water charges in Hubei) and these constituted the second tier.[17] A third tier of peasants' burden comprised fees imposed by sub-provincial authorities, which were, in theory, illegitimate. These were described as the 'local add-ons', as shown in Table 3.1. These figures were normally not reported, thus not available, if not for a local survey conducted on the eve of the tax reform in 2002 (Author's interviews, 2004). Furthermore, the first- and second-tier revenues reported in Table 3.1 would need to be adjusted downwards by approximately 20 per cent to as high as one-third to take into account the failure in tax collection, as part of the 'abandoned land syndrome' and outgoing migrant labour.[18] The impact was that the actual burden reduction, based on revenues actually collected before and after the reform, would be smaller than the official rate.

Bearing in mind these complications, the official burden reduction rate of some 60 per cent (as in Table 3.1) was still three times as high as the national requirement.[19] The local leadership also closely followed the reform-related performance indicators the provincial government imposed, and won the 'distinguished performance' provincial award (*shuigai xianjin danwei*).[20] However, as noted above, the considerable success in burden reduction also brought the issue of sustainability to the forefront. If Xian-an could, and did, cut rural extractions by more than one-half in a single year, what other things had it also done, or needed to do, if such initial achievement was to last?

High compensation

This question is partly answered by the remarkably high compensation rate, measured in terms of the proportion of transfer payments to the lost revenue from *legitimate* burdens, that Xian-an had obtained subsequent to the tax reform. Table 3.2 gives the details.

Table 3.2 Transfer payments under rural tax-for-fee reform in Xian-an (million yuan)

	2002	2003
Reduction of total burdens R (A + B + C) (over 2001)	30.0	32.1
Reduction of legitimate burdens R (A + B) (over 2001)	14.4	16.3
Transfer payments (TP)	16.3	19.5
TP as % of R (A + B + C)	54.3%	60.7%
TP as % of R (A + B)	113.0%	119.6%

Source: Author's interviews (2004).

Two observations flow from Table 3.2. First, the loss in revenue in terms of 'legitimate burdens' was more than compensated with inflows from central and provincial coffers, at 120 per cent in 2003, and 113 per cent in 2002. These were extraordinarily high levels of compensation, bearing in mind that Guangdong Province, whose provincial budget was three times as large as Hubei's – and thus was in a much better position to give more compensation to localities – in 2003 reported a compensation rate of *just* 70–95 per cent (Author's interviews, Guangzhou, 2004).

Second, despite the high compensation rate, there was still considerable shortfall of some 40 per cent if local add-ons were included in the calculation. Available information indicates that *total* reduction of burdens, which would include the 'illegitimate' local add-ons, amounted to some 30 per cent of pre-reform local expenditure, almost doubling the share of 'legitimate burdens'.[21] It was plainly clear that the rural tax reform posed a substantial pressure on local government finances, given the historical existence of local add-ons, and the exclusion of these in the calculation of compensation through transfer payments.

Table 3.3 shows the three categories of transfer payments the county received under the rural tax reform. First is a fixed amount of 'regular' transfer payments coming largely out of central coffers. Its intended purpose was to make up for the *structural* shortfall of local revenue resultant of reform, since the reform mandated a slash of fees formerly authorized by central authorities. Its calculation followed a standard, nationally devised, formula taking into account the gap between 'regular' revenues and budgeted expenditures at the township and village levels, and covered basically the loss of revenue from those 'legitimate' burdens.[22] 'Non-regular' revenues – those illegitimately imposed local fees and charges – were not included in the calculation and would go uncompensated.

A second, smaller category is 'transitional' payments, aimed at facilitating the process of downsizing in local governments. As mentioned previously, the rural tax reform package required local governments, as a collateral measure, to reduce staff numbers and cut administrative costs. In practice, downsizing incurred *more* cost, as departing staff were generally paid in full (salaries plus allowances) during the first 3 years of absence, if not even more.[23] A survey of records found that the central government had provided for special subsidies to sweeten the process as early as 2001. Central documents issued in late 2001 prescribed that central

Table 3.3 Rural tax-for-fee transfer payments, Xian-an (million yuan)

	2002	2002 (%)	2003	2003 (%)
'Regular' payments	11.3	70	11.3	58
'Transitional' payments	2.2	13	2.2	12
One-off payments	3.2	20	6.0	30
Total	16.7	103	19.5	100

Source: Author's interviews (2004).

coffers would subsidize, for 3 years, the payroll expenses for 'streamlining' (*fenliu*) staff who were formerly employed within the official establishment (*bianzhine*), while provinces were to shoulder the costs of those staff employed extra-establishment (*bianzhiwai*).[24] Implementation was apparently slow, however. Ministry of Finance officials still expressed reluctance to commit central funds to that effect as of 2002/03. 'It was up to the localities', one senior national finance official had said, 'to cut costs to cater for the loss of income previously obtained with problematic means' (Author's interviews, Beijing, 2002). At the provincial level, the mentioning of central transitional payments had to wait until 2003 in a provincial report on the reform (Wang 2003: 9–10).[25]

The third category, the 'one-off' payment, was solely financed within the province. In Xian-an, as Table 3.3 shows, this was an even larger sum than the transitional payments. It was also the only variable category out of the three, with the amount in 2003 doubling that in 2002.[26] Its share of the total transfer payments soared from 20 per cent in 2002 to 30 per cent in 2003. Despite its rising importance, this third category was not mentioned in provincial official documents until late 2003.[27] There were also no clear guidelines to govern its allocation. Local officials explained that the 6-million-yuan sum in 2003, attributable to several sources, was generally a result of lobbying and bargaining with provincial officials.[28]

> Provincial officials did not tell us how they came to this figure [the 6 million yuan]. There was no pre-set, and transparent, formula to do the calculation. If there had been one, all localities would have tailored their work according to the criteria in order to secure the monies. The province could not, then, be able to honour the commitments. It simply did not have sufficient monies to give to all those who met the required standards. Indeed this 'one-off' payment is very much an uncertainty. We don't know for sure whether it will still exist this year, much less how much we can secure …
>
> (Author's interviews 2004)

The rule of the game was, therefore, particularistic lobbying through achieved results. Superior levels were persuaded that good work in policy implementation merited additional rewards, though they retained the liberty to change the criteria. As it turned out, Hubei Provincial Government announced a separate category of 'merit-based' payment applicable to *all* counties as from 2004.[29] The criteria of award remained opaque, but the payments were now universally applied to all localities, or at least the existence of the payments itself was made known to all. To this extent, Xian-an's successful implementation of government reforms, and lobbying for fiscal support in return, has had an impact on higher level policy.[30]

Cadre reforms: building capacity or cutting costs?

What kind of government reforms had brought such substantial fiscal reward to Xian-an? Commencing in 1999, Xian-an's government reforms quickly attracted national and provincial attention. In 3 years, state-salaried personnel went down by 25 per cent, and bold moves were initiated to adjust the role and structure of township governments.[31] These reforms formed the backbone of the latest local government reform at the township level across Hubei Province as from 2004.[32] However, as the following discussion points out, the important implication of these government reforms did not reside in the direct savings to personnel expenses they may bring, but in their perceived potential, as reflected in the discourse on the reform, in reconstituting local officials from 'targets' to *agents* of change.

Downsizing had, traditionally, been held to hold the key of success of rural tax reform, and government reforms in general. The reason behind this almost sole focus on downsizing was the perception that overstaffing was *the* problem in government, so that downsizing became a natural response. Along this line, *the* question for sustainability of rural tax reform became this: could local government be made slimmer, so that peasants' burden would not rebound? But as noted previously, to the extent that downsizing had aimed at cutting bills, this had more often than not failed. The 1998 State Council downsizing was an utter failure in this respect – central expenditure on staff-related items *increased* in the few years after downsizing, rather than decreased.[33] Studies on local government also discovered a similar phenomenon: reform costed (Li 2004). A senior central official in charge of the policy admitted to the author that despite official rhetoric, downsizing exercises nationwide had, by and large, failed to produce genuine saving.

> The reality is, we have found out, after the three-year transitional period, the state coffers still have to pay the streamlined [*fenliu*] staff, though the original plan was to have zero staff costs by then. It is thus unrealistic to expect direct saving from reducing the number of serving staff. Saving may be achieved only when there is a high level of political mobilization – under such circumstances people may feel obliged to leave without compensation. But this is quite out of the question given the socio-political climate of the present day.
>
> (Author's interviews, Beijing, 2004)

Reflecting the focus on payroll was the discourse on 'subsistence finance' (*qifan caizheng*). Since the 1990s, it was commonplace to find reports complaining of the large portions of local government budgets being 'eaten up' by payroll bills and staff-related costs, leaving too little monies for investment (e.g. Wang 1998; Liu 2000; Gao *et al.* 2003; Wang 2004). These reports invariably focused on the dwindling share of 'productive' expenditures (*shengchanxing zhichu*) in the local budget, as against administrative and policy expenditures (*xingzheng shiyexing zhichu*).[34] However, it is misleading to take the ratio between these two broad categories as an indication of the size of state-salaried personnel, and of the efficiency of government. A closer look at the statistics tells that staff costs formed part of the 'administrative and policy' expenditures only. For instance, of the total local education expenditure in 2001, payroll costs for teaching and administrative staff at schools accounted for 62.7 per cent, with the rest being housekeeping (*gongwu fei*) costs (8.8 per cent), operational (*yewu fei*) costs (6.5 per cent), purchase of equipments (7.1 per cent), minor renovation (8.7 per cent), reception and entertainment (0.4 per cent) and others (5.7 per cent).[35] On the whole, payroll accounted for around 55–60 per cent of total provincial budgetary expenditures.[36] Nationally, the share of state payroll costs in the gross domestic product (GDP), at 8.5 per cent as of 2002, was on a par with a sample of OECD and developing countries.[37] Ultimately, the concern in question thus appeared to be not one of overstaffing but of non-performance of existing government personnel. This observation was confirmed in the author's discussions in China:

> The issues are more complex than mere downsizing. There are too many and too few [people] in the government at the same time – too many at the time of distributing benefits, but too few when assigning tasks. Motivated and capable staff is in short supply.
>
> (Author's interviews, Beijing, 2002)

If downsizing cannot possibly cut costs, what benefits, in terms of improving government efficiency and performance, may it bring? On this point, Xian-an's former Party Secretary, Song Yaping, had this to say, shortly after he was promoted to the provincial government,[38]

> Lack of economic development is often not due to the relative lack of resources – natural resources, capital, etc., but to an out-of-date government system wherein the government is used to perform many [unnecessary] tasks. We are stuck with a large fleet of state salaried personnel ill-adapted to the needs of a market economy. But the crux of the matter lies less in having 'too many' cadres but in what they should do. After months of investigation in my early days in office [in Xian-an], I concluded that to achieve development we had to first reform ourselves: our government system, our job as government, and our cadres.
>
> (Author's interviews 2004)

Government reforms in Xian-an thus focused firmly on reforming – not just reducing – the cadres. Some headcounts were slashed through downsizing and administrative restructuring, as elsewhere nationwide, but a lot of emphasis was placed on changing the 'outlook and mindsets' of cadres. This they did through an innovative scheme of 'selective exposure inculcation'.

Sending-off cadres to coastal cities

From 2001 to 2004, over 800 cadres were sent to various coastal cities to work for 2 years.[39] The scheme of sending cadres to 'stand on their own feet' in coastal cities attracted the attention of the national media a few months after the first batch of cadres left home. Unlike previous cadre training programmes, the 'sending off' programme did not arrange 'postings' for cadres. Instead, participating cadres were expected to join the fleet of migrant workers in the cities they went to, securing jobs on their own. Two among the first batch of 187 sent-off cadres talked about their experience in a popular programme of Central Television in June 2001. One cadre, a township party secretary before he left for Shenzhen, described his experience as commensurate with a 'cultural shock':

> How I eventually secured a job there [in Shenzhen] taught me an important lesson: that we have to work our way to success. Success does not come easily. But when it does, after much frustration and numerous reattempts, you understand that it is really *yours*, and you deserve it. One can't feel more satisfaction. I was quite confident when I first arrived there. I thought of landing a job at a senior management level in an enterprise, possibly as the assistant to the General Manager, or as Deputy General Manager. I applied for four jobs at that level at Shenzhen's labour centre on my first visit. I waited for several days and there was no reply. My friends then told me that employers were looking for a helping hand, not a boss. I gathered, not without some struggle, that I needed to reposition myself. I then deleted my record as the Township Party Secretary from my resume and adjusted downwards my expectations in the job applications. I revised down for several rounds more before I successfully secured my present job of administrative manager.[40]

Another cadre, also a township official, elaborated on what he perceived as the major difference between work at home and in Shenzhen:

> In Shenzhen, we realize what our limitations are. The gap in standards between home and there is stark and clear. Back home, we used to have a lot of meetings. When we had to get something done, we called together a bunch of cadres and formulated a plan. We then assigned various tasks to others. The next step was to convene another meeting after some time to hear reports and examine the progress of implementation, and if necessary to revise the work plans. We spent a lot of time talking and reviewing. Work in Shenzhen is quite different. There we not only plan, but also execute the tasks ourselves. We have to think carefully and in great detail during all stages of market research, operational planning, implementation, and

evaluation. It is a lot tougher compared to what we were used to. The lesson is: if you cannot deliver, others will quickly take over your job!

(Xian-an District Party Committee Secretariat 2003: 152)

The sent-off cadres thus learned from their 'near-real-life' experience of being a 'free-floating' individual, unprotected by their units, looking for jobs in competitive labour markets in the more developed regions of China. To ensure maximal effect of 'training', the scheme had four major parameters.[41] First was the self-help principle in finding a job. There was no prearranged posting or secondment between units. Second, the scheme cast a wide net and was intended for all cadres on the state payroll, with the exception of school teachers and medical personnel, who were under 40 years of age and had a post-high school qualification.[42] Third was the voluntarity principle. Cadres joined the scheme through voluntary application, with each unit distributed a quota of available places in accordance with their pool of eligible cadres. Fourth, cadres were expected to return to the original units after 2-year 'training'. To symbolize this continuous relationship and to cushion the harshness of the new environment, a basic monthly living allowance of 150 yuan was paid to participating cadres throughout the 'training' period.

Xian-an's leaders admitted that many cadres found the scheme harsh and difficult to live with. Internal investigations discovered about 5 per cent, or 34, of the 646 participating cadres between 2001–3 did not leave home. Some started small businesses in the vicinity; others simply stayed idle. On the other hand, some successfully 'transformed' cadres opted not to return after the 2-year 'training'. As of 2003, 47 had extended their 'training' for more than a year, after the original 2-year term had expired. Table 3.4 gives more details.

While some former cadres chose to stay in their new positions in the coastal cities – they had apparently adapted to their new roles – the majority did return to Xian-an after 2 years. Table 3.4 shows that 165, or 72 per cent, of the first two batches of 227 sent-off cadres returned. A considerable share of these, especially those of the first batch, was subsequently placed in strategic positions at district and township levels.[43] Those extending their stay also outnumbered those

Table 3.4 Sent-off cadres (2001–4)

Joining the scheme		Due to return (as of 2/2004)	Returned	Extended 'training'	Staying home
2001	187	Yes		47	
2002 (1)	40	Yes	165	18	
2002 (2)	203	Yes	Being arranged		
2003	216	No			34
2004	200	No			
Total	846	430	165	65	34

Source: Author's interviews (2004).

opting to stay home, suggesting that the scheme had so far attracted more motivated cadres than unwilling participants.

After five batches in a row, the scheme was tightened up in early 2004. First, to raise the quality of participants, the voluntarity principle was to be more strictly applied. Units would face a severe penalty should they use the scheme to penalize 'unpopular' cadres. Second, to motivate quality cadres to join the scheme, returning cadres would be given priority, where applicable, in job assignments to positions of leadership. In view of the dwindling pool of eligible cadres, those who had participated would be eligible for a second round.[44] Third, overstayers would not be paid the monthly stipend 3 years after the original training term ended. These cadres would remain on the official establishment and they could, theoretically, return to retire. Fourth, to improve communications with the sent-off cadres, a website was launched and individual electronic mail boxes were installed.

The scheme contributed to some direct savings. The sent-off cadres, during their 'training' period, were temporarily taken off the strength of their units. Each participating cadre was entitled to an annual stipend of 1,800 yuan, against an average annual payroll of 10,000 yuan had they not joined the scheme. The average balance of having 400 cadres 'sent off' (an average of 200 participating cadres every year, for 2 years) meant an average annual saving of 3.4 million yuan, or 1.7 per cent of total fiscal expenditure in 2003.[45]

There were also indirect economic gains. Returned cadres brought home extended social networks and investors. In 2003, investment projects directly attributable to returnees brought in capital of 75 million yuan. More indirectly, but no less unimportant, was the publicity generated by media attention on the scheme, through nationally televised programmes and press reports. The following reflects the sentiment:

> The Central Television has followed our scheme for a full three years since 2001. It released recently [in early February 2004] a four-part documentary totalling 80 minutes. This was great publicity for us. If one minute of advertisement time on national television programme costs 60,000 yuan, we have earned a great deal.
>
> (Author's interviews 2004)

Cutting costs or recruiting new investors *per se* were welcome, and these were readily employed in official publicity on the reforms. Notwithstanding such material benefits, senior leaders stressed in interviews that the intended objective of the scheme was more about enhancing cadres' capacity to command changes required for the new market economy and new tasks of government. The sentiment against a pedantic calculation of costs and gains was apparent in Party Secretary Song's remarks, made in the context of social insurance reform, another major measure in the local reform programme:

> We know the government needs to pay its share of contributions to the social insurance scheme, as employer for state salaried personnel. Doing so has

cost us additional expenditures. But one should not see this as something negative. When assessing reform we should not focus merely on flows of monies, and on annual budgetary balances. We need to embrace a broader vision, and *there are different ways to do the calculations*. For instance, what if we do not establish social insurance, and thus avoid the additional budgetary expenditures now? The government would still have to pay for pensions when cadres retire in the future. With the insurance scheme in place, all of us start contributing to retirement funds from now on. More importantly, because we have erected a safety net in advance through social insurance, it is easier to conduct other reforms, like downsizing, thus making it possible to gain many other benefits.

(Author's interviews 2004, emphasis added)

Mr Song was explicit that the major objective of sending cadres away was *not* about downsizing, though the programme also contributed to that effect. It was meant, in his words, 'to inculcate a new mindset, and change the attitudes, or orientations towards work and perception of risks amongst the cadres'.

We need to prepare our people if our reforms [fiscal, government, etc.] are to succeed. The big context is the development of market economy. Our government institutions, and people, must change to cope with, and fit into, the needs of market economy. Downsizing is part of the change but a narrow and sole focus on the size of government and downsizing can mislead us. What is critical is what the government does; whether it is delivering the 'right' services or adding nuisances/stumbling blocks. Sending our cadres to work in the coastal cities – where the market economy was the most developed in China – will help to achieve the transformation of government – make sure the government do the right thing – through changing the mindsets of our people.

(Author's interviews 2005)

Did the scheme achieve its desired objectives? It could be premature to attempt assessment given the recency of the reform. The elusive nature of the objective – changing the mindset and attitudes of cadres – also makes assessment difficult and vulnerable to criticism. The following remarks by a first-batch returnee, who had hence been promoted, give some indication as to how at least some participants, or the more successful ones, perceived the results, and the challenge, of the reform:

Our [government] reform is not, ultimately, about downsizing; or how many cadres were sent off to work in the coastal cities. It is about enhancing change in how people think. I can observe some differences during our chats with outsiders. We are less interested in knowing your rank, but more in what you have done in your work – like what kind of development you have helped to bring to the locality under your jurisdiction, this sort of thing …

On this the differences between returnees and those who do not have similar experience are obvious. The world 'out there' is large … My two-year experience as a sent-out cadre has left a deep imprint on me. Those were the days when I felt the most free and 'light-hearted' in all my life – I finished my duties and there was no excessive supervision, eyes looking from behind my shoulders. After work I could do whatever I wanted, without fear or apprehension. This has a great impact on how we returnees, or at least myself, see work and life. Before when we received an instruction we tended to implement it hierarchically. If you didn't oblige you'll have trouble keeping your job. Now we place more emphasis on communication and feedback. First we'll ask what resources and from whom we could have to help with this work, and what are the consequences if it fails to work out well. We are more ready to listen and enquire into the details of a situation – in other words more 'humanized' and less 'crude'. I could see this new attitude in work has already contributed a lot to the relatively smooth progress in our downsizing and restructuring reforms. We are not a well-off county and cannot afford generous sweeteners. Last year in the middle of a restructuring exercise I stayed up 'til the early hours talking to a few colleagues who had yet to agree to the plan. When one colleague eventually agreed to sign the chapters he asked why I hadn't left and had some sleep. It was hard for an individual to say 'goodbye' to a unit where he has worked for decades, and naturally people needed time to give considerations to it. We should have a lot more patience.

(Author's interview 2005)

Conclusion

Much in the explanation of institutional change involves accounting for sustainability, and the lack of it (or more precisely the discontinuation of a previously sustained pattern). Friedland and Alford (1991: 256–9) premise such processes on the contradictions between institutions. As institutions operate on different logics, the conflicts arise when institutions interact and propel political struggles between groups and organizations that lead to changes within each of the institutions. The interaction between the market and the family, in different institutional fields, is one example: 'Capitalist markets may depend upon families in order to minimize the cost of supplying a labor force, but at the same time, the labor market may undercut the capacity of families to support reproduction' (Friedland and Alford 1991: 256). Interactions between the institutions of family and the market serve to produce, sustain or cause further changes in each of them. In interactions between segments of the same field – fiscal institution for example – reform initiatives by Chinese county-level leaders to rationalize sub-county segments of the fiscal system may undercut the county's fiscal autonomy efforts targeting higher levels of the system (Li 2005a: 101–2). Institutional change is endogenously embedded in the interaction between parallel institutionalization processes, mediated by conflicts in interests therein.

The story told in this chapter suggests that sustainability of rural tax reform in a central China county is likely to be contingent, if partially, upon some specific developments in the arena of government reform. Burden reduction could not be sufficiently sustained through changes within the fiscal field alone, and increasing transfer payments in particular, because of the limited capacity of the central state coffers and the 'insatiable' demands for local expenses under the current interest configuration. Neither could downsizing be a solution, if only that downsizing costs more than is saved. Pilot cadre reforms in Hubei pointed to a possible opening to sustaining changes in the rural fiscal arena from developments *outside* the fiscal institution. The 'sending off cadres' programme cherished an ambitious if also elusive agenda: to change 'targets' of reform, as local officials often so described themselves, into *agents* of reform. There were initial indications that the scheme had had some impact in this respect. Returning cadres came to perceive their roles somewhat differently, and were more efficient in delivering their duties. If behavioural change requires more time to mature, changes as reflected in discursive communications are easier to note. The scheme had injected new *expectations* on, as well as self-perceptions of, the returned cadres and increasingly on the entire fleet of cadres – and thus pressure to meet them. Nationwide the focus of reform had moved to reforming the government itself, as pressure to sustain early achievements in the rural tax reform was mounting. The Xian-an reform had in this context, having secured endorsement from the provincial leadership, contributed to deepening government reforms throughout the province, as well as attracting national publicity. The task was daunting and the stakes were high. The wider application of local experience was often slippery as what worked for a locality, given the multiplicity of contingency factors, may not work for the rest. That said, this chapter shows the processes in a locality, unfolding over two institutional fields, whereby the challenge of sustaining change in an entrenched state practice could *possibly* be met.

4 State and market in public service provision

Opportunities and traps*

International experience tells that public services often fail to work for those in need. A recent edition of the World Development Report series, *Making Services Work for Poor People*, identifies three interrelated 'legs' of accountability relationships upon which effective service delivery for poor people hinges (World Bank 2003: 6–10) – relationships between, respectively, citizen and policymaker, policymaker and service provider, and citizen/client and service provider. First, when setting policy objectives, policymakers need to know what are in demand by citizens: what, and how much, is preferred under what circumstances. Second, policymakers need to convey effectively their policy decisions to service delivery agents, and monitor their performance. Third, users of services need to be sufficiently motivated and feel able to provide feedback on service delivery performance. Adequate incentive structures need to be in place in all three 'legs' to make things work for the poor: service delivery agents will care about their clients; the poor will bother to apply effort to demand improvements instead of withdrawing from the system and policymakers will seriously examine users' feedback in the interest of improving the services.

The Chinese situation scores badly against these expectations. The authoritarian political system has so far thwarted the development of 'voice' mechanisms vital to the demand-side information. Policies are often decided behind closed doors despite the 'mass line' rhetoric which claims that official policy is a result of refining the demands of the people. The consequence is that the need for public services by the rural population – the peasants – has scarcely been researched and documented.[1] An indication of the dearth of demand-side knowledge is the recent, and belated, effort by the central government to gather information on peasants' needs, when 'touch-base' surveys on peasants' needs for services were hastily commissioned *after* the promulgation of a new policy in March 2006 to 'Construct the New Socialist Countryside' to increase rural services and spending (Author's interviews 2006).[2]

Even when policymakers get their objectives roughly right, implementation has been a major problem. Agency control is at best uneven, relying on costly methods to achieve compliance (Tsai 2007). On the client–agent front, the local rural public service units (PSUs) assigned the role of delivering public goods to rural residents often fail to do their job. As part of the authoritarian state bureaucracy, PSU officials tend to act more like 'masters' than service providers, and are more interested in imposing fees than in providing service. Two books have received international attention and become 'underground' best sellers in China – one by former township party secretary Li Changping in 2002 (*Telling the Truth to the Premier*) and the other by rural researchers Chen Guini and Chun Tao in 2004 (*A Survey of the Chinese Peasants*) – which contain vivid and compelling accounts of the abuses of local officials and PSU workers.

Serious as these problems of accountability deficit are, they are nevertheless not unique to the Chinese situation. Poor people in many developing countries have complained of the deplorable treatment they are offered (World Bank 2003: 4). Complicating things more is that while increased wealth and more public spending on service provision help, neither alone is sufficient to bring about desirable changes to benefit services to the poor (World Bank 2003: 35–42). More deep-seated changes in institutional arrangements (budget, political, administrative) are required. International experience shows that while such changes are difficult to come by in the first place, they are even more difficult to sustain over time.

Against this context this chapter looks in detail at a local reform programme in central China which, through institutional changes adjusting the role of government and the market, sought to align the incentives of rural service providers and to improve agency control by policymakers. The chapter will examine the processes and context of reform – why the attempt was made; who were behind it and how resistance to change was dealt with. Two thoughts underline the emphasis on *process*. First, there can be no success in bringing changes if people dare not try. Understanding how actors *initiate* change is, therefore, in itself important – part and parcel of understanding how successful changes may come about. Second, we may get to know more about *what* reforms can work to bring about improved services for the poor through a close examination of how reforms, in actual cases, made progress, and how resistance to change was overcome.

The rest of the chapter will proceed as follows. The next section outlines, briefly, the policy background of the PSU institutional reform, and in particular the burden-reducing rural tax reforms preceding it. I shall then discuss the objectives and reform designs of the PSU reform in Hubei Province of central China. The processes leading to the initiative will be dissected and major actors identified. I conclude with some preliminary observations on the reform's future prospects and implications for institutional reforms in general.

Chinese rural tax reforms and 'hollowing out' of local governments

During the past two decades, there have been various attempts to reform the Chinese public service sector. The efforts were, however, mostly piecemeal initiatives of individual ministries and local governments in 'lack of a well-developed overall strategy and coordination' (World Bank 2005b: 4). Results were at best mixed as new issues of equity and access problems emerged. Against this, the need to improve public service provision in the countryside has lately gained added urgency in the Chinese policy agenda. Looming large in this renewed salience are the rural tax reforms implemented nationwide since 2002, and subsequently the spectre of a 'hollowing-out' of rural local governments in the aftermath of the tax reforms.

The Chinese government started to contemplate the need to revamp the rural tax regime around the time of 1998, after nearly a decade of increasing tension between peasants and the grassroots-level governments and years of local reform experiments (see Chapter 1). The reform package addressed the underlying institutional problems superficially, however, if at all, and local officials, and those at the township level especially, were made the scapegoats for what went wrong. Cash-strapped local governments had historically relied on various kinds of local fees and surcharges to finance the bulk of local spending, including paying for the salaries of officials. Under the reform, such fees were no longer allowed, and local governments were also under severe pressure to downsize to reduce the demand for revenues to pay for staff. A stringent system of top-down monitoring was put in place to ensure local compliance, with the dispatch of provincial inspection teams to each and every county (see Chapter 6). The consequence was that the official target of burden reduction was achieved quickly, exceeding original expectations both in terms of speed and magnitude. At the same time, however, fears emerged as to how long such results could last, and rural public services were further depleted – causing outcries about the 'hollowing out' of local governments (Fu 2001; Heimer (Edin) 2004; Kennedy 2007; Li and Dong 2004). In some cases, maintaining the basic operation of government – such as paying for basic staff salaries, transport expenses, telephone fees for government offices – had become a challenge (see Chapter 6).

Ironically, as the reform to reduce state tax extraction on peasants succeeded in its original objectives, it also deepened the crisis in local governance as the supply and the quality of rural public services, which had been at a low level, received another blow. It was in this context that the central government eventually had to pick up the bill – through taking up more responsibility for some services which were hardest hit, for example, education and basic health care, culminating in the adoption of the 'Construct the New Socialist Countryside' new policy initiative in 2006.

The emphasis of rural policy from then on shifted from one of burden reduction to one of increasing rural public spending. In the 2006 national budget alone, 340 billion yuan was allocated to rural public services, an increase of 42 billion yuan from 2005. In 2007, rural public spending further increased to over 430 billion yuan and to 562 billion yuan (budgeted) in 2008.[3] The challenge is tremendous, however, given the breadth and depth of the 'service deficit' after long years of neglect. Increasing central spending on rural services requires a suitable administrative capacity at the local level to match. The pressures from the earlier rural tax reform had, however, ill prepared local governments for the new task. An obvious question is: can township governments pull themselves together to meet the additional demands upon them for more and better services, having been severely demoralized and stripped of personnel and local revenues? Conversely, can the new central resources made available in the 'new countryside' programme be put to their intended purposes to improve public services, rather than squandered by self-serving local officials? Given the deep-seated deficiencies in the system – weak agency control, lack of accountability to citizens and clients, passivity and helplessness of the clients – worries abound that the latest drive to improve rural public services, largely through an increase in public spending, may degenerate into yet another wasteful campaign of the 'Great Leap Forward' genre (Guo 2006; Li 2006a, 2006b). The stakes for institutional failures were high.

Public service unit reform: separation and agency control

Hubei Province in central China had seen high burden levels and was hard hit by the rural tax reforms.[4] It was thus perhaps not surprising to see reform experiments aiming at the deep-seated incentive and control problems, as pressures and difficulties *sometimes* motivate action (and innovation) (Chapters 1 and 3). The PSU reform started in early 2003 as a district-initiated experiment in Henggouqiao Town in Xian-an District, some 70 kilometres from Wuhan, the provincial capital.[5] The reform involved converting state-run public service agencies (in Chinese, *zhan-suo*, literally meaning (service) 'stations') at the township level into non-state-owned market entities, to which the township government would 'contract out' the delivery of rural public goods. Seen as a way to improve rural service provision at little additional cost, the reform was subsequently endorsed by provincial leaders and implemented throughout Hubei Province, in phases, from 2004 (Li and Yuan 2007).

Two key features of the Hubei reform are: (1) conversion of the state PSUs into non-state market players; (2) funding of rural public services being output based instead of input based. Through a structural separation of the township government as policymaker and non-state units as service provider, it has been argued, the government is more likely to focus on outcomes and goals and be less distracted by problems in delivery and implementation, resulting in more effective monitoring over the service delivery units (World Bank 2003: 98).

New market players

Arguably, the key measure in the reform was the conversion of 'ownership status' of the state PSUs. All township service units were to be first abolished, and then re-established as non-state 'service centres'. When this transfer from state to non-state units was completed – and workers in the new units were no longer government employees – township governments would, after a review of the scope of services, re-delegate the service delivery functions formerly performed

Table 4.1 Scope of Hubei public service unit (PSU) reform

	Henggouqiao Town	*Xian-an District*	*Hubei Province*
PSU staff nos.	141	1,065	70,000 +
Nos. of PSU	12	About 150	About 10,000

Sources: Author's interviews, Hubei (2004, 2006); Yuan (2009).

by the state agencies to the newly constituted units. A contract would be drawn specifying the scope and details of services, and how the units would be compensated.

When the reform started in Henggouqiao Town in 2003, 12 PSUs with a total of 141 staff members were affected. These comprised all service units directly under the town government with the exception of the medical centre, namely construction, housing management, husbandry and veterinary, transportation, justice, agricultural technology, agricultural mechanics, water works, rural economic management, family planning, cultural services and broadcasting. Education has been managed from the county level as from 2002 and thus was not included. Within a year or so, the reform was extended to cover 1,056 staff members in over 150 township PSUs across Xian-an District and subsequently across Hubei Province, affecting over 70,000 PSU staff (see Table 4.1).

A full metamorphosis, as envisaged in the reform design, comprised the following phases.[6] First was 'setting the ground'. A leading official from the township government was sent to the service agency to oversee the process. Account books were checked and assets and liabilities recorded. Pre-existing management problems in the agency were taken note of, and dealt with wherever possible. Extensive communications were held with existing staff to convey to them the reform plan, and what next to expect. 'Excessive' personnel who had joined the agency workforce without proper approval, that is, those 'temporary employees' without formal state cadre status, were 'counselled out'. The objective, in this initial phase, was to 'prepare the ground' for reform through rationalization. In the second phase, the scope of public service functions of the agency was clarified, given the often murky boundary of public *vis-à-vis* profit-making services in the actual operation of the units. The legal responsibility to provide the public service to the community was then 'transferred' to an office within the township government. Third was abolition of the township service agency. With its public service duties transferred away, the agency as a state unit was formally abolished. Fourth was the change of status of the agency personnel. Compensation akin to 'severance payments', based on the length of service and level of pre-existing pay, was calculated and dispensed to the permanent workers, whose status as government personnel ended at that point. Fifth was the formation of new non-state legal entities, either as enterprises or social organizations. To facilitate their development and to 'sweeten' reform, assets of the former agencies, such as buildings and equipment, might be 'lent', or simply assigned, to the new units.

Sixth was the contracting out of public service delivery from the township government to this newly constituted organization. A contract was drawn up specifying expected outputs, funding level and methods of disbursements, assessment criteria and timing and so on. Apart from fulfilling the public service duties, the new agency was encouraged to undertake other market-oriented activities to buttress its income.

The most difficult part in the above process was the fourth step – individual workers severing their government cadre status permanently. For many, the status of government cadres brought them not only a stable job and source of income but also substantial formal powers, informal influence and perks. Resistance to change came from both sides of the employment relationship: service workers did not want to leave the government ranks; and already hard-pressed county and township leaders did not want to spend their stringent budgetary resources on the 'severance payments'. Indeed, the provincial government waited until 2005 to offer county governments a subsidy of 4,000 yuan for each township public service employee leaving the government ranks, as a move to mitigate resistance to reform across the province, which was about one-fourth of the average severance payments paid eventually. In the face of the lack of fiscal support from above and yet the political pressure to implement reform, local officials resorted to all kinds of tactics, from delayed and phased implementation to half-baked implementation.

In Xian-an District, of the total 1,000 plus PSU workers affected by the reform, just under half (48 per cent) left the ranks of government in accordance with the original reform design. Many workers (44 per cent) adopted the 'traditional' methods of downsizing used in previous rounds of administrative reforms – so-called 'streamlining' (or, in Chinese, *fen-liu*). Streamlined workers continued to receive about 60–70 per cent of their basic pay for 3 years during which they are expected to find alternative employment or start their own businesses. About 7 per cent of workers went into various retirement arrangements.

In other counties, the difficulty in implementing reform was even more marked. In an extreme case, almost none of the PSU workers underwent the formal severance process in Jianli County,[7] where peasant burdens used to be very high. The staff were treated as 'streamlined' (*fenliu*) staff, as in previous downsizing exercises, and continued to work in the reconstituted PSUs. A hybrid situation existed: non-state-owned PSUs and staff retaining their status as government employees and still drawing salaries from the government coffers.

Funding sources and mechanism

A problem with rural PSUs in China and elsewhere in the developing world is the low quality of service despite a massive body of staff. This has produced a vicious cycle: with salaries consuming most of the resources available and little left to pay for necessary operational costs (such as equipment, running costs), workers find their hands tied in doing their job. Morale is low; 'ghost workers'

Table 4.2 Family planning services: performance criteria, Town X, County Y (2005)

Item	Content	Weight (%)
1	Report monthly to Town Government of work progress through written reports	12
2	Publicize family planning policy and knowledge on eugenics, birth control and health care, reaching 80% of households	20
3	Regularly survey the 'prospective target' of family planning services; deliver post-operation after-care services	28
4	Distribute free medicine and birth control devices, reaching 80% of households	20
5	Train staffs on policy and technical know-how	20
	Total (%)	100
	Contracted, and paid, funding	RMB 46,700

Table 4.3 Water works and irrigation services: performance criteria, Town X, County Y (2005)

Item	Content	Weight (%)
1	Advise government on flood preventive work	12
2	Revise and improve the flood prevention plans; on duty round the clock during the flood period; ensure smooth and effective communication with all relevant parties, especially during flood period	18
3	Implement anti-drought services for agriculture	10
4	Manage irrigation and water works facilities	10
5	Formulate plans, design, organize construction works, and manage the water works infrastructure and roads leading to villages	15
6	Protect and manage water resources, prevent pollution to water resources; ensure safety in drinking water	10
7	Provide technical advice and services on water works matters; arrange technical training activities at least once per year	8
8	Mediate disputes over water works within the town; ensure safety in water works	10
9	Other matters related to water works services delegated by the government	7
	Total (%)	100
	Contracted, and paid, funding	RMB 99,400

abound, as many collect pay without effective work. Finding a way to motivate performance hence underlies the second key measure in the Hubei PSU reform: public monies would henceforth finance the delivery of service directly rather than pay for maintenance costs of an agency. In the reform discourse, the phrase 'fund the service, not the personnel' (*yang shi* or *yang ren*) was coined in relation to output-based contracts. Tables 4.2 and 4.3 show the expected outputs in two service units, namely family planning (and birth control) and water works services.

The contracts sent a message that the newly constituted non-state service centres, while entrusted by local government with public service delivery, would have their performance watched closely. Any awarding of public funds was henceforth to be based strictly on performance. This was not easy to achieve, however. In many areas of public service, it is difficult to specify *what* exactly needs to be done, not to mention to decide whether a service has been delivered or performed effectively. Such insusceptibility to measurement and clear-cut specification is a characteristic intrinsic to the nature of the work involved (some classic examples are policing, teaching, counselling, learning to drive) which Scott (1998) describes as practical knowledge or 'mētis'. The World Bank (2003: 52–3) has noted the absurdity of being 100 per cent specific in the design of public service contracts, as previous 'work-to-rule' strikes by public service workers in various countries have amply demonstrated. In the Hubei cases described above, it might be more appropriate to quantify output requirements in family planning and birth control services than in the case of water works. But even in family planning, the assessment criteria apparently followed an implicitly 'negative' approach – whether rules were contravened, or some quantitative yardsticks had been met – rather than focusing directly on the quality of services. For example, the service contract required the family planning service centre to submit 12 written reports, one each month, to the Town Government on work progress (Table 4.2, performance item 1). This carried a weight of 12 per cent in the total performance required, with each monthly report accounting for 1 per cent. On the other hand, how well or badly the reports were written would not, apparently, affect the assessment. In water services, there was a sliding scale of incentives, according to which unsatisfactory work performance would lead to a cut in funding. But it is not clear how judgements regarding performance were made, what criteria were adopted and so on. Township governments were required to conduct periodic users' surveys to assess the views of residents as part of the assessment of the service centres, but how vigorous these surveys were conducted and how reliable the results were is an open question.[8] In any event, as noted in Tables 4.2 and 4.3, the contracted service amount was paid in full in both cases. The question arises as to what this implied for service delivery. To what extent did the contract have a genuine impact on service performance? How did the impact work out exactly? Was it achieved through more vigorous monitoring despite the generic difficulty in assessing service provision? No easy answer is readily available to these questions.

In this connection, one should bear in mind that government funding accounted for only a portion of what had kept up the provision of essential rural services before the PSU reform, as well as part of the total budget of the reconstituted service centres post-reform. Township PSUs had been starved of public funds and left to live on arbitrary extractions using their leverage of being part of the state apparatus. Indeed, malpractice and corruption had become so prevalent that rural PSUs were infamous for collecting fees without delivering any

Table 4.4 Budgetary funds for township public services: Xian-an District (million yuan)

	(Pre-PSU reform) 2003	*2004*	*2005*
Personnel/service contract funds	1.68	2.11	2.53
Other personnel costs[a]	1.43	n.a.	n.a.

Sources: Author's interviews, Wuhan (2006); Yuan (2009); Xian-an District Fiscal Finance and Government Establishment website (available at http://www.hbcz.gov.cn/421202/, accessed 20 December on 2005).

Note
a These refer to staff costs for those not in active deployment, including pension payments for retirees and staff not assigned positions.

meaningful service. Solving this problem of excessive extraction had led to the rural tax reforms across China since 2002, as noted above.

With many fees abolished and remaining fee incomes more tightly supervised, rural PSUs faced a fiscal crisis. The change in funding mechanism outlined above, as part of Hubei PSU reform, was intended to improve the efficacy of government funding in rural service delivery. At the same time, the converted service centres were encouraged to develop new, and related, services using a market approach to buttress their incomes. The idea was that since the new units were no longer part of the government, they would need to provide services that met a genuine demand in order to earn more income. From the perspective of the end users, this meant that a wider spectrum of services might be made available, with some services financed largely by public funds under service performance contracts, albeit often still requiring a fee, and others purchased at full cost.

Field research has indicated the fluidity in the relative balance of various funding channels and immense difficulty in obtaining a 'full' picture across the board. In some parts of Hubei Province, the county government has, apparently, stepped up funding to rural service provision by a quite considerable degree (see Table 4.4). Budgetary funds to rural services increased after the PSU reform in Xian-an District by 50 per cent between 2003–5, excluding the personnel costs for retirees and other non-active staff. Regarding the sharing of expenditures on rural services between the district and the township, information available on 2005 suggests that about 60 per cent of the 2.53 million yuan funding came from the district-level budget, with the remainder coming from the township.

No direct information is available for other years, but the township was likely to shoulder a higher portion of a smaller sum total before the PSU reform, a time when higher level governments had yet to pay attention to rural service provision. A Xian-an District government document prescribes a total of five avenues of rural service funding as of 2006: (1) district budget provision; (2) provincial subsidy under the PSU reform; (3) funds from the rural tax reform transfer payments; (4) special earmarked grants from above; and (5) township 'own funds'.[9] Of these, avenues (2) and (3) are new features arising from the PSU and rural tax reforms. Article 5 of the document also pronounces the District government's commitment to increase funding to rural public services in the future 'if its general

Table 4.5 Husbandry, veterinary service centre, Town Y, Xian-an: income sources (2004)

Income sources	Yuan	% share
1. Public, of which	61,200	46.6
1.1 District government	4,200	3.2
1.2 Town government	12,000	9.1
1.3 Public service fee incomes	45,000	34.3
2. Private (market)	70,000	53.4
Total	131,200	100.0

financial situation permits'. During an interview with a senior provincial official, it was mentioned that the Hubei provincial government had recently required the counties to maintain county budgetary provision to rural services at or above the 2004 level as a precondition for qualifying for special subsidy from the province.

Thus apparently rural service funding in the province was on the rise after 2005 as a result of policy encouragement and direct fiscal injection at the provincial level. A report from the Provincial Fiscal Bureau notes that total rural service funding at the county level increased by 27 per cent in 2006 over 2005, to 455 million yuan (Fu 2007). In addition, the provincial government also dispensed an additional 200 million yuan as special subsidies to the counties (avenue (2) as above) to encourage the implementation of the PSU reform, at a rate of 5 yuan per peasant, on average. This was doubled to 10 yuan per peasant in the 2007 budget, costing the provincial coffers a total of 350 million yuan.

Despite the increase in budgetary provision, fees collected directly from users remained an important source of public funding. As the case of 'husbandry, veterinary' service centre (see Table 4.5) indicates, budgetary provisions from the district and township levels together accounted for 12.3 per cent of total funding in 2004, the first year after PSU reform, while incomes from 'public service fees' accounted for 34.3 per cent. Thus, despite the drive to abolish 'illegal' fees, public service provision still depended quite considerably on fee collection, albeit that these remaining fees were, theoretically, legal and closely monitored.

Moreover, altogether, public funding (including public service fees) comprises only under half (46.6 per cent) of total funding of the husbandry and veterinary service centre, the rest being 'market-based' incomes from new services, such as the introduction of new breeds of pigs, transportation logistics and market networking across localities (Li and Yuan 2007). Traditional services performed by the centre and funded by public funds are related mostly to public health (e.g. vaccinations), while new, market-based services are all economic/business oriented.

'Killing two birds with one stone': reform under and despite pressure

How did this process of change, as outlined above, come into being? I argue that the turn to the market – the main feature of Hubei's PSU reform – was largely a result of agency interaction with local pressures. In 2003, Xian-an was still recovering from a breakdown of rural credit associations in the late 1990s when it found itself in the trough of the rural tax reform. Xian-an was a 'high-burden' locality and was thus hit hard by the burden-reduction reforms imposed from above in 2002. Centrally authorized extractions, covering various agricultural taxes and the 'five and three township-village level levies', were on average 160 yuan per capita in 1999, against the provincial average of 129 yuan (Chapter 1). Despite the increase in central transfer monies, almost half of the 'lost' revenues from peasants went uncompensated, since central transfer payments covered largely the centrally and provincially mandated fees and taxes only. A net shortfall of some 30 million yuan was reported in 2003 against the pre-reform total revenues, and accumulated debt at the township level amounted to 226 million yuan (Yuan 2008).

The township PSU reform came to the fore in 2003 amidst a series of interrelated government reforms engineered, since 2000, by then District Party Secretary Song Yaping.[10] From the beginning, the reform had two parallel goals – to 'kill two birds with one stone'. On the one hand, there was the imminent pressure – real or political – to downsize. On the other, the condition of public services in the countryside had been extremely poor. As local governments faced additional hardships during the rural tax reforms, rural services were under even greater threat. As a senior district official described it, the township PSU reform had emerged as a result of a confluence of ideas and opportunities posed by parallel reform processes:

> Secretary Song believed that to solve the many problems in our villages, and to develop our economy, of fundamental importance is to reform the practice of the government ... The functions of the government had to change. Just when we were contemplating how and what to do, there came the national rural tax reform. Then those familiar consequences: our township cadres could no longer collect fees as they did before; the township could hardly maintain its normal functioning. These new circumstances presented us an opening to launch the [township service unit] reform.

Song himself made clear in interviews that his eyes were set on *developing* the market, and that stripping the township service units of their government status was a step in that direction:

> Downsizing [the public sector] is not my major objective. What I think matters is changing the functions of the government. The development of [a] market economy requires it.
>
> Our township public service units are products of ... the planned economy. As they stand now they will not live up to the current needs ... Now we are abolishing them altogether, and converting them to autonomous agencies in society. They can then do whatever they like to follow the market needs ... This PSU reform is the first step to foster commercialization and the market in the countryside.

We can draw two observations from the above. First, the township PSU reform was part of an integrated programme of reform engineered by a local leader in whose mind the market occupied a central place in the order of development. Where the market was weak or had yet to exist, as in service provision in the Chinese countryside, one way to develop the market was through converting non-performing state service units into private, market players. On the other hand, the *immediate* context of reform, namely the immense fiscal pressure on township governments and the political pressure from the central government to downsize, was critical to putting reform ideas into *practice*. Despite Song's dismissal as 'not being the major objective', the renewed pressure to downsize, or the rhetoric of it, in the aftermath of the burden-reduction reforms served to attract allies at *higher* levels to the township PSU reform, for precisely the reason that the reform caused the most controversy among local officials: it promised to cut staff! At a time when people were increasingly weary of the prospects of successful downsizing through conventional methods, Xian-an's PSU reform rekindled hope once again of the possibility of reducing personnel expenditure.

This perhaps explains how Song's reform experiments could find an ally at the apex of the provincial leadership. Provincial Party Secretary and Politburo member Yu Zhengsheng soon became an ardent supporter shortly after he arrived in Hubei as its top official. Yu was instrumental in Song's promotion to the provincial government in late 2003 and the subsequent provincial approval of the reform.[11] The statement below, made during a visit to Xian-an in March 2004, is suggestive of Yu's attitude:

> Township comprehensive reforms hold the key to sustaining the achievements of the rural tax reform – keep the peasant burden low. *And the critical part in township reforms lies with the public service units.* We *need to find a way of developing rural public services*, and yet without risking the rebound of the peasant burden. (Emphasis added)[12]

It is apparent that given the national policy of burden reduction, provincial leaders were under pressure to reduce extractions from peasants and *keep* them low. At the same time, the heat was on the townships. 'Township comprehensive reform' was hailed as holding critical importance to sustaining a low level of burden. However, as Chapter 3 notes, national policy had given little guidance *how exactly* to reform townships – apart from a reiteration of the need to downsize, the limits of which even central officials had by then realized. As the impact of fee reduction on local budgets was felt, local governments were pressured into finding new means to maintain a minimal presence and functioning with reduced resources. In 2002, there was, therefore, a market for innovative reform ideas.

Xian-an's township agency reform thus met a need at the time. Song's articulation and the elegance of his ideas linking government downsizing with market development enhanced the reform's appeal to the provincial leaders. Its greatest attraction, to provincial leaders, was a promise of a new path to downsize and reduce personnel costs. Paradoxically, however, this has also been the source of most resistance. There were two dimensions to this resistance. First was affordability: were there the resources to pay for the one-off severance payment? Second was doubt about its effectiveness: could the payment serve its intended purpose – could downsizing be *made* effective?

Full compensation per member of staff, including social insurance payments, was, on average, 25,500 yuan. Depending on different estimates of numbers of eligible staff, the cost of reform ('one-off' severance payments plus social insurance payments) varied from 1.7 billion to 7.2 billion yuan across the province. As noted above, the provincial government had been slow to shoulder this burden, expecting the counties and the townships to pay for most of the cost. However, cash-strapped local governments were equally unwilling to accommodate even the smallest estimate. Even Henggouqiao Town of Xian-an, where the reform was first piloted, did not complete the step of permanent severance until the district government promised to pay the costs involved. A town official described their considerations in 2003 as follows:

> The district government did not issue any policy document on the PSU reform. There were only oral instructions from Secretary Song that the reform must severe the government-cadre status of the personnel. But we could not do it since no monies were made available to us to pay the required compensation. We needed a few million yuan to pay the outgoing staff, covering the one-off severance payment, pension and medical insurance payments, etc. We simply could not implement the reform in one go without new resources.

As a chosen location for pilot reform, there was no turning back. What Henggouqiao Town did eventually was to implement the reform in two phases. In early 2003, the state-owned service units were abolished and non-state service centres came into existence, except that the former PSU staff still remained in the government ranks. The same local official as above explained how they did it:

> We are now implementing the reform with a contingency plan. We'll regroup the service agencies and combine some of them. The government status of the agencies will be abolished, but the original status of the staff as government personnel will not be affected. We'll have the new 'service centres' set up and start running business first. Then wait for opportunities [to gain] fiscal support from above.

Eventually, in 2004, the district government provided the funds for severance payments, and the reform was 'completed' in Henggouqiao. Across the Xian-an District, a total of 7 million yuan was paid to 518 staff as 'severance payments', representing an average of 14,000 yuan per person (Yuan 2008). Xian-an's leaders had a large stake in seeing through the reform that they had initiated. In any event, the provincial government in 2003 awarded Xian-an with 6 million yuan of additional transfer monies for its government reforms (Chapter 1). Other counties were much less enthusiastic and most waited for provincial monies before initiating any action. In 2004, seven counties were given a total subsidy of 120 million yuan to spearhead the reform. In 2005, as mentioned above, all counties received a provincial subsidy of 4,000 yuan for each PSU worker leaving the government ranks, with a total provincial outlay of 1.26 billion yuan.

For the reformer Song Yaping, worries over reform costs were entirely unnecessary. In his words to the author, in 2005:

> How much does it cost to keep a staff? Take an average annual payroll of 12,000 yuan per person. Then there is the indirect cost, such as office expenses, which is about 5,000 yuan per person per year. On the other hand the severance cost is at most 25,000 yuan, which is less than 2 years of staff costs! Cost is not a problem. That is why Xian-an did it and other bolder leaders, like those in Jingshan County, have also done it, even without fiscal support from the province. It makes good business from the perspective of the public purse.

If cost is not the real issue, then what is? 'People's mind-set', Song concluded, in 2006:

> People lacked confidence and were often besieged by a pervasive sense of insecurity, so that they were worried about resistance from staff. They thought our staff could not make it to the market. They thought our people could not survive [other than] as government cadres, and thus this reform – severing the employment relations – would not work. The [severance] monies would only be wasted, as the staff would eventually press for a return. Many localities have hence adopted a wait-and-see approach, and have not implemented the severance arrangement.

Apparently, the 'confidence' deficit was also found among central officials. A senior central official said the following in an interview:

> Now it is too early to talk about a possible national extension of Hubei's model. The effect of the reform is as yet unclear. First it is uncertain if the reform will foster genuine competition in service provision, and thus improve service quality. If no real competition exists, if the services are simply delegated to the same batch of people who have been around before reform, the current reform is unlikely to lead to significant improvement in public service provision. The severance arrangement, which is peculiar to Hubei's model, also raises new questions. The measure requires injection of new resources but now peasants' fees and taxes have been cut the central government is already spending more on the villages [*vide* the special central transfers on rural tax reform and funds for the 'New Countryside' projects]. We need to be very careful if still more new monies are needed. The

current thinking is that, with the New Socialist Countryside plans, new monies will be spent on direct services to the peasants, like roads, energy, water, the impact of these are more direct and easier to see. We're thus putting less emphasis on making changes in the institutional front at this stage. But sure Hubei may still proceed with its institutional reform using provincial resources. The central government will wait and see ...

(Author's interviews, Beijing, 2006)

In October 2006, the State Council issued a directive on 'rural comprehensive reforms' focusing on rural education, county–township fiscal management and township government reform (State Council 2006). While the directive confirmed the earlier experiments on education and rural finance (largely the centralization of township management functions to the county, first started in Anhui), Hubei's PSU reform – as an important pilot measure in the third area – was conspicuously not mentioned. A general reading by local officials in Hubei and other provinces was that the central government had 'cold-shouldered' Hubei's experiments (Author's interviews, Hubei and Hong Kong, 2007).

Conclusion

By 2006, central policy seemed to have come full circle since national burden-reduction reform commenced a few years ago. Drastic measures to reduce state extractions on peasants had led to calls for radical institutional reforms – to the extent that the entire layer of township government might possibly be done away with. The pendulum started to swing back, however, when it had made the farthest swing. As burdens reduced, concerns emerged over the 'hollowing out' of local government and amidst these came the new plan to construct the 'New Socialist Countryside'. With the current emphasis on direct services, interestingly, as the above remarks by a central official suggest, the latest policy turn seems to have had an effect of *redefining* the problem in the countryside, as well as what constitute possible solutions.

International experience reminds us, however, that too often increased public spending alone is insufficient to meet the challenge of improving public services for those in need. In many cases, deep-seated changes in institutions – how public monies are allocated and spending monitored, whether the needs of the clients are adequately surveyed and fed to the decision-making process, and how service providers with the necessary capability and aptitude are trained and put to work – are required, or at least some of them. Where does the township PSU reform stand in this process, and Hubei's experiments in particular? Problems in rural services in China are embedded in a whole range of institutional and historical arrangements, and the PSU reform described in this chapter is only a small step in tackling the 'thick' institutional 'base' and offers, therefore, a partial solution at best. Taking this first step is important, however, if through it people's *awareness* of the need to tackle *other* institutional reforms is also raised. This last effect has worked better among officials at the lowest level of the state hierarchy. Township officials in Henggouqiao were quick to point out the need for reform at higher levels of government and the limitations of a bottom-up approach to government reform, when the PSU reforms were piloted in 2003:

> What do we need to do next? Reform the upper levels! If government reform is confined at the township level, it won't last long. As long as our upper levels don't change as well, they will make demands on us in the old way, and we will still have to comply, even though these do not fit in our reformed system. We still have to creatively make ways for these demands. These adaptations may work for a while, but will eventually weaken our reform … Then reform will succumb to pressures from the top … Right now reform has only taken place at the bottom. The upper levels [county and above] have not changed at all. They are just watching us … *But government reforms are not like enterprise reforms. For the latter a decentralized approach has worked. This won't work for government reforms.* There is a need for more and better coordination and leadership. (Emphasis added)

Township officials looked for leadership in two directions. The first was a vision of reform that would extend government reform beyond townships to all levels. Second, they demanded strategic decisions on which specific reform models should be adopted. Local experiments had been helpful but national and provincial leaders needed to take responsibility at some point – not so much to promulgate a unified model nationally but to analyze and assess the local reform experiences for wider implementation. To an extent this step has been taken up at the provincial level in Hubei. As noted above, the central government has so far remained non-committal. Perhaps the difficulties in township reform, as seen from the experiments in Hubei so far, have had the ironic effect of alerting the central government to the fact that there is *no* easy solution when it comes to government reform.

In the midsummer of 2006, given the lukewarm central response to Hubei's institutional reform efforts, Song Yaping – the main architect of Hubei's reforms – made an assessment regarding the PSU reform's prospects:

> Institutional reform takes time and needs the right context to proceed. At this juncture, the 'right' context [of extending the reform] is not there. The 'New Countryside' plans focus largely on the material side, not on the institutional … But there is a limit [to which] our traditional government structure can work, especially given the new demands. That is why I believe the time will come when Hubei's township institutional reform will be seen as useful again.

Perhaps the difference between central and local thinking should not be overstated. A senior central official's remarks made at roughly the same time came very close to Song's, if with a slight twist:

We anticipate the townships will soon face more challenges. They have already had a hard time from the rural tax reform. With the additional demands from the New Socialist Countryside policy, the challenge is even greater. The fact is that provision of public goods in the countryside was, historically, not impressive. Maintaining the provision at the pre-existing level with reduced means will be hard, but relatively manageable since the standard has been low. If expectations are raised, however – as is now the case with 'the New Countryside' plans – the conventional system will find it really difficult to cope ... We in the central government are aware of the ongoing local experiments [in Hubei] ... We shall wait and observe how they go ...

(Author's interviews, Beijing, 2006)

The Chinese experiment on adjusting the mix of state and market elements in rural public service provision outlined in this chapter suggests a dialectical process of policy evolution. Institutional reforms to align actors' incentives are complex, and resistance to change commonplace. Governments are often tempted to look for quick 'fixes', placing hopes on, say, a bigger budget or a good year in the economy, as in the current case. Since 2006, township institutional reform has entered an impasse in China, as national attention has shifted to direct rural services, and hopes for service improvement placed on increased funding. I argue, however, that the impasse may likely be temporary, as maintaining the status quo will not work. The pre-existing system has not performed previously and cannot possibly perform better now with additional demands from more spending projects. Further change will likely come when local failures to deliver, under the pre-existing institutional framework, become a conspicuous fact rather than a theoretical possibility, or when local implementation of institutional reform has brought more fruit, despite the absence of national approval, as has happened in previous waves of policy evolution.

5 Path dependence, agency and implementation in local administrative reform*

How do policymakers make up their mind as to whether or not a policy proposal should be adopted? What are the major considerations at work? The policy sciences literature, drawing on insights from diverse disciplines, has taken a somewhat eclectic approach to answering this question (including how this question is put). Various subgroups have placed emphasis on, for instance, conflict/power, learning, history, ideas and the role of policy implementation (Deleon and Martell 2006; Pierre 2006; Grin and Loeber 2007), with each exhibiting various degrees of generality.[1] The conflict/power model is the most commonly used approach. It sees policymaking as the product, as well as manifestation, of the dominant power structure(s) and conflict contestations in the wider social and political systems, including the bureaucratic machinery wherein the deals are struck. Alternatively, those models that see policies as a product of learning generally adopt a more 'rational' view of decision making, though some policy learning theories also explicitly incorporate power contestations as part and parcel of the learning process (Bennett and Howlett 1992). Policy learning theories also discuss the role of history in policy formulation, as history is implied in the concept of learning. What remains unclear is the kind of history that is relevant, the extent to which history is relevant and how exactly the past's influence on the present and the future is affected (Hirsch and Gillespie 2001). The implementation studies literature, on the other hand, has consistently argued that what is going to be implemented *will* have a major impact on what *was* (and will be) decided as a policy. The future, namely what is going to take place during the post-policy-formulation phase – the implementation process – will counteract with the past and lead to, or constitute, *new* changes in policy (Winter 2006).

This chapter focuses on the question of policy formation. It does so by examining the case of decision making in relation to the recent developments in Chinese township administrative reform. It suggests that the influence of past trajectory – that is, history of the reform – on subsequent decisions in the same policy domain is critical. In particular, the memories of *failed* reform attempts in the recent past have led to an inclination among policymakers to focus on costs of reform at the expense of potential benefits while considering new measures.

At the same time, negative experiences also reinforced a predisposition, or a theory of agency, among central government actors (and also those at lower government levels) who tended to see stakeholders as either resisting change stubbornly or waiting to benefit from reform passively, rather than being capable of bringing about change and bearing risks as participative agents would do. In turn, this perception of how other actors may respond led national policymakers to adopt a passive stance, whereby they were reluctant to express explicit support to emerging local reform initiatives, let alone foster their successful implementation. History, learning, agency and implementation all played a role in policymaking.

The main part of this chapter is divided into several sections. The next section outlines the trajectory of Chinese township administrative reform during the last two decades, including its wider contexts and remaining problems. Then the chapter discusses a critical juncture of decision making more recently to examine how decisions at the national level were made, or not made, despite a pressing need for change. By laying out *how* things have happened as they did, the chapter highlights the possibility for improved decision making – enhanced state capacity – *via* a heightened awareness and agency of the actors to act *differently*.

Chinese township administrative reform: a trajectory of frustrations

The Chinese township administrative reform seemed unable to make genuine progress despite repeated attempts to achieve change over the last two decades. Occupying the lowest level in the five-tiered Chinese government hierarchy, the township has been subjected to a series of cyclical downsizing and expansion as waves of national administrative reforms have come and gone.[2] Township reforms started as early as 1986, 2 years after the township was established as a formal level of government. Then, the objective was to strengthen the structure and functions of the township government, and powers were decentralized from the counties. The expansion of government led, however, to a subsequent call for downsizing in the early 1990s, as reform shifted to the interface between government and enterprises in order to 'claw back' the reach of the government into the economy. Despite the rhetoric of economic reform calling for a smaller government, however, little was accomplished (Burns 2003). At local levels, there was a phenomenal increase in township personnel nationwide from the mid-1990s as local governments enjoyed increased discretion over recruiting additional workers, whom they paid with 'informal' local tax and fee incomes. Some efforts to downsize and contain the growth in staff were made in the late 1990s after the central government ordered, in 1998, the number of core central government staff to be reduced by one half within 3 years. Results have not been satisfactory, however. At the turn of the millennium, an average township government in central China was estimated to employ at least 350–550 salaried workers paid through various channels of public monies, as opposed to fewer than ten in the mid-1980s (Wu 2006: 15–17).[3]

Explaining the failure of successive administrative reforms in the Chinese government requires a separate effort that is beyond the scope of this chapter. Indeed, one may deduce from the brief account above that the several rounds of reform since the 1980s were driven by different concerns and objectives. For instance, the reforms in the mid to late 1980s had township government expansion, not downsizing, as an intended objective. This was in contrast to administrative reforms in the early to mid-1990s, which were more motivated by a desire to speed up economic reform and growth. More recently, apparently similar downsizing reforms that were carried out after 2000 were driven by a fiscal crisis *within* the government, especially at the county and township levels. It therefore seems inappropriate to treat township government reforms as a single genre to be evaluated against one set of criteria.

Chapter 2 has noted how township governments faced renewed pressure to restructure and downsize since 2000 as a result of the national policy of reducing state extraction. Under the measures that were promulgated in 2000 and adopted nationwide since 2002–3, county and township governments were deprived of their most lucrative sources of fiscal revenue. Staff pay had always accounted for the lion's share of the meagre budgets of township governments (Yang 2003; Chen 2004; Ai and Zhou 2007), and many turned to informal sources such as unauthorized fees and charges. From the perspective of the central government, however, cutting the cost of township government – which had daily, and direct, contact with rural residents – was instrumental to the success of its efforts to reduce rural taxes and ameliorate state–society tension.

It therefore came as no surprise that the central government explicitly required township governments to downsize by 20 per cent in its 2000 plan to reform the rural tax regime (see Figure 2.1). The saved staff costs were, according to the reform documents, to compensate for the shortfall of revenues subsequent to the reduced taxes. As these documents stated,

> After the implementation of the rural tax reform, the reduced revenues of county and township governments are to be met by a corresponding decrease in local expenditures through the following ways: adjusting the functions of the county/township government, streamlining government structure and organization, rationalizing the establishment of township government departments and service agencies, tightening up the management of personnel establishment and having more dual appointments of Party and government personnel.
>
> (CCP Central Committee, State Council 2000)

The measures relied upon in this round of administrative reform were, however, no different from the previous rounds.[4] Despite official reports claiming success, a decrease in staff numbers often did not imply any savings in total staff expenditures, largely because the reduction figures masked *increases* in personnel elsewhere in the public sector, and also because the downsizing measures called for new expenses as sweeteners (see also Chapter 3; Burns 2003). For instance, in one province, downsizing turned out to be largely rhetorical:

During the five months of intensive downsizing 'campaign', the total number of township government bureaus in County A was reduced by 60 per cent, from 160 to 64. Leadership positions (positions at the level of township heads and party secretaries, including deputies) went down by 17.4 per cent from 482 to 398. The number of township service units was down to 202 from 339, and staff numbers down 65 per cent from 2,195 to 770. These impressive figures however masked important continuities. The 'outgoing' leaders were merely given alternative job titles to produce a smaller statistic for the leadership positions, and all kept their original perks and pay levels in their new positions. Reductions in the number of units often meant the amalgamation of several units into one, with little change to the functions of the units and little done to reduce overlap of duties or improve efficiencies.

(Li and Wu 2008: 148)

The central government, as the major driving force of successive downsizing reforms, has belatedly admitted that previous attempts to downsize government had not worked.

The reality is, we have found out, after the three-year transitional period, the state coffers still have to pay the streamlined [*fenliu*] staff, though the original plan was to have zero staff costs by then. It is thus unrealistic to expect direct saving from reducing the number of serving staff.

(Author's interviews, quoted in Chapter 2)

Yet new measures have been slow to materialize.

A lack of new initiatives

It is perhaps plausible to surmise that there have been few policy innovations in administrative reform because there is, in fact, *no* strong demand for imminent change. Given the failures of previous administrative reforms, the Chinese Government has, apparently, yet to find the costs of failures 'unbearable'. Burns (2003: 777) points out that the CCP has an entrenched interest in maintaining a high level of government employment and in rewarding supporters through providing state sector jobs. While the logic of economic reform and fiscal pressures had demanded downsizing measures (out of a concern for cutting slack staff and raising labour productivity), the traditional need to maintain, if not expand, political patronage apparently pulled the party-state in a diametrically opposite direction and compromised its efforts in administrative reforms. Recent developments in township administrative reforms also appeared to lend support to this observation.

As mentioned above, township administrative reforms were included in the national rural tax reform package in order to keep local tax fees at a low level. Many Chinese townships had relied on a variety of local fees and taxes to finance their core functions and staff bills, and abuses were common. A direct response of the central government, when it started to move to contain rural state extraction, was thus to constrain local staff growth and to cut down current staff levels, so that township governments would face less demand from within its workforce to increase local revenues to pay their wages. However, as explained above, downsizing proved to be tricky. If downsizing failed to save costs, then the central government would have to increase transfer payments to local governments in order to compensate for the shortfalls in local revenues which townships were now forbidden to collect. From 2002 onwards, the central government had indeed done just that: central transfer payments specifically for this purpose reached RMB 24.5 billion, 54.6 billion and 78 billion in 2002, 2004 and 2006, respectively (Chen 2003; 'Xianxiang caizheng' 2005; 'Jinnian' 2007). However, as the actual shortfall far exceeded the increase in incoming central transfers, as noted in Chapter 3, and a substantial portion of the incoming monies from the central government failed to reach the township government owing to fund diversion and 'taxing' by intermediaries at provincial, municipal and county levels (Ou 2008), many township governments faced immense difficulties in terms of continuing their normal operation and maintaining a minimal level of public services. There were reports of closures of local village schools in parts of China as early as 2003, and many township governments could not pay their staff on time and ran into new debts (Fan and Shi 2005; Fagaiwei 2006).

Faced with these problems, the central government was compelled to move beyond its original narrow focus on downsizing. Starting from 2003, official statements and policy documents have demanded efforts to be spent not only on administrative restructuring and downsizing but also on adjusting the functions of township government, rationalizing public service agencies and altering the state–market mix in public service provision in the countryside.[5] In 2006, a decision was made to centralize the management of township finance at the county level, which was first piloted in Anhui Province, the birthplace of rural tax reforms, a few years ago (Wang 2006). This development reversed the trend, in evidence since the mid-1980s, of strengthening the capacity of the township, to manage its budget independently. Apparently, since the township had been weakened during the rural tax reform as a result of the reduction in local revenues and government capacity, a judgement was reached at the higher levels that further centralization would help, not hinder. The relatively stronger county governments were to take up duties that were previously the responsibility of the township authorities, thus relieving some of the pressure on the latter.

Also in 2006, the State Council held a meeting at which it prescribed a three-pronged approach to deepening the administrative and organizational reforms in township governments. This consisted of, 'adjusting the functions of the government (*vis-à-vis* enterprises and society), reducing government personnel and expenditures and strengthening rural administration and public service provision' (Wen Jiabao 2006). Despite these repeated calls for administrative reforms to go beyond a sole focus on downsizing, there was, however, a conspicuous absence of guidelines setting out specific measures. A State Council Document (State Council 2006) issued a few months after the meeting, presumably designed to codify the meeting resolutions and to elaborate on implementation measures, also failed to offer any new measures.

A local proposal

A closer look reveals that the central government had been offered suggestions on township administrative reform from local governments but decided against their adoption. Discussing the local initiatives in this context presents us with a window into central government decision making. The relevant question, for our purposes, is not whether the central government *should* adopt a local proposal as a national policy, but *how* the central government arrives at a decision either way. What considerations have gone into the decision-making process?

Earlier it was noted that local governments were required to implement downsizing and restructuring. Most localities simply paid lip service and followed the traditional method of 'streamlining', with little impact. Hubei Province in Central China, on the other hand, experimented with a more radical approach by adjusting the state–market mix in rural public service provision in favour of the market. Government public service units (PSU) at and below the township level were abolished, and then re-established as non-state-owned service centres. These new units were then expected to function independently of the government, which could outsource specific public services to them through performance contracts. The quality of service was expected to improve, and it was expected that government staff costs would be reduced in the medium to long term, if not immediately (Chapter 4).

Lacklustre central response

Hubei started its reform with the policy of establishing township PSUs in some localities in 2003, and implemented it province wide from 2005 to 2006. The main thrusts of reform – enhancing the role of the market in rural public service delivery as well as providing a new way of downsizing township government – appeared to be simply following through the call for 'deepening' reform contained in national policy documents. This appears to have contributed to the confidence among Hubei's reformers that their initiative would, eventually, be adopted nationally (Author's interviews, Hubei, 2004, 2006). However, when the State Council issued yet another directive on 'rural comprehensive reforms' in October 2006, not a single word in the Directive referred to Hubei's PSU reform. This was despite the fact that one major emphasis of rural comprehensive reforms was to be, explicitly, township administrative reform. This conspicuous omission was generally interpreted by local government officials, and Hubei officials in particular, to mean that the central government had 'cold-shouldered', if not outright disapproved of, Hubei's reform. The question remains: why was the central government not more positive towards Hubei's reform given its repeated calls for new initiatives in township administrative reforms?

Preoccupation with costs

As mentioned previously, there has been renewed pressure for local administrative reforms in the aftermath of the rural tax reform. A senior official in the central government in charge of administrative reform emphasized to the author at an interview that rural administrative reform was now a *must*:

> Why do we need to reform township PSUs? Because the way they are used to operate no longer suits the needs of peasants and their super-ordinates at the upper levels in the current political circumstances, namely delivery of services! There has got to be change one way or the other.
>
> (Author's interview, Beijing, 2006)

Why was better delivery of rural public services important now, if not before? Another senior central official, who had played an active role in recent rural policy formulation, had this to say:

> Since the outbreak of SARS (Severe Acute Respiratory Syndrome) in 2003, public awareness of the importance of the narrowing urban–rural divide in public services has surged tremendously. It is now no longer a topic of discussion in elite circles only, but part of the public discourse. Urban residents now recognize that rural public service provision also affects their own safety and interests, not just the well-being of their rural fellow citizens.
>
> (Author's interview, Beijing, 2006)

The problem was that the central government was uncertain about how to proceed with local administrative reform, despite a perceived need for it. When asked what problems the central government had found with Hubei township's PSU reform, the central official in charge of administrative reform elaborated on the costs, and risks, that Hubei's reform was likely to incur:

> Hubei's reform will require additional fiscal expenditures to pay for the 'severance payments' and associated costs for the laid off PSU staff, in order to mitigate resistance of the outgoing workers. However, first, it is unclear how much this bill will amount to. Hubei once mentioned 1.8 billion yuan. I have no clue as to how they arrived at this figure. In any event, the central government cannot be expected to foot the bills for excess staffing at local levels. Moreover, the central coffers have already increased transfer payments to local levels during the rural tax reform, and cannot afford to spend more on [the staff costs of rural] local governments.
>
> (Author's interview, Beijing, 2006)

Closely related to concerns about costs are reservations on feasibility, in other words, doubts that the intended outcomes may materialize. There are two major uncertainties. The first is about whether Hubei's reform can downsize government more effectively than more traditional methods. The second is whether the reform can effectively improve the quality of service delivery in the countryside.

> First, the laid off staff may still refuse to leave government for good after they are paid the 'severance payments'. If they fail to make a good living, or feel aggrieved for whatever reason, they may well demand to return to government ranks, as in the case of staff laid off through the traditional method of 'streamlining'. The government will be under tremendous political pressure to take them back in. The chance of staff not seeking to return is contingent on many factors, the most important probably being economic – that is, whether they have successfully found a better job and improved their standard of living – rather than changes to arrangements of the laying off process, namely the differences between the traditional streamlining method and Hubei's reform. If that is the case, why bother to pay more? Secondly, assuming that the PSUs are eventually converted to non-state-owned service centres, it is highly uncertain that these service centres are capable of delivering genuinely improved services to the rural population. The design of the reform will give an advantage to former PSU staff, relative to 'outsiders', in staffing these service centres [in order that the former PSU staff will not fiercely oppose the reform]. In that case, it is likely that there will be little market competition from the supply end. With more or less the same batch of people manning the 'new' service centres, it is questionable that services can be much better. In any event, there is likely to be a lack of alternative service providers with the required training in the countryside to compete with the former PSU workers. A *de facto* monopoly of services will not be conducive to service improvement. If the market is unlikely to be in place or to work, we shall still have to rely on more traditional methods, namely administrative supervision and monitoring, in order to maintain service standards. If that is the case, why take the extra efforts to embark on Hubei's reform, which, after all, is about introducing market forces to the government sector of rural public services?
>
> (Author's interview, Beijing, 2006)

Targets, not agents, of reform

Fuelling, and mediating, the reservations described above are the dominant images among central and local officials of reform stakeholders as 'targets' of reform, rather than participative agents. PSU workers were, for instance, generally portrayed as those at the 'receiving end' of reform measures. Given their vested interests, they were *expected* to resist reform. Indeed this perception has even infiltrated 'reformers' in Hubei, where township government officials often referred to PSU workers, and indeed themselves, as 'targets of reform' in day-to-day conversations.[6] Similarly, peasants were generally regarded as passive recipients of government services who may welcome or resist reform but who were not capable of contributing to it. During interviews, officials often made remarks about the attitudes of peasants towards reforms. A Hubei county-level leader once said,

> Since 2002 our rural tax reform has substantially reduced peasants' burden, but peasants still hold a different attitude [they remain unsatisfied].We'd better cut taxes down to one cent, and even distribute monies to them! ... We keep the interests of the peasants in mind all the time in designing reforms ... however, peasants don't feel gratified yet. For example, now we no longer demand water fees, but they want even more benefits!
>
> (Author's interview, Hubei, 2004)

In the eyes of officials across different levels, peasants were merely recipients of government policy. Worse still, peasants were critical. While officials were adamant about their concern for peasants' interests, and often complained of the difficulty of satisfying their 'insatiable' wants, they had applied relatively little thought as to how to incorporate peasants into the process of reform itself in order to make things work.

For instance, the market emphasis of Hubei's PSU reform called for the systematic collection of user feedback in order that the township government may adequately monitor the delivery of services. In practice, the participation of peasants in reform appeared to be very limited. Notwithstanding the official requirement, local officials had little to tell the author when asked about how they obtained feedback from peasants, suggesting their lack of consideration, and even awareness, on the matter.[7] Another indication of this lacklustre attitude towards peasant participation is related to a prescribed measure in the national rural tax reform on village fee collection. Village committees are required to convene general meetings of villagers to approve their spending plans before collecting any fees annually (Ministry of Agriculture 2000). Intended to constrain excessive local taxes and fees through popular participation, this reform measure (in Chinese, *yi-shi-yi-yi*, meaning literally deliberation on each and every item) – a form of participatory budgeting at the most grassroots level,[8] was severely criticized by local officials nationwide as unenforceable and undesirable, and has since remained largely on paper (Yang *et al.* 2005; Feng 2008). Apparently, peasants are, as always, *not* expected to take any active, positive, role.

Conclusion: moving beyond the trodden path?

This chapter suggests that decision making in the Chinese administrative reforms has been heavily influenced by past reform trajectory. Previous negative experiences have led to an almost sole emphasis on costs when considering new reform measures. Despite repeated calls for new initiatives, policymakers often turned their back on proposals when they were put forward, leaving local experiments to 'float or sink' on their own.

There are, no doubt, good reasons for prudence. Indeed, still vivid memories of major policy disasters in the Maoist period suggest that it is wise to err on the conservative side. Adoption of a policy option is a serious matter, and conventional wisdom requires localities to prove their measures beyond reasonable doubt before national adoption. The trajectory of administrative reform in China suggests, however, that where interest contestation is intense and resistance to change entrenched in the dominant power structure, the taken-for-granted rule of proving feasibility from the bottom up becomes an elusive possibility in practice. What is apparently lost in the contemplation of actions within the central policy circle is the multitude of options in between the poles of adoption and negation.

To improve future decision making, it may be advisable to obtain a broader view of the possibilities allowed by a local measure as well as to identify possible costs and sources of resistance. One possible route is through adjusting the dominant image of reform stakeholders and fostering more participation and collaboration among them. Indeed, a closer examination of the Hubei PSU reform implementation has revealed, tentatively, that the reform was able to go ahead *because of* the agency of PSU workers (Li and Yuan 2007). Once the county and township leaders made clear their determination, as line managers at upper level government, to convert the township PSUs into non-state-owned 'market players', a significant number of PSU workers were capable of coming to grips with the situation quickly, despite initial grudges. Furthermore, they took initiatives independently in order to make the new system work, and also to earn new revenues for themselves. Ideas mushroomed and new services were launched. If such initiatives come with the risk of new abuses (for instance possible diversion of public resources to 'market'-based new services), the problem lies more in the shortfall of agency of the *upper levels* of adequate oversight (including the lack of measures allowing bottom-up monitoring), than in the passivity of the 'targets of reform'.

Bremer (1984) argues that, in seeking to develop the capacity of policy analysis, it is futile to focus on the institutional, or 'internal', capacity in most developing countries, given the many limitations in the organization, culture and sheer resource levels in developing countries. The gap is simply too large to be 'fillable', and the task too complex and embedded to be disentangled. Instead, she suggests an alternative strategy to improve policy analysis through building 'process capacity'. Simply put, it involves getting other actors and organizations *outside* the traditional circle of government policy analysts to conduct policy analysis *for* the consideration of the policymakers. The task of developing the government's capacity of policy analysis thus becomes one of developing the capacity of the government to identify suitable external agents to conduct the analysis, and to critically appreciate and make use of the analysis during the formulation and adjustment of policies. Zhu and Xue (2007)'s discussion of Chinese policy think tanks points to the beginning of such a process of developing the 'process capacity' in contemporary China.

This chapter suggests that the processes of building 'process' and 'internal', institutional, capacities for policy analysis are not exclusive to one another.

'External' agents of analysis and, indeed, of execution, need first to be 'recognized', and appreciated, before their analysis can ever be 'made use of' by 'internal' policymakers during the decision-making process. Otherwise their very existence, as co-analysts of policy, may not even be taken note of. This calls for the development of the capacity of the 'internal' actors to see the roles of, and respond to, the 'external' actors appropriately – as partners in the process of policy analysis and deliberation. In addition, the constitutive role of policy implementation in policy analysis, as this chapter has highlighted, points to the presence of a pool of policy analysts within the policy circle, namely the implementers at the various government levels. There is, in other words, no shortage of agency and analysis capacity within the existing system, if only it is given its due recognition.

6 Working for the peasants

Strategic interactions and unintended consequences*

How should we interpret such recent rural policy developments as reforms to reduce peasant tax burden, initiatives to construct the 'New Socialist Countryside' or the quest for a 'Green GDP' index?[1] Official rhetoric inside China has depicted them as a succession of coordinated central measures with coherent objectives, namely social harmony and sustainable development.[2] This chapter cautions against such an interpretation. Focusing my analysis on the rural tax reform, arguably the beginning of this policy shift, I contend that it is misleading to see the burden-reduction reform as a 'central project' *intentionally* reaching out to help the once-neglected rural population. I argue that subsequent developments were more the *unintended* consequences of strategic interactions between central and local state actors. The story is more nuanced and complex than the official account admits.

National policy on peasant burden reduction was engineered around 1998, when the views of then Party Secretary General and State President Jiang Zemin and then Premier Zhu Rongji converged on the need to tighten controls on local extraction.[3] Six years later, Premier Wen Jiabao described the ongoing burden-reduction reform as a two-phase process, 'a result of central government's planning'.[4] The first phase, from the release of the original reform package in 2000 to its implementation in 2003, involved the reduction of the fiscal burden and the rationalization of the rural tax regime. The extensive range of local fees charged to peasants at the township level, with many imposed by the county level and above, was placed under tight scrutiny and many items were abolished, while the rate of the formerly nominal Agricultural Tax was raised to compensate townships in part for the lost income.[5] Then, with the release of Central Document No. 1 (2004), the reform entered the second stage, in which the burden was further reduced through the progressive abolition of Agricultural Taxes, while measures were introduced to raise peasants' income, for example, through direct subsidies to grain-growing peasants.[6] As the Chinese economy develops and the national financial situation improves, the central government gains a larger capacity to address the needs of the rural population, and considerable resources have been allocated to these matters.[7] Numerous studies have elucidated the historical and institutional embeddedness of the 'peasant burden' problem (Bernstein and Lü

2003; Unger 2002; Tao and Liu 2004; Yep 2004: 43–70; West 1997). The consensus is that fees proliferated out of historically grounded institutional mismatches, in particular between the growing needs of local bureaucracies and their limited ability to finance themselves through existing fiscal channels, and not exclusively because of local corruption. The fiscal system had evolved incrementally as the country edged away from central planning. During this process, necessary local (and rural) services were left largely unfunded while the size of township administration snowballed, partly as a result of the policies, regulations, appointments and actions of higher levels of government, and partly as a by-product of lacklustre economic development and thus shortage of non-farming job opportunities. Locally imposed fees proliferated to fill the gap. Heavy local extraction on the peasants was, therefore, institutionally embedded and rooted in national policies and practices, and its correction required more than a focus on the local levels.

Fieldwork of this study was done in five townships across three provinces (Hubei, Anhui and Guangdong). From 2002 to 2006, I made 19 trips to the research sites to conduct interviews, group discussions, elite surveys and field observations during various stages of the reform process. This chapter draws mainly upon the data on Hubei and Anhui. Anhui was the site of pioneering tax-for-fee reforms during the 1990s; Hubei endured a number of highly publicized cases of heavy peasant burden leading to tension between peasants and local cadres.[8] Both are central agricultural provinces. In Hubei, research was conducted in the Yining District of Yichang Municipality and the Xian-an District of Xianning Municipality. Yichang is a mountainous area where the Three Gorges Main Dam is located, and where local fiscal rationalization experiments in the late 1990s had some national influence,[9] whereas Xian-an is known for its pioneering local government reforms before and during the rural tax reforms. The Anhui localities we visited were more 'average' and less 'glamorous' with respect to local initiatives. They include an agricultural town in mountainous Qianshan County in southwest Anhui, a better-off town with some industrial activities in Shucheng County, a nationally designated 'poor county', and the pioneer site of 1978 rural reform in Feixi County, not far away from the provincial capital.

Our research team conducted over 150 interviews with some 105 respondents. About 80 per cent of these were local officials in Anhui and Hubei involved in the implementation of reform, and the rest were officials and researchers in Beijing close to the reform formulation and analysis process.

The design of tax reform

When it came to the design of reform at the national level, the social contexts of rural governance were conspicuously lost. Earlier, Chapter 2 has noted policymakers' narrow focus on fee reduction, paying insufficient attention to deeper, institutional issues. While a range of 'supplementary measures' was set up with the purported objective of *keeping* extraction low, they invariably targeted the local implementers, whether through tightening up local expenditure (acting on the demand side for more state extraction) or forbidding new revenue items (acting on the supply side).[10] The remedy prescribed for an earlier failure of control was, therefore, yet more control, though it was not clear how it could possibly work better this time.[11] In the formulation of a national reform policy, a complex issue was reduced to a simple logic: peasant burden had become excessive because top-down control had slackened, and townships had become 'overstaffed'.[12] No reference was made to the otherwise-established knowledge that townships, and public goods in rural societies, had long been grossly underfunded in the state budget. Similarly, no questions were raised about why townships became 'overstaffed' in the first place.

The reforms soon ran into difficulties, and studies blossomed to evaluate their implementation (Li and Wu 2005: 44–63; Xiang 2004a), sustainability (Chapter 3) and impact on the 'hollowing out' of township-level governments (Kennedy 2005; Tian *et al.* 2003: 33–6; Zhu 2002: 13–20).[13] Townships of average to low income were so deprived of fiscal resources that they could hardly carry out their 'normal' activities as government.[14] In some places, education, road building and other basic government services were severely diminished. Views were highly polarized. Many scholars suggested cutting bureaucracy by making the township a branch office of the county government, whereas others fiercely disagreed.[15] Questions were raised as to whether the central government had *intentionally* weakened the township or even pre-planned the demise of township government from the beginning of the rural tax reforms, as part of a 'master plan' to eliminate a major cause of excessive extraction (Kennedy 2005). An affirmative answer would be in line with a 'top-down' conception of the reform process.

There are *prima facie* indications of a top-down 'central project' to weed out the townships. Ongoing reforms designed to contain extrabudgetary and off-budget local revenues, for example, have tightened up fiscal monitoring from above. In some provinces, the salaries of state workers, such as schoolteachers, had already become a county responsibility *prior to* the rural tax reform (Li 2005a: 87–108). Various components in the public finance reforms, such as centralizing local government accounting services, also seemed to have contributed to the weakening of the township as a level of government.[16] The tax-for-fee reforms – by capping extraction and eventually erasing the majority of fees – deprived many agricultural townships of their historically central function: to collect taxes and fees.[17]

This picture, however, is less neat and tidy if the agency of local actors is considered. Rather than dictating the reform, the central government failed to act at critical junctures, and relied on provinces and localities to fill the gap. Whatever effects the rural tax reform had on rural services, these were a product, somewhat unintended, of strategic interactions between central and local state actors.

Top-down pressures

While petty state functionaries at the grassroots level are sometimes seen by local populations as embodying the 'state' (see Gupta 1995: 375–402), central leaders find it useful to their legitimacy to distinguish between themselves and their local agents. In the search for scapegoats, they often reinforce or even generate perceptions that blame policy failures on implementation details and front-line state workers, rather than on inadequacies of policy design. A process of this kind took place in relation to peasant fiscal burden. The centre suggested that predatory and inefficient local officials had caused excessive burdens. This attribution of blame matched well with the popular perception that the central government had promulgated all kinds of good policies, only to have them distorted or ignored by local implementers. In a 2004 survey, Lianjiang Li found that the lower one goes down the state hierarchy, the lower the trust rural residents have on officials.[18] Attributing blame to local officials has worked to the benefit of the central government, allowing it additional space to review and correct failing policies. Ironically, the central government needs the independence of local cadres for this process to work. Local cadres implement risky policies so that the centre can claim those policies that work and scapegoat lower levels when these policies fail.

This policy process was not simply a matter of a wicked centre wishing to abandon its responsibility. It also reflected policy contention at the highest levels. A veteran provincial level official involved in the reform process offered the following observation:

> We in the provinces know very well that the tax-for-fee reform is merely the starting point, a window from which gradually to dismantle the multi-faceted institutional and policy constraints against the peasants. But the reform process was first complicated by power struggles amongst the top leaders (in particular between Party General Secretary Jiang Zemin and Premier Zhu Rongji), and then caught up in bureaucratic meddling and departmental interests. The Ministry of Finance, in charge of the reform since 1998, had, for instance, little expertise or interest in rural governance and the peasantry. They had thus adopted a pedantic approach to the issue of reducing the peasant burden, seeing it narrowly as a question of improving fiscal implementation and rationalization. They had not taken the broader picture of the national fiscal system and rural–urban resource allocation into consideration.[19]

One notable indication of this gross neglect at the centre was the needless policy reversals that resulted from too much haste in the implementation process. On 15 February 2001, the official Xinhua news agency issued a press release that immediately made the headlines: the central government was about to extend the reform to the whole country by 2002.[20] Two days after the announcement, a national agricultural work conference was held in Hefei, capital of Anhui Province. Among the participants were some 48 provincial/ministerial level officials from 20 provinces.[21] The meeting served to strengthen the message sent initially by the Xinhua release: a major rural reform was imminent. However, it then became clear that the necessary groundwork had not been laid. During the

Hefei meeting, Finance Minister Xiang Huaizheng said nothing new, apart from reiterating the Xinhua announcement and requiring the provinces to provide cost calculations. The latter suggests that the central government had imposed a time frame of reform *before* provincial leaders were consulted and costs calculated. Moreover, in early March, before provincial leaders had returned their cost calculations, then Premier Zhu Rongji announced the reform to people's deputies and the press during the annual meeting of the National People's Congress. Zhu went on record saying that the central government planned to allocate 20–30 billion yuan annually from the central coffers to cover the reduced income caused by the rural tax reform, or more if necessary. When questioned whether this was sufficient, Zhu was ambivalent: 'I may be able to be more specific at next year's (post-NPC) press conference'.[22]

It is surprising that the central government should declare a major policy in such an authoritative and open forum as the National People's Congress Annual Plenum, with the presence of national and international media, without proper preparation. As if to confirm these oral commitments, the State Council issued a directive nine days after Zhu's press conference, in which provincial governments were allowed 'to decide for themselves' whether to implement the rural tax reform, subject to the approval of the State Council.[23] Despite the soft wording, the directive was widely perceived as a signal to launch reforms quickly. At this point, however, provincial governments had not yet finished with their cost calculations. Had the central leaders waited a little longer and seen the provincial estimates first, they might have avoided the subsequent embarrassment of having to reverse the March directive with a new one in April. One possible reason is that central leaders had underestimated the complexity of the issues involved, thinking that provincial calculations – when they came – would only make changes at the margin. The central government was apparently too confident of its own estimate (20–30 billion yuan), made by central fiscal officials largely in-house and drawing on, by and large, official statistics of agricultural tax revenues and the centrally endorsed township and village fees only.[24] There was no intention to include in the calculation all the other miscellaneous local fees that, being unauthorized, were to be simply abolished. Local governments were expected to absorb the forgone revenues from these 'illegitimate' fees by cutting 'unnecessary' expenditure – for instance, by downsizing local bureaucracies.[25] The gap between these expectations and the practical situations in many townships was wide and, as noted previously, the actual situation in the townships was in fact well known among segments of intelligentsia and policy circles. The Ministry of Finance had relatively limited knowledge of the complexities of rural affairs, as rural affairs had not traditionally been in its portfolio.[26] The ministry's 'blind spot' was ignored and existing knowledge elsewhere was not solicited, despite the fact that a major policy was at stake.

Considerable elite competition and tension between Jiang Zemin and Zhu Rongji might have contributed to this oversight.[27] After nearly a decade of local experimentation with lukewarm support from the centre, tax reforms had finally secured a heavy push from Jiang Zemin in September 1998, when in a high-profile visit to Anhui Province, Jiang spoke in favour of continuing the reform experiments. Jiang's explicit support at that juncture was critical, since local reform experiments in Hebei and other provinces had been suspended a few months earlier due to incompatibility with a new national policy on the circulation of agricultural products, backed by Zhu Rongji.[28] After Jiang's new stand on the tax reform, Zhu swiftly became a stout supporter.[29] At the Party Central Committee Plenum of October 1998, rural tax reform was officially endorsed as national policy, and a three-man team was formed within the State Council to formulate a detailed reform package.[30] Subsequently, Zhu repeatedly urged the team to adjust their planning schedules and speed up implementation. When the team proposed a three-stage work plan (proposals, consultation and pilot implementation) and suggested full implementation by 2002, Zhu responded 'the three phases can proceed simultaneously rather than consecutively, and why wait until 2002? We should aim at starting reform in several provinces by next year [1999]!' (Chen and Chun 2004: 354).

When provinces returned their calculations in April 2001, 2 months after the Hefei conference, the total annual bill that the central government was asked to foot amounted to 100 billion yuan.[31] With the impact of the Asian Financial Crisis,[32] this amount exceeded the centre's capacity, and led to an embarrassing slowdown: a new State Council directive was issued abruptly on 25 April, exactly 1 month after the 24 March directive, to announce a 'temporary halt to reform extension'. For a while, the international media abounded with reports that the Chinese burden-reduction reforms had been aborted.[33]

Elite competition and bureaucratic boundaries worked against proper reform preparation at the central level, despite a long gestation at the local levels and the availability of better knowledge elsewhere. The resulting reform package reflected a very partial, and lopsided, understanding of the issues involved, and aimed at making local governments absorb most of the costs of reform. Provincial governments were naturally opposed to this and therefore lobbied hard for central transfers.

Local reactions

Central–provincial bargaining over reform costs delayed implementation of reform for more than a year. Momentum was regained in 2002. Twenty provinces had implemented the reform by the end of 2002, and by late 2003, virtually all 30 had done so. In 2002, new central subsidies allocated for the 'tax-for-fee' reform amounted to 24.5 billion yuan. This rose to 30.5 billion and 52.4 billion yuan in 2003 and 2004, respectively.[34] By spring 2002, tax reform seemed worthwhile to many provincial governments. As one provincial official explained:

> It is pretty simple why we started. The central government promised us additional subsidies to kick-start the reform. Why not snap up the new monies? Reform or not, these new resources will add to the local coffers. The provincial government cannot lose out one way or another by joining.

Once reform appeared inevitable, provincial governments set their eyes on maximizing their gains. In any event, the bulk of actual reform costs could be pushed further downwards, to counties and townships, and the province could even profit by 'taxing' central subsidies.[35]

Branded as inefficient, corrupt and unruly, officials at township and village levels became the 'object' of burden-reduction measures, while also bearing the brunt of responsibility for implementing the reforms. The reforms got a sceptical reception among county and township officials. Provincial leaders in Hubei, for instance, publicly acknowledged that local cadres were 'confused' about the need for this reform, and early starters in 2002 had run into considerable difficulties.[36] County and township officials lacked a sense of urgency, it was argued, and during preparatory work were interested more in calculating costs – and bargaining for more fiscal compensation from above – than in working out expenditure cuts.[37]

It quickly became clear to county and township officials, however, that resisting implementation was out of the question. Heimer describes how higher levels use the cadre responsibility system to make township officials implement reform measures that are against their interests.[38] Essentially, this involves placing mandatory requirements in the 'performance contracts' that county governments sign with the townships. In 2003, these requirements included meeting specific tax reduction benchmarks and avoiding overt conflicts arising from the implementation process.[39] Provinces also stepped up their monitoring of reform implementation. In the agricultural heartlands, where levies were known to be high, provincial inspection teams were dispatched to all counties.[40] The teams would normally stay in a county for a week to visit households and grassroots cadres across townships and villages. Information was collected first-hand on as many as 45 benchmarks, ranging from the degree of burden reduction, methods of implementation, imposition of new fees, and township administrative structuring and downsizing.[41] For instance, as a result of provincial inspections in early 2003, one county in Hubei was criticized for failing a number of performance indicators. These included reducing the tax burden to a level below both the 2001 level and 100 yuan per acre. The county was relatively well off and county fiscal officials attributed their failure to insufficient consideration of local conditions in the central reform requirements and resistance from local (township and village) cadres.[42]

Such stepped up vigilance served to convey a clear message: county and township officials had to treat the reform seriously and meet the required targets. As provinces competed to outperform the centrally prescribed benchmarks, the collection of local fees declined nationwide.[43] In all the townships and counties we visited during the course of our fieldwork, the fiscal burden appeared to have dropped considerably, notwithstanding problems over the quality of reports and statistics.[44]

How did county and township officials manage to meet the target, given the entrenched nature of the burden problem documented extensively in the literature? Mostly they managed by simply reducing the services provided by local governments. A leading cadre in a moderately industrialized town in Anhui Province said,

> Well, we can only do what our means allow us to. The burden level *must* go down, and we are left with much less than what we need even just to maintain the basic operation of government. Despite the increase in transfers, these cannot compensate for what we lost from fees. With less disposable resources we can only do much less.

This town is the site of the only foreign joint venture in Shucheng County, Anhui, and had good access to inter-provincial roads.[45] It was thus better off than neighbouring towns, and the county had also recently increased fiscal extractions from the town. But even in this 'better-off' town, the entire annual budget of 1.7 million yuan, including incoming fiscal subsidies, was sufficient only to pay for staff salaries and basic social security.[46] Developing the local economy further would have required new investments in road building and farmland irrigation. When monies were tight, development was simply out of the question. 'The farthest we can set our sights on these days are minor projects of a "remedial" nature', said the Party secretary. The officials elaborated that they had planned minor public works valued at some 0.6–0.7 million yuan (over a year), but as a result of the reduced income, they could only afford a third of them.

Such was the situation that a town with some industrial income and foreign investment was seen by the county as a 'milk cow'. In townships more dependent on agriculture, the 'minimalist' approach to public expenditure often meant despair and resignation. In another town in a hilly region of Anhui Province,[47] town leaders were preoccupied not with choosing which public projects they could afford but with meeting the basic expenses that the routine operation of a government office would have taken for granted.

> Now we have even less for local use than before [the tax-for-fee reform], since the payments from above are less than what we used to collect from below. Moreover, previously we would decide how much to collect from the peasants based on how much we needed to spend. Now everything is fixed above and we have had less revenue. How does this affect us? First, there is the historical debt accumulated from previous projects, education and other items. I don't know how we can possibly repay it. Second, we are running into new debts, as sometimes we are forced to borrow money to pay for tasks that must be done as a matter of necessity, despite the dire post-reform fiscal situation. Third, we have numerous funding 'gaps' in the day-to-day running of government offices, including staff salaries, operating costs such as transport expenses, telephone and internet connection fees, and reception expenses. These are major concerns to us since they recur on a daily basis.

In this town, some components of staff salaries had historically relied on extrabudgetary income. As extrabudgetary fees were now prohibited under the reform, the town became heavily reliant on incoming transfers, which amounted to over half of its total outlay. Fiscal dependence appeared to have made township cadres more receptive towards further centralizing measures.

> I heard that the county level will soon take over the payroll management of all township cadres. Last year they did that to our teachers. Well, is it good? Yes, even though this will signal the substantive 'death' of the township as a level of fiscal finance, if not in name. The township has *never* been an independent level [of finance] in the past anyway! The biggest benefit of this change is the prospect of evening out cadres' salaries across different townships. The long-standing inequity of differential pay levels between richer and poorer townships would then be rectified. This is fairer and good for morale.

This attitude of welcoming the 'demise' of one's level of government was not peculiar to this town, or to specific individuals. The Party Secretary of another average-income, and until recently largely agricultural, township in Anhui Province sent a similar, and stronger, message when I asked him to comment on the impact of the tax reform:[48]

> The current situation in our country is that the upper levels (central and provincial) are flooded with resources, whilst the local levels are left to struggle. The lower in the state hierarchy you go, the more difficult the situation is. We at the township level have the most to do, but the least to spend. This is irresponsible, as I see it. The result? Numerous tasks are left undone. It is futile for us even to protest. Nobody will listen. What makes it worse is that if anything within our township goes wrong, superiors will *not* examine why and how. They do not care whether we have done our duties properly. *They will just hold us responsible* – because things under our jurisdiction go wrong! This is what we call the 'leadership responsibility system'. Nobody would seriously care to find out if we have the resources or power to perform the assigned duties to start with. We are just to take the blame, we are the scapegoat ... What could we in the township do to make our lives easier? Not much, really. Everyday we walk a tightrope. Our people often say: we can only work with what we are given. *Now we are just hoping for 'peace' – if we escape major problems by the end of a day, then we congratulate one another for making it through one more day* ... What do I think about abolishing the township as an independent level? Well, I'm for it. Since 2004 it is the county that manages our budget.[49] If we go one step further and make the township a branch office of the county, the upper levels will have to take over our current responsibilities. That would be a relief! We would then be free of the burden of worrying over insufficient resources or being held responsible for tasks that are beyond our means. We can then focus our work on implementation.

The speed with which the national reform achieved its intended objective – as seen in high burden-reduction rates – has brought to the foreground a central issue: whether villagers can prosper simply with a reduced level of extraction. As noted earlier, it was widely acknowledged within academic and policy circles that burden reduction should be sustainable. The embedded nature of the burden issue, however, was lost in the policy phase. What needed to be 'fixed' were problems in the implementation of policies at the lower levels: counties and townships. Local officials were left with little choice but to comply, given their subordinate status in the state bureaucracy, and they coped by passively 'sitting through' their job. With resources barely sufficient to pay for salaries, public services were minimized, if provided at all. Some townships found it difficult just to maintain the government. Ironically, 'to maintain the basic operations of grassroots-level government' was one of the three main objectives of the rural tax reform.[50] Without a sufficient budget, and banned from entrepreneurial activities, commercial or fiscal, township officials learnt the security of dependence, and thus tacitly embraced the 'demise' of townships as an independent level of government. The collective response among township cadres to the enthusiastic debates among academic and policy analysts on their future prospect was one of resignation: *'we have never been independent'*.

Conclusion

This chapter suggests that the central state has, as a result of elite competition and bureaucratic politics, simplistically attributed the hardships of rural life (low household income and low levels of public goods provision, and so on) to excessive *local* extraction. In turn, this extraction was explained by overstaffing and spending abuses in townships and villages. A complex and multifaceted issue was reduced to one of maladministration and bad institutional designs at local levels. The beauty of this schema, from the perspective of central state actors, is that it absolved the central government of responsibility for rural suffering. Supervision of local agents thus became a central aspect of the national reform programme. A scapegoat was found, and then hunted down, and reform objectives – bettering the situation of the peasants – were proclaimed accomplished.

Township cadres, the objects of the reform, defended their past practice and demanded that superiors play fair by paying for its costs. They then utilized their advantage as implementers by tailoring reform details to their needs, maximizing job security, and minimizing responsibilities. Paradoxically, the cumulative effect of the implementation manoeuvres has been to *foster* the centrally defined objectives of the reform, as demonstrated in the higher-than-expected burden-reduction rates and the faster-than-scheduled pace of reform implementation nationwide. As reform approached its completion, local state actors also tacitly accepted their dependency, leading to a collapse of township governance. When local officials were deprived of the motivation, authority and resources to assume responsibility for local governance, upper levels were left with a choice between taking new measures or ignoring the need for action. Subsequent attempts to shift upwards the fiscal responsibility over education to the provincial level, and the

'Construct the New Socialist Countryside' Programme, suggest that more duties are being assumed by central and provincial governments in making up for the public goods 'deficit' in rural areas.[51] Whether these will eventually work *for* rural residents and have any meaningful impact on the quality of rural governance remains to be seen. What this chapter shows is that changes in rural fiscal practices were not the result of a central plan, but the outcome of a complex process that no one had designed.

Conclusion

The previous pages have told the story, or stories, of a reform seeking changes to the practice of local state extraction in the Chinese countryside. What insights does this discussion bring to existing knowledge about institutional change and policy process, in particular on institutional entrepreneurship and the transition from deinstitutionalization to reinstitutionalization? Is the rural tax reform in China at all a coherent programme working towards an objective and change target which is identified a priori and defined relatively clearly? This conclusion revisits the main empirical findings of the book to highlight the messages they bring to our theoretical understanding of policy process and institutional change.

The institutionalism literature has suggested that institutional entrepreneurs may be found at either 'central' positions or the 'periphery' of the institutional field (Hardy and Maguire 2008: 201–2). Actors at the periphery are more prone to innovate as they have more access to alternative practices and ideas, are less embedded in existing practices and less constrained by interests and powers of the system. On the other hand, central actors possess the resources to make changes, when and if they want to (Greenwood and Suddaby 2006: 40). In the case of state extraction practices discussed in this study, change efforts have emerged as a result of actions, and interactions, of *both* central (national government) and peripheral (local government) actors. Institutional entrepreneurship is found to be a complex *process*, with heterogeneous actors constructing, and narrating, a multitude of accounts, each of which prescribes a different definition of 'the problem', its causes and preferred remedies. Specifically, local officials have shouldered the brunt of policy failures, facing dual pressures from above and rural constituents from below. These intense pressures have given rise to incentives among *some* local government actors to innovate. As noted in Chapter 1, a few town-level officials were critical to the emergence of local experiments on rural tax reforms, despite the huge political risk involved. In contrast, leaders at the more upper levels, from county to national, were characteristically 'slippery', preferring to have subordinates act rather than sticking out their own necks. The obvious question is why should those local officials who had volunteered their initiatives have bothered at all, in view of the non-committal stance of many of their superiors? Why did the rule of collective actions on commons *not* apply in these instances?

When confronted with anomalies, there is often a temptation to dismiss the evidence and interpret the anomalies as a latent variation of the rule. A commonplace tendency in explaining local agency in an authoritarian regime has been to attribute local actions to decisions at the 'top', so that local innovations become merely the disguised outcome of implementation of intentions and ideas higher up in the state hierarchy. Heilmann's (2008a, 2008b) notion of 'experimentation under hierarchy', for a recent example, stresses the role of national guidance in local experiments, although the explicit objectives of the work are to assess the relevance of local policy experimentation in the Chinese economic reform, not to define the nature of local agency. The local processes of rural tax reform experiments described in this book suggest that central–local interactions have followed a different pattern. Local actors have experimented with new policies *despite* their lower status in a hierarchical structure, *not* because of it. Organizational seniors were found reluctant to demand their subordinates to innovate, lest that they then had to be held responsible for the risks. A combined effect of bottom-up pressures, personal history, local culture and contingency explains how the several individuals situated at the lower echelons and periphery of the policymaking hierarchy had initiated the local experiments that precipitated the nationwide reform of burden reduction a few years later.

Having established the relevance of local agency, our discussion also stresses that local agency *alone* does not suffice for *sustaining* change. Without timely endorsement at a higher, and ultimately, national, level, isolated local experiments, however instrumental they are in *initiating* change, will not persist. Central actors play three essential roles as institutional entrepreneurs, in a context of multilevel, multi-actor governance: (1) assessing alternative local options; (2) conferring legitimacy status to local experiments and thus consolidating their continual existence; and (3) diffusing tried local policies through nationwide implementation. Not until nationwide diffusion takes place does a local experiment acquire a secure status in the process of institutional change.

However, that the central government has a role in sustaining change which has started locally does *not* imply the existence of a linear progression between local experimentation to national policymaking *as a matter of practice*. National decision-making as it occurs often follows its own logic; critical decisions on policy have sometimes been based *not* on a careful assessment of local experiments, but on other considerations not immediately related to the policy in question. Chapter 6 notes that after almost a full decade of official rhetoric on the severity of peasants' burden and years of local reform experience, reform at the national level came to fruition only in the context of power dynamics between top leaders. In 1998, rural tax reform entered the national policy agenda not because the plight of peasants had significantly deteriorated at that point, warranting that action no longer be delayed, but because power competition between Jiang Zemin and Zhu Rongji had led one to embrace the reform so as to undercut the other, and the other was then forced to jump on the reform bandwagon to pre-empt damage.

Counting costs and benefits plays a major part in the policymaking process. Chapter 5 shows that national actors' calculation was tainted by their *previous* experiences with reform, and by their predispositions to see other stakeholders as resisters to change rather than allies to work with. This suggests the possibility of improving policymaking through cautioning policymakers of the risk of path dependence, and by fostering cooperation with other actors. The crux is whether, and how, embedded agency is possible. Can actors disembed themselves from the structure constituting their beliefs, values and knowledge and act otherwise (Seo and Creed 2002; Garud *et al.* 2007)? Oliver (1992: 581) has suggested several scenarios wherein embedded agency may likely emerge: (1) a decline in functional necessity or performance of the practice/institutional arrangements; (2) a weakening of the political interests supporting the institutions; (3) a loosening of the cultural consensus perpetuating the institutions; and (4) a thinning out of the interactions sustaining institutional coherence. In this study, the rural tax regime has failed to perform its basic function of extracting sufficient revenue to finance-approved government services (scenario 1). Over time, the tax regime lost its legitimacy as it was equated with government exploitation and abuses against the peasants (scenarios 2 and 3). Mediating this process of delegitimation and shifting cultural consensus were changes in the interaction patterns among the multiple groups of actors in the multilayer governance system (scenario 4). While central actors blamed local governments for the performance crisis, local governments also accused the upper levels of acting irresponsibly and scapegoating the subordinates for policy failures. The system was pulled from different directions as actors adopted adaptive coping strategies to defuse the effects of efficiency gaps and mutual accusations. Power competition then sealed the fate of the regime as leaders used its *discontinuation*, *vide* the adoption of the rural tax reform, to pursue their personal interests and other agendas (scenario 2). Embedded agency of heterogeneous actors has taken place amidst a combination of multiple co-evolving processes.

Process-centric

Hardy and Maguire (2008: 211) group the literature on institutional entrepreneurship into two broad types: (1) an 'actor-centric' approach highlighting the role of individuals or organizations as 'entrepreneurs', with emphasis on their special qualities and intervention strategies towards a goal of change; (2) a 'process-centric' approach seeing entrepreneurship as a collective process involving multiple actors, whose actions and interactions give rise to change processes as, partly, an unintended consequence. The discursive looms large in the second approach, as actors construct and communicate their conceptions of the problem and prescriptions of remedy to other actors as part of the 'struggling' process. The analysis in this book falls in line with the 'process-centric' approach.

Despite this distinction, actors are central in all processes, and differences between the approaches are a matter of degree. Throughout the chapters, there are abundant descriptions of actors: their definition of the problem, their ideas of reform, their efforts to recruit allies and overcome resistance, their self-collections and assessments of the change process, challenges and achievements. One key actor discussed is Anhui agricultural technician He Kaiyin (Chapter 1), whose resilience in winning allies for his reform ideas was critical in translating a general discussion into a policy programme. Another is Hubei district-level party secretary Song Yaping, whose ambitious comprehensive reform programmes bridged the boundaries of multiple fields pertinent to improving the performance of rural governance (Chapters 3 and 4).

This book has focused not only on the impact of the agency of these key actors on the reform process but also, if not more, on the *linkage* between the agency of the key actors, the embedding historical organizational socio-economic contexts, and the agency of the other actors (their perceptions of the problem, remedy and the contexts underlining the perceptions) with whom the key actors worked, or struggled against. In fact, appreciating the meanings and significance of the ideas requires an understanding of the contexts wherein the ideas have emerged. To fully grasp the entrepreneurship of He Kaiyin, for example, it is insufficient to elaborate how resilient He was when persuading officials to put his reform ideas into policy action – what he said and what he did in the process of persuasion. His early life experiences played a critical part in cultivating his capacity to withstand frustration and in strengthening his determination to persist in the face of setbacks. Similarly, Song Yaping's reform ideas can be comprehended only in the context of Song's adventurous experiences in southern China as a 'free floating' worker, as well as the challenges facing Xian-an District at the time when Song arrived as district party secretary. Placing the contexts and processes at the centre stage of analysis, and including both the accounts of key actors and counter accounts of others to reveal both the intended and unintended dimensions of the change process, characterizes the 'process-centric' approach of this study.

Dual policy process

On policy and its process, our discussion confirms an old wisdom: the 'stages' model is a heuristic device rather than actual description of the policy process. Policymaking and implementation interweave at the level of activity, as well as interact as processes (Lasswell 1956). The designs and contents of the rural tax reform have changed substantially over time to respond to new problems identified during the course of implementation. More importantly, policy evolution has emerged as a result of interactions of actors from varied levels of the political system and organizational hierarchy, with each level (except the very top) engaging in both policymaking activities as well as implementation.

This book has elaborated a dual policy process with features of the 'Garbage Can' and Rational Models, two diametrically opposed analytical policy models in the policy science literature. Against a linear progression from problem definition, goal setting, option identification to cost-benefit analysis of the options in the Rational Model, 'Garbage Can' Model maintains that policy starts from available options (or solutions) searching for a problem when the situation is complex and ambiguous, or technology is uncertain (Cohen *et al.* 1972). The Central Narrative of rural tax reform portrays a neat sequence comprising problem identification, local experimentation, national policy adoption, implementation, feedback and then policy adjustment, with a heavy dose of a rational decision-making process led largely by the central government. Upon closer inspection, however, national policy is found to be more an outcome of available policy options meeting the political needs of central leaders, mediated by truncated notions of problems.

Figure 7.1 portrays the policy process up to the point of national policy adoption in two versions, one reflecting how the policy was formulated as reported in the Central Narrative, and the other following more closely the actual policy trajectory as events unfolded. The nature and scope of the problems identified were substantially different in the two versions, with corresponding impact on the options being conceived and considered. There are no clearly defined 'goals' nor cost-benefit analysis in the 'Garbage Can' version, which are central features in the Rational Model. Cost-benefit analysis is subsumed in the identification of options in the Garbage Can Model: available options in the form of working local measures are regarded, implicitly, having passed the cost-benefit test. At the same time, specific policy options (the 'garbage') are sought out when they are perceived to meet the relevant interests or concerns of the critical actors. The direct linkage between interests as inputs and policy instruments as outputs makes unnecessary the independent identification and analysis of problem and goals in the Garbage Can Model.

Notwithstanding their obvious differences, the two models are useful as heuristic tools only. Each model assumes some elements of the other and is thus at least partially mutually constitutive of one another. For example, while the Central Narrative adopts the Rational Model in portraying the evolution process from problem identification to policy design, the *specific definition* of problem in the Narrative was in fact mediated by interests of the dominant actors (Chapter 6). It has thus taken up the 'truncated' definitions in the Garbage Can Model rather than the more comprehensive definitions and analyses in the Rational Model.

From deinstitutionalization to reinstitutionalization

Can reform last and the reduced burden level stay? The success of reform is contingent on effective deinstitutionalization of the pre-existing pattern of practice as well as the reinstitutionalization of the new mode of practice. Deinstitutionalization refers to the process 'by which the legitimacy of an established or institutionalized organizational practice erodes or discontinues' (Oliver 1992: 564). The erosion of legitimacy may occur as a result of 'organizational challenges' – in this case, the local and national reform measures, or the failures to reproduce previously legitimated actions. As a process of 'destructing' the status quo, deinstitutionalization is the first and prerequisite step of having sustained change: the old form of existence needs to cease before a new form can emerge, *and then* stay. We may thus envisage,

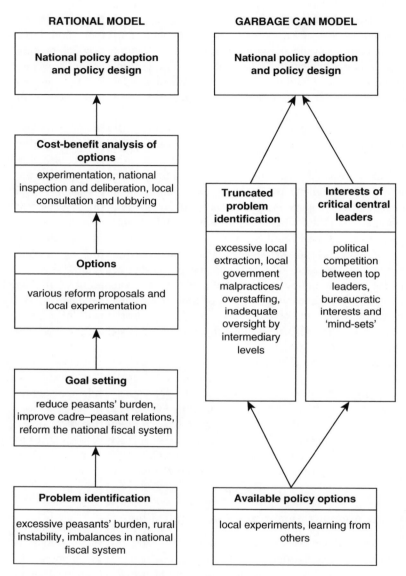

RATIONAL MODEL

National policy adoption and policy design

↑

Cost-benefit analysis of options

experimentation, national inspection and deliberation, local consultation and lobbying

↑

Options

various reform proposals and local experimentation

↑

Goal setting

reduce peasants' burden, improve cadre–peasant relations, reform the national fiscal system

↑

Problem identification

excessive peasants' burden, rural instability, imbalances in national fiscal system

GARBAGE CAN MODEL

National policy adoption and policy design

Truncated problem identification

excessive local extraction, local government malpractices/ overstaffing, inadequate oversight by intermediary levels

Interests of critical central leaders

political competition between top leaders, bureaucratic interests and 'mind-sets'

Available policy options

local experiments, learning from others

Figure 7.1 Rural tax reform: dual policy processes.

analytically, a three-step process for institutional change: (1) deinstitutionalization of the old established practice; (2) emergence of new actions; and (3) the institutionalization of the new actions, or 're-institutionalization'.[1]

This conclusion so far has focused on the first and second phases: deinstitutionalization and emergence of new actions. For the new actions, and their effects, to *last*, a reverse process of *re*institutionalization is required, wherein the new actions and effects acquire a status of 'taken-for-grantedness' – much as the status of the previous, old pattern *before* the deinstitutionalization process had set in – and no longer necessitate continuous interventions to sustain their continuance (Jepperson 1991: 151; Berger and Luckmann 1967: 80). The literature on institutional logics has stressed the contribution of contradictions between the differential institutional logics across multiple institutional fields to *generate* institutional change (Friedland and Alford 1991; Clemens and Cook 1999; Seo and Creed 2002). The emphasis is largely on the processes leading to deinstitutionalization as the contradictions between diverse and conflicting institutional logics precipitate political contestations between actors, which destabilize the cultural consensus underlining the status quo. Chapter 3 suggests that the interaction of actions in differential institutional fields may also lead to *re*institutionalization. Changes in the human resource management field are found to have had positive effects towards sustaining the change effects in the rural tax reform, which actions taken within the fiscal institutional field alone were found insufficient to sustain. Here what is emphasized is the *plurality* of institutional fields that serves to *consolidate* ongoing changes, through interactions of changes across different fields of actions. Differential institutional logics thus may complement, as much as contradict one another. Actions taken in one institutional arena embedded in a web of related and diverse institutional arrangements may work to reinforce actions in a related arena, and help towards institutionalizing the latter. The interrelatedness of institutions does not only contain seeds of contradiction and work towards *de*institutionalization but also seeds of co-development to foster *re*institutionalization; both processes are integral to completing the change process.[2]

Embracing, and transcending, contingency and uncertainties

This book has charted the twists and turns in the change processes of a recent phase of an old practice in China: state extraction from the rural population. It illuminates a complex picture of pluralist stories told by diverse actors involved in the parallel processes, full with rhetoric and translation, interest and struggles, evolving objectives, shifting grounds and unintended consequences – the 'accessories' the institutionalism and policy science literatures have identified in the change baggage. Elaborations in the theoretical literature over the recent few decades have called for empirical work to test the theoretical propositions and to stimulate further theoretical inspirations, and many have noted the practical difficulties faced in in-depth empirical studies (Greenwood *et al.* 2008: 25). Fully aware of these challenges and having faced a lot of them, this book seeks to contribute towards filling this empirical gap.

Several findings stand out. One is the complexity of change process and plurality of actors involved in the process or, more precisely, processes. This requires analysts to go beyond any single account of the events to reach for alternative accounts and to interpret their interactions. National level actors, actors at the intermediary levels and local actors engage in a continuous process of strategic interactions. While national policymakers blamed local actors for bad policy implementation, they were slow to recognize their due share of responsibility and relied excessively on local levels for bearing the costs of change. Local actors were both innovative and passive. They were mostly passive and often resigned to their fate of serving as scapegoats of upper level decisions. But at times, when pressures built up to crisis level, the need to respond to top-down demands led a few to experiment with changes proactively, often with minimal or nil support from upper levels. While these local innovators were still motivated by a desire to deliver better their jobs as *subordinates*, instrumental to the process of innovation was the bottom-up pressure from the society in which these local, and often grassroots-, level officials were embedded. With no lower level to pass along their responsibilities, town-level officials were in an unenviable position of having to face up to the challenges of real-life governance and to deliver minimal results which their upper levels could more easily choose to evade. Obviously, the vast majority of local-level officials just got by and did not seek change. But in this study of the rural tax reform, it was a group of town-level officials who turned ideas of reform into actions.

One major challenge of this study is to face squarely the limits to this enterprise to get to know about policy process and institutional change. Indeed another main finding of this study is the centrality of uncertainty and contingency in the change process. Most local officials did not bother to innovate, but a few did and their agency set off changes, subsequently, on a larger scale. What explains the occurrence of agency as and when it takes place? The complexity of the change process means that multiple 'parallel' processes are involved. These processes are related to a varied degree. Moreover, it is not possible to anticipate in advance whether, and how, these developments will 'co-evolve' to a point that brings forward a certain situation. To a large extent, we are able to *identify* what constitutes the 'relevant' processes only *post hoc* – after their co-evolution has come to a situation that we can then know of their relevance to the subject of inquiry. However this does not imply total chaos in the world of social analysis, and that serious academic work is the same as guesswork. What we need is to register uncertainty and contingency, know their relevance to our work as social analysts and use an appropriate method that allows us to take account of the parallel processes that *may* be relevant to our analysis. The following has been said towards the end of Chapter 1,

> ... it is futile to look for parameters defining 'conditions' of sustainability. Eager to anticipate the chance of success (or failure) of ongoing change processes as we may be, we cannot possibly foresee what may happen tomorrow and the day after tomorrow from what has happened today and yesterday. The possibilities of contingencies and the existence of parallel, diverse processes are real and abundant, so that what has taken place – which we as analysts take note of – will only have a *partial* influence on future events. It could be that just round the corner, a process that seems

totally irrelevant as of yesterday will 'co-evolve' to a point of relevance — but we could only know that *after* such co-evolution happens, at a later point of time. That does not imply incessant chaos and volatility in our vision of the future, however. To the extent that we cannot predict what will happen tomorrow, we know *by and large* how things will be, and the manner and processes whereby change may happen, or not happen, by taking a closer look at the past. We know there will be contingencies. We know we are all influenced by history. We know we can all make a difference, if we want to. As a result life has its side of 'stability' and 'certainty', as well as being dotted by 'surprises', nice or bitter. A 'back along the timeline' account reveals all these dependence-stability influences and agency processes in their full manifestation, and thus enables us to ground the eclectic observations that shape the future. The work of social analysis is to reveal in full how ambiguities work, not to explain them away and replace them with self-imposed simplicity.

Appendix

A chronology of major events and actors

Year	Actor(s)	Event(s)
1988 (October)	Central Rural Policy Research Office; He Kaiyin, Anhui Provincial Government General Office Research Center	National essay contest in commemoration of rural reform of 1978; He's award-winning essay called for deepening of rural reforms. The essay was published in central 'internal intelligence' bulletins and circulated among senior national officials, along with other award-winning essays
1990 (February)	He Kaiyin	He published another paper advocating reform through an Anhui-based Xinhua journalist. The paper caught the attention of several national officials and Anhui Provincial leaders. Anhui Provincial Government called a meeting of rural policy officials to discuss He's ideas but no further action was taken due to unfavourable reform climate at the time
1991 (February)	State Council Research Office; Premier Li Peng; He Kaiyin	An official at the State Council Research Office told He that Premier Li Peng was interested in He's reform ideas. However due to the straitened national situation at the time, Li could not commit any support, whether in terms of resources or policy. He also refused to put his words of support on record
1991 (April)	He Kaiyin; provincial leaders in Anhui, Henan, Hebei	In another paper on rural reform, He elaborated his ideas on rural land and tax reforms. The paper was reprinted in 'internal intelligence reports' of several major national dailies, catching the attention of some provincial leaders in Anhui, Henan and Hebei

(Continued)

Appendix (Continued)

Year	Actor(s)	Event(s)
1992 (Spring)	He Kaiyin; Du Rensheng, Director of the former Central Rural Policy Research Office; Wang Zhaoyao, Party Secretary of Fuyang Prefecture, Anhui Province	He and Du met at a land meeting in Anhui. Du was impressed with He's rural reform proposals. Du introduced He to Wang, who was also at the meeting. Wang was then under pressure to adopt reform of some kind in Fuyang, which was designated a national rural reform experimental zone since 1987. After the meeting, Wang took He to Fuyang to explore reform possibilities
1992	Party Secretary Liu and Mayor Li, Xinxing Town, Woyang County, Fuyang Prefecture, Anhui Province	Xinxing became the *first locality* to implement rural tax reform, despite the reform being previously vetoed by the County People's Congress. The Xinxing reform started the era of rural tax reform as a practice. Some neighbouring localities followed suit and started their experiments
1993	Various counties in Hebei, Anhui, Guizhou, Hunan provinces; Wang Zhaoyao; Ma Yeming, Mayor of Taihe County, Anhui	More counties started piloting rural tax reform, with the support of local, and sometimes, provincial, leaders. Wang Zhaoyao (Fuyang prefecture party secretary) was promoted to Vice-Governor and Deputy Party Secretary of Anhui Province. Ma Yeming met He Kaiyin in a provincial agricultural meeting and together they worked out a rural tax reform proposal for Taihe, which Wang recommended to the Provincial leadership for approval
1994	Anhui Provincial Government; Hebei Provincial Government	Anhui Provincial Government officially approved the piloting of rural tax reform across all townships in Taihe County, despite initial differences in opinions among the leaders. At the same time, Hebei Provincial Government announced an extension of the reform in Hebei province
1995 (April)	Wang Yuzhao, former Anhui Provincial Governor and Deputy Director of Economic Affairs Committee of National People's Political Consultative Conference (NPPCC)	Wang Yuzhao had played an instrumental role in Anhui's 1978 rural reform and been supportive of He's ideas, the two men being colleagues in Anhui in the late 1970s. Wang led a study delegation to Anhui to assess the need for rural reform. He was invited to accompany the visit. The study report argued in favour of reforming the rural tax collection system in order to contain peasants' burden within a reasonable limit

Year	Actor(s)	Event(s)
1996	Various provincial and local leaders; Vice-Premier Li Nanqing; NPPCC Chairman Li Ruihuan	Wang's report on rural tax reform was endorsed by Li Ruihuan and forwarded to State Council and Central Committee for consideration. The pilot reform extended to 50 counties in seven major agricultural provinces. Li Nanqing inspected pilot reforms in Henan Province and Fuyang Prefecture of Anhui Province and compiled a report in favour of reform for circulation to other central leaders
1997 (January)	Central Rural Work Conference; Vice-Premier Wen Jiabao	Wen stated the central leadership's position on rural tax reform: the local pilots had achieved desirable results and useful experiences and could hence continue. However, implementation across the board was premature, given its complexity and impact on other arenas and systems such as the national fiscal system and grain procurement system
1998 (June)	Premier Zhu Rongji	Zhu approved a State Council Order on grain procurement. The new arrangements contradicted with the rural tax reforms being piloted in six provinces, grinding reform to a halt. Fuyang Prefecture of Anhui became, apparently, the sole locality still piloting the reform
1998 (September)	Jiang Zemin, Party Secretary and State President	Jiang threw himself behind rural tax reform and spoke favourably of a national policy during a high-profile visit to Anhui
1998 (October)	The Third Plenum of the Fifteenth Central Committee, CPC; Zhu Rongji and Jiang Zemin; three-man team (Finance Minister, Agriculture Minister, Head of the Central Leading Group on Economics and Finance)	Premier Zhu Rongji announced the Rural Tax Reform as national policy at the Third Plenum. A three-man team was formed within the State Council to formulate a detailed reform package. The team proposed a three-stage work plan (proposals, consultation and pilot implementation) and suggested full implementation by 2002. Zhu urged for a faster pace, with implementation in several provinces in 1999
1999 (March)	Premier Zhu Rongji, at NPC Annual Plenum	The Government Report states the Government's decision to launch the rural tax reform in order to 'relieve peasants' burden from its roots'. Reform was to be piloted in Anhui Province in 1999 before extension nationwide

(Continued)

Appendix (Continued)

Year	Actor(s)	Event(s)
1999 (April)	3-man team	The team submitted to the State Council a report to guide reform implementation, based on studies and investigations of local reform piloting experience
1999 (November)	Zhu Rongji, at Central Economic Work Conference	Zhu reiterated the Government's determination to implement rural tax reform, and announced a new schedule: piloting in several provinces in 2000, and nationwide implementation from 2001
2000 (January)	State Council, 57th Premiers' Work Meeting	The meeting approved the major reform parameters recommended by the three-man team, including setting the rate of Agricultural Tax at 7%, and local surtax at 20%
2000 (March)	The Central Committee, CPC and State Council	Central Document No. 7, 'A decision on launching pilot reforms to rural fee and tax system', announced the national reform package and piloting reforms throughout Anhui
2000 (April onwards)	Ministry of Finance, and other central ministries; Jiangsu Province	Promulgation of a series of related regulations and guidelines on various dimensions of reform: tax rates of various special agricultural products, abolition of township- and village-level fees, adjustment of county–township fiscal relations, improving township governance, etc. Jiangsu provincial leadership opted to commence reform using its own resources
2001 (March 15)	Premier Zhu Rongji, at a press conference during NPC Annual Plenum	In answering to a question from a reporter, Zhu stated that the central government was prepared to spend 20–30 billion yuan per year to compensate for the shortfall of local revenue as a result of the rural tax reform, which would raise Agriculture Tax rate from 5% to 8.4% (including local surtax) and abolish most fees charged at the township/village levels. The rural education financing and administration system would also be reformed as part of the package

Year	Actor(s)	Event(s)
2001 (March 24)	State Council	State Council Notice No. 5 (2001), 'On further improving the pilot work of the rural tax-for-fee reform', prescribes that provincial governments may proceed to implement the rural tax reform after seeking endorsement by State Council. The message was, in effect, that nationwide implementation of reform could now proceed
2001 (April 25)	State Council General Office	Another State Council directive, 'A notice on some issues on the pilot work of rural tax-for-fee reform in 2001', announces a halt to reform extension. Anhui and Jiangsu continued with reform. It was widely reported in international media that the Chinese rural tax reform had 'aborted'
2001	*Rural tax reform special transfer payment*: As the original plan to extend the piloting to most provinces nationwide in the year 2001 was dropped, central special transfer payment paid out at the end of 2001 was 3.3 billion yuan (0.28% of total central budgetary expenditure of 1176.9 billion yuan), against the originally planned amount of 20–30 billion yuan	
2002 (April)	State Council General Office	'A notice on expanding the pilot work of the rural tax-for-fee reform in 2002' signals the resumption of reform momentum. Twenty provinces implemented the reform on a province-wide basis before end of the year
2002	*Rural tax reform special transfer payment*: 24.5 billion yuan was paid out during the year to 20 provinces, 1.73% of total central budgetary expenditure of 1411.8 billion yuan, an almost 6.5-fold increase over 2001	
2003 (March)	State Council	State Council Notice No. 12 (2003), 'On implementing nationwide the pilot work of rural tax-for-fee reform', announces that all provinces were to pilot the rural tax reform in the year of 2003. The notice also highlights the need for measures to prevent the burden level from rebounding
2003 (March)	Anhui Provincial Government	Anhui Provincial Government Notice, 'On the pilot scheme of shifting the Special Products Tax to Agriculture Tax', sets the scene of the subsequent national abolition of the Special Products Tax, and exemplifies how local actions may contribute to national policy evolution

(Continued)

Appendix (Continued)

Year	Actor(s)	Event(s)
2003 (May)	State Council General Office	State Council General Office Notice No. 50 (2003), 'Opinions on the work to alleviate peasants' burden in 2003', relays detailed instructions from various central ministries including the abolition of related fees, stepped-up oversight arrangements, and new control measures such as the 'one fee' system for schools, and quotas on the maximum newspaper/magazine subscription fees per village/township. This regulation, for the first time since reform commenced, requires provincial governments to report to the State Council the local fees that they had abolished or retained, and instructs explicitly of the criteria on fee screening
2003	*Rural tax reform special transfer payment*: 30.5 billion yuan was paid out during the year to provinces nationwide, 1.94% of total central budgetary expenditure of 1566.3 billion yuan, and 24.5% more than the payment in 2002	
2004 (January)	The Central Committee, CPC	Central Document No. 1 (2004) 'The Central Committee of the Party and State Council's opinions on several policies on enhancing peasant income'. The reform entered the second stage, with the progressive abolition of Agricultural Taxes and introduction of other relief tax measures. Peasants' incomes were also boosted through various direct subsidies
2004 (March)	Premier Wen Jiabao, at NPC Annual Plenum	Wen announced plans to phase out Agriculture Tax in 5 years in his Government Report
2004	*Rural tax reform special transfer payment*: 52.4 billion yuan was paid out during the year to provinces nationwide, 2.86% of total central budgetary expenditure of 1827.4 billion yuan, and 72% more than the payment in 2003	
2005 (March)	Premier Wen Jiabao, at NPC Annual Plenum	Wen stated in his Government Report that the government would complete phasing out Agriculture Tax by 2006, 2 years ahead of the original schedule. By end of the year, 28 provinces had stopped collecting revenue from Agriculture Tax

Year	Actor(s)	Event(s)
2005 (December)	The 19th session of the 10th Standing Committee of NPC	Agriculture Tax was officially abolished *vide* a resolution
2005		*Rural tax reform special transfer payment*: 66.2 billion yuan was paid out during the year to provinces nationwide, 3.26% of total central budgetary expenditure of 2024.9 billion yuan, and 117% more than the payment in 2004
2006		*Rural tax reform special transfer payment*: 78.2 billion yuan was paid out during the year to provinces nationwide, 3.33% of total central budgetary expenditure of 2348.2 billion yuan, and 18% more than the payment in 2005
2007–		From 2007 onwards, annual national budget reports no longer listed separately the rural tax reform transfer payments, apparently due to routinization

Notes

Introduction

1 An early reference to the political implication of peasants' burden can be found in a notice by CCP Central Committee Secretariat, State Council Secretariat (1993), which complains of the ineffective local implementation of previous central directives on peasants' burden and warns of the repercussions of the aggravating burdens on agricultural production, as well as social stability of the countryside and the entire country. In June 1996, then General Secretary and State President Jiang Zemin raised the stakes further during a site visit to Henan villages (see quotation; Jiang 1996) to a matter of life and death of the Party. A similar tone and reference to 'long-term stability and peace' was found in a central committee document on peasants' burden issued a few months later (CCP Central Committee, State Council 1996).

2 These figures were 53.6 per cent and 30 per cent as of 2009.

3 *Jingjixue Da Cidian* (Dictionary of Economics), Shanghai Cishu chubanshe, 1992.

4 See 'The legislative plan of the Tenth National People's Congress Standing Committee', available at http://news.xinhuanet.com/zhengfu/2004-01/09/content_ 1268128.htm; and Ding (2004), accessed on 24 March 2011. The proposed law did not appear on the legislative plan of the 11th National People's Congress, http://big5. xinhuanet.com/gate/big5/news.xinhuanet.com/legal/2008-10/29/content_10272646. htm, accessed 24 March 2011, consisting of 64 items of legislations.

5 On the definition of peasants in the proposed law, Professor Xiang Jiquan, a renowned rural expert, and his collaborators suggested in their proposed revisions to the draft bill that the concept of peasant should be broadened to include not only the non-residing peasant workers but holders of urban household registration status but currently resident in the countryside to engage in agriculture, forestry, fishing and related economic activities (Xiang and Chang 2007: 3).

6 These various views of reservations arose among a widening and yet largely 'elite' policy community including prominent scholars working on administrative reform and rural issues, and lawyers who had assisted peasant workers in litigations (Wang 2007).

7 The Ministry of Finance and some local governments had conducted individual studies and surveys to estimate the *san luen* local levies in the early phase of the national reform, but these studies were not conclusive and not systematically followed up and continued.

8 Alvin So explains this 'split state' phenomenon where the local is predatory and the central benign as a consequence of neoliberal project since economic reform (So 2007).

9 The central tenet of the ANT, developed by a group of sociologists and philosophers of science, is that an actor in a day-to-day sense, for example, a teacher, or a computer, is actually constituted of multiple heterogeneous elements interacting with one another, or working together as a 'net', hence the term 'actor-network'. The elements include

both the human and non-human kinds. The major *problematique* is to explain how the movements of elements become 'stabilized', and then forgotten and 'put away' in the 'black box', which people then denote as the 'actor'. To find out how movements stabilize, ANT suggests a simple way: open the black box and observe how the elements had previously interacted (Latour 2005).

1 Path creation? Processes and networks

* This chapter was originally published in *Policy and Society*, 25, 1 (2006): 61–84, and has been updated for the current volume.

1 Hence is the adoption of the term, 'breakthroughs', to denote those rare, and often cherished, occasions. A celebrated book describing a sample of contemporary innovations in Western societies is aptly titled, *Breakthroughs!* (Nayak and Ketteringham 1986).

2 Adcock *et al.* (2007) gives an excellent 'back the timeline' historicist account of the shifting constitution and evolving agenda of various strands of new institutionalisms.

3 Earlier, Granovettor (1985) has pointed out the dual features of the embedded agency: the pervasive presence of agency and its limits. As much as new ideas have roots in the pre-existing structure, they are of sufficient difference to make a meaningful deviation from it.

4 See http://www.lancs.ac.uk/fass/centres/css/ant/antres.htm for a handy bibliography of the relevant literature.

5 The formulation on this point in Latour (2005: 27) is 'no group, only group formation'.

6 See Law (1992) for a concise introduction to the main concerns and genesis of ANT, and Latour (2005) for a 'comprehensive' statement of the ANT position against 'mainstream' positions.

7 Chinese Academy of Social Sciences rural issues researcher Yu Jianrong once protested, along a line similar to ANT, against the obsession with theoretical construction/application in many rural studies in China, arguing for a return to the actors – through letting the peasants speak and tell their own stories, to arrive at a more relevant understanding of reality. See http://www.sachina.edu.cn/Htmldata/news/2005/04/273.html, accessed on 26 November 2005.

8 Rural tax-for-fee reform (*feigaishui* in Chinese), experimented in Anhui, Henan and Hebei since the early–mid-1990s to reduce tax abuses on peasants, became national policy in 2000. By 2002, about two-thirds of provinces implemented the reform and all by late 2003. A principal measure of the reform was to wipe out, almost entirely, the local fees and charges which township governments – the bottom-level of local government – had historically relied on to supplement the shortfalls of resources provided for in the state budget.

9 These include my own contributions (Chapters 2, 3 and 6 of this volume, and Li and Wu 2005), which look into the central–local dynamics of implementation, wider implications for political administrative reforms, and sustainability processes. Bernstein and Lü (2003) and Yep (2004) write on the broader historical and institutional context of the reform.

10 Latour (1987: 1–17, 21) argues, with numerous real-case thought experiments, that the best – feasible, effective – way to open a black box to understand how something now there had made it is to travel 'back in time' to see what was happening before that something took place, instead of engaging in analysis of the finished product as it is. No matter how logically rigorous the analysis in the latter case may be, it is by nature a static exercise and could not have revealed the dynamic story of how change happens.

11 Garud and Karnoe (2001b: 12) summarize the challenges facing entrepreneurs in effecting innovations. On the importance of 'drama' in drawing support to innovations, see Lampel (2001).
12 He and Wang (1990: preface), and Chen and Chun (2004: 246). The eight other co-organizers were: Ministry of Agriculture, State Commission for Economic System Reform, State Council Research Center for Economic, Technical and Social Development, State Council Rural Development Research Center, Chinese Academy of Social Sciences, *People's Daily*, *Economic Daily* and *Peasant's Daily*. The initial pockets of family-based decollectivization in isolated villages in Anhui and Sichuan were spontaneous, bottom-up, initiatives by the production teams. Its subsequent contagion to more localities across counties and provinces involved both bottom-up pressures and the connivance and at times active encouragement and protection of middle- and senior-ranking officials at county and provincial leaders. Kelliher (1992) gives an excellent account of the interactive processes involved.
13 The most obvious indicator of remaining, if not new, problems in agriculture and rural economy in the late 1980s was the reversal of the upwards trend in agricultural production after the peak in 1984, and the decline in growth rate of rural income during 1989–91 (average rural household income growth rates over the previous year during 1988–91 are 17.8 per cent (1988), 10.4 per cent, 4.7 per cent and 3.2 per cent (1991), in accordance with Agriculture Yearbook, various years). Others included tension between stable supply of food and agricultural raw materials for urban-based industries on one hand and making agriculture more profitable so as to make it sustainable and improve rural living, and the dilemma between the difficulty of raising productivity over fragmented, small portions of land and the difficulty of finding alternative sources of income for the voluminous rural population.
14 The book is He and Wang (1990), which is the 'official' publication of the contest and includes the texts (some of which are extracts) of all the 135 essays winning the 'excellent chapter' award. He's essay is included (extracted: 241–6), while also available in full length in He and Sun (2000: 51–67).
15 He and Sun (2000: 7). These included the internal version of the prestigious academic journal *Jingji Yanjiu* (*Economic Research*), which published the essay in full, two lengthy interviews in the journal *Ban yuan tan* (*Biweekly discussions*), internal version, *People's Daily* (the internal supplement), and a State Council internal bulletin, *Juece chankou* (*References for Decision-Making*).
16 The Central Document No. 1 (1985) on 'Ten policies on further enlivening rural economy', promulgated 1 January 1985, officially marked the second stage of rural reform, after the first stage reform centring on decollectivization. See http://past.people.com.cn/GB/shizheng/252/5580/5581/20010612/487222.html, accessed on 14 November 2005.
17 The Third Plenum of the Twelfth Party Congress convened in October 1984 announced the speed up of comprehensive economic reform with cities as the focus. See http://past.people.com.cn/GB/shizheng/252/5580/5581/20010612/487216.html, accessed on 14 November 2005.
18 The 'Decision of the CPC on economic system reform', promulgated at the 1984 Third Plenum was full of references of the new wealth in rural China, as a result of progress in agriculture and development of rural industries; see http://www.people.com.cn/GB/shizheng/252/5089/5104/5198/20010429/467457.html, accessed on 14 November 2005.
19 This could be discerned from reading the speech by Vice-Premier Tian Jiyun at National Agricultural Conference in November 1988, accessed at http://news.xinhuanet.com/ziliao/2005-02/25/content_2619183.htm on 15 November 2005. While emerging problems over agricultural production and prices were noted, and the tone had turned more cautious, the central theme was still that more fundamental rural reforms needed to wait given their implications for the urban sector.

20 Examples of essays proposing a similar idea of land tenure market include one by a rural expert from Sichuan Academy of Social Sciences (Guo 1990: 157), one from Hubei Academy of Social Sciences (Xia 1990: 18) and State Council Rural Development Research Center Experimental Zone Office (1990: 60–1).
21 Decollectivization was still hotly debated in some quarters during the late 1980s and into the early 1990s, when several collectivized 'models', like Tianjin's Daqiaozhuang and Henan's Nanjie, were heralded as espousing the vitality and relevance of socialist ideals. See Xiang (1999) and Qiao (2004) for analysis of this alternative phenomenon to the mainstream trend of decollectivization.
22 According to He, the first pocket of *dabaogan* occurred not in Xiaogang of Fuyang District, as is often said in official and popular reports, but in a commune called '12 1/2 li' in Leian County. He was pretty close to the party secretary, Wang Yemei, of Leian County at that time. Author's interviews 2004; Chen and Chun 2004: 246.
23 Wang was party secretary of Tao Xian Prefecture during the early days of family farming reform, whom He had worked closely with during the *dabaogan* reform (Author's interviews 2002).
24 Chen and Chun (2004: 246) and Author's interviews (2004).
25 About a year before the Thirteenth Party Congress was convened in October 1987. Political reform was prominently debated as part of the agenda. Also attracting a lot of attention was inflation, price reform and reform of urban-based state-owned enterprises.
26 Chen and Chun (2004: 257–8); Author's interviews (2004).
27 Wen (2001) argues for the need to understand the 'logic' of reform policy cycles in China in line with economic cycles. What Wen did not address is that the two cycles are interactive and partially mutually constitutive, so that one also needs to bear in mind the 'openness' of history and that what had happened was not necessarily the 'inevitable'.
28 The provinces of Hebei and Henan started piloting rural tax reforms along the lines of He's reform ideas in 1993–4, with explicit support from their provincial leaders (Chen and Chun 2004: 288–9, 291–7).
29 During January to February, 1992, Deng Xiaoping went on a tour of the 'windows' of the post-1978 reform policy and the major economic cities in the country, including Wuhan, Shenzhen, Zhuhai, Shunde and Shanghai, in which Deng pressed on the need for more opening and reform. This 'southern tour' had the effect of causing an immediate change of the conservative policy climate prevailing since 1989.
30 The policy to set up 'experimental zones' was made in early 1987 as part of the moves to explore the ways to continue with rural reform. Nineteen zones were approved within 2 years and Fuyang Prefecture in Anhui was one of them. Areas of experiments include land tenure and management, sale and distribution of agricultural produce, rural economic co-operative organizations, township enterprises, and rural credits and finance (State Council Rural Development Research Center Experimental Zone Office 1990).
31 Chapter 6 of this volume elaborates further the theme of responsibility shirking, arguing that, in the case of rural tax reform, eventual shouldering of state responsibility for rural welfare, a process in the making, was taking place as a result of mutual shirking of responsibility by central and local officials to one another.
32 As to why Wang was more willing to commit than Li Peng or Anhui's provincial leaders, who had also shown interest in the reforms, probably the experimental reform zone status of Fuyang had led to a different risk assessment, since the pressure in making new reform progress was more focused there than in the central and provincial government. Doing nothing 'new' could be interpreted as a failure to perform, while the rule of bureaucratic survival in higher levels is the avoidance of mistakes, and thus the less risk the better.

33 They visited Yongshang County and Woyang County. See Chen and Chun (2004: 271–4). The major difference in He's rural tax-for-fee reform design, as compared to the national reform package adopted in 2000 formulated largely by Ministry of Finance officials on top of local, including Anhui's early pilot reforms, was that the tax-cum-fee levy will be paid in kind (agricultural produce) in He's design rather than in cash. He regarded his design as having an added advantage over the MoF design in that it was better aligned to the underdeveloped sales market of agricultural produce, and thus simpler and easier to implement, as well as less susceptible to abuses. See He and Sun (2000: 79–84). He's 'follower' in Hebei province, Yang Wenliang (see note 34), said in an interview in 2001 that the tax-in-cash system had major problems which He had intended to avoid in a 'tax-in-kind' system (W. Yang 2001).

34 Yang Wenliang worked in Hebei Provincial Government Research Office. Hebei was to become another province piloting rural tax-fee reforms in 1993, apart from Anhui (Chen and Chun 2004: 274, 291–7).

35 The Three Gorges Dam project and the controversies in planning processes historically offer a very good example. The debates in the late 1950s in particular sent out a strong flavour that the project at that time verged on the edge of a major planning failure. See Li (1996: 1–29).

2 Differentiated actors

* This chapter was originally published in *Modern Asian Studies*, 40, 1 (2006): 151–74, and is reprinted here with slight revisions. An early version was presented at International Conference on 'Theoretical Issues in the Study of Rural and Small-Town China', 14–15 November, 2003, University of California, Berkeley.

1 A sample of major works in this genre include Lieberthal and Oksenberg (1988), Lampton (1987), Lieberthal and Lampton (1992), Goodman and Segal (1994); as well as earlier classics like Barnett and Vogel (1967), Schurmann (1968), Donnithorne (1967) and Goodman (1984).

2 For a succinct review of the recent trends of the implementation literature, see Hill and Hupe (2002).

3 A group of literature in this genre is the three volumes published as a result of a series of annual workshops between 1995 and 1998 under the project 'China's Provinces in Reform', exploring the complexities of continental China and the role of the provinces and sub-provincials as generic actors in the polity. The project was organized by the Institute for International Studies at University of Technology, Sydney (UTS), and later by the Centre for Research on Provincial China, a joint institution of UTS and the University of New South Wales. The Centre publishes the journal *Provincial China* first started by UTS in 1996. The three volumes are: Goodman (1997), Hendrischke and Feng (1999) and Fitzgerald (2002).

4 The group of articles on the 'Open Up the West' campaign/policy appears as Vol. 178 (June 2004) *The China Quarterly*. Authors include David Goodman, Heike Holbig, Nicolas Becquelin, Eduard Vermeer, Christopher McNally, Lijian Hong and Tim Oaks. For earlier works on the need to disaggregate China, see Goodman and Segal (1994) and Goodman (2000: 4–18).

5 A similar observation along this line was made in other contexts. For instance, over the discussion of philosophy of social sciences, Roy Bhaskar and Tony Lawson noted that a major reason for the continuing survival of the positivist conception of social sciences was 'the inability of its opponents to sustain in a sufficiently coherent manner' (the key components of the critique). Margaret Archer pointed out that the Collectivist Account of the structure–agency question is kept defensive against, and supplementary to, the Individual Account due to a failure to advance coherently an

independent ontology of social structure. See Bhaskar and Lawson (1998: 3) and Archer (1995: 46–9).

6 Some examples of recent work adopting a dualistic framework, sometimes implicitly, are Heimer (Edin) (2003: 35–49), Tsui and Wang (2004: 71–90) and Su (2002).

7 For an extensive critique of the dualistic approach and an argument for the non-dualistic alternative, see Li (1997: 49–65). In a further development, Li (2005a: 87–108) attempts to locate endogenous forces of change.

8 In early 1993, tens of thousands of villagers in Xian-an Township, Yanshou County in Sichuan Province protested against the imposition of local levies of some 70 yuan per person to pay for the construction of a road connecting the county to Chengdu, the provincial capital. Local officials staged a clamp down, resulting in persistent resistance from the peasants for some time, and subsequently drew the attention of the central government and the international community to the heightening tension between peasants and local cadres in China. See http://bjzc.org/bjs/bc/02/6320/8/2004, accessed on 12 August 2003 for an account of the 1993 events, and Pou (2003: 42–3), for an interview of the peasant leader of the 1993 resistance.

9 According to official income statistics, rural to urban income per household widens from the lowest at 1:1.86 in 1985 to 1:3.11 in 2002. The widening gap was reversed briefly during 1995–7, when the ratio dropped from 1:2.86 in 1994 to 1:2.47 in 1997. The ratio was 1:2.57 in 1978. See National Bureau of Statistics of China (2003: 344). In 2003, the gap widened further, as rural income per capita increased by 4.3 per cent in 2003, against 9.3 per cent for urban dwellers. *China Daily* 28 April 2004.

10 An estimate purportedly by the Party Central in 2002, as reported in a Hong Kong source, put daily demonstrations, rallies and other collective activities in cities at an average of 120 cases, and 160 cases in the countryside, excluding visits to the 'Receiving the Public' section of the various government departments. See *The Trend* 4 (2002), 12–14. A semi-official study on the subject gives a long list of 'direct causes': heavy peasants' burden; reform to state enterprises (and the consequent massive urban unemployment); maladministration over land, finance and enterprises; malpractices in village elections; tensions over lineage, religion and ethnic groups; and general law and order issues. The report quotes also an equally handsome list of deep-seated causes: bureaucratism, breakdown in grassroots level governance structures, poverty, transitional problems in economic development and reform, implementation failures and the absence of 'self-corrective' mechanism in the political system. See Chinese Public Administration Society Project Group (2002: 6–9). A body of literature has emerged to study this phenomenon. See for instance O'Brien (1996: 31–55); O'Brien and Li (1995: 757–83).

11 The year 1998 saw two major developments in political development in China's vast countryside. Village elections were formalized and given a strong boost from the top *vide* the amendment to the 'Village Committee Elections Organizing Law', in trial since 1987 (see the 1998 Law at http://www.npcnews.com.cn/big5/chapter12/1/class001200006/hwz64679.htm). Not only were elections prescribed, the operation of village-level administration should also follow rules of transparency and democratic management, *vide* Central Committee of Party and State Council, 'A Notice on the implementation of transparent administration and democratic management institutions in village level', No. 9 (1998), at http://202.99.23.199/home/begin.cbs, accessed on 8 September 2004. For discussion on the background and pre-2000 developments, and assessment of the significance, of the elections, see a group of articles in *The China Quarterly*, 162 (June 2000) by Kevin O'Brien and Lianjiang Li, Robert A. Pastor and Qingshan Tan and Jean C. Oi and Scott Rozelle.

12 Data obtained from surveys of some 6000 rural households in ten provinces indicate that rural extraction in terms of formal agriculture taxes, local administrative fees and education charges increased in all provinces since 1993, the year of peasant resistance

in Sichuan. For instance, well off Guangdong sees the proportion of total fee burden to rural household income rise from 7.95 per cent in 1993 to 9.67 per cent, while poorer provinces rose even more from 9.85 per cent to 13.05 per cent (Shanxi in West China), and from 10.83 per cent to 18.7 per cent (Sichuan). In Anhui where pilot reform started in a few localities since mid-1990s, the rise was from 9.71 per cent to 13.9 per cent. See Tao Ran, Liu Mingxing, Zhang Qi, 'Zhongguo Nongcui Shuifei Fudan: Yige Zhengzhi Jingjixue di Kaocha' (The peasants' burden in China: A political economy analysis), at http://jlin.ccer.edu.cn/download/2002926522340.doc, accessed on 30 May 2003.

13 Nevertheless, new initiatives were attempted recently to make the political approach work. See a document jointly issued in July 2004 by the Central Committee of the Party and State Council, 'On enhancing and improving the institutional arrangements on transparency and democratic management in village level governance', at http://202.99.23.199/home/begin.cbs, assessed on 8 September 2004. New institutional details were prescribed to clarify the respective jurisdiction of the local party branch and elected village committees, and to regulate the operational details of transparent administration.

14 For the announcement, see 'A Decision of the Chinese Communist Party Central Committee on Important Issues on Agriculture and Rural Affairs', passed at the Third Plenum of the Fifteenth Central Committee, 14 October 1998. The Third Plenum was explicitly referred to in the Central Document No. 7 (2000) announcing the launch of national pilot reform. Also see J. Wen (2000: 211).

15 The three members are Xiang Huaicheng, then Minister of Finance, Chen Yaobang, then Minister of Agriculture and Duan Yingbi, then Director of Central Leading Group on Finance and Economics. See State Council Office (1998: 91).

16 Interestingly, the wider institutional roots of the peasants' burden have been well noted by mainland researchers, though this recognition has not been translated into reform design. See for instance Chen (2002a: 135–7), He (2002: 2–5) and S. Zhang (2002: 2–13). Chen Xiwen is the vice-director of the State Council Development Research Center, and the Secretariat of the Central Leading Group on Economics and Finance, and thus a key figure in the formulation of central rural policy. He and Zhang are both scholars at the influential Chinese Academy of Social Sciences.

17 Under the 'Target Responsibility System' of cadre appraisal first instituted in the mid-1990s, specific indicators were designed to assess job performance. Jobs that were regarded as the highest priority would cost the officials their position if they failed on these. Reduction of peasants' burden was added to fertility control as jobs on that 'pass or perish' list, as per State Council Notice No. 5 (2001), 'On further improving the pilot work of the rural "tax-for-fee" reform', 24 March 2001, section 5. For discussion of the Target Responsibility System, see Heimer (Edin) (2000).

18 Guangdong reportedly achieved the highest burden reduction rate amongst all provinces in 2003. See a report in *Guangzhou Daily*, 9 February 2004, 'Guangdong's peasants' burdens cut by 74 per cent, topping the list in the country'.

19 Author's interviews with central officials involved in the formulation and implementation of the reform package, Beijing, 2003–4.

20 This is obtained from author's interviews with central officials on establishment control at Beijing, and with the 'targets' of the exercise, local officials at the township and county levels in Hubei and Anhui, 2003–4. The 20 per cent figure is stated in Central Committee and State Council, 'An opinion on consolidating the establishment at the city/county/township levels', Document No. 30 (2000), 26 December 2000.

21 These include 39.6 billion yuan of designated transfer payments announced in the 2004 Budget by Finance Minister Jin Renqing in March 2004 (http://big5.xinhuanet.com/gate/big5/news.xinhuanet.com/zhengfu/2004-03/18/content_1371660.htm, accessed on 7 September 2004), an additional 10 billion yuan of direct subsidies to grain growers,

and additional subsidies (of unspecified amount subject to central–local negotiation) to selected provinces piloting the stepped up reduction/suspension of Agriculture Tax in 2004.

22 An example was a July 2004 report by the National Development and Reform Commission, which reported 20,000 cases of illegal rural fees, totalling over 400 million yuan, discovered during a national survey of rural fees in the first half of 2004. The survey focused on fees on education, marriage registration, fertility control and immunization of pigs, as reported in *China Youth Daily* (Beijing), 23 July 2004, accessed on 20 August 2004 at http://www.ccrs.org.cn/NEWSgl/ReadNews.asp? NewsID=8374&BigClassID=8&SmallClassID=9&SpecialID=0.

23 'Opinions on policies to enhance the income growth of peasants', jointly issued by Chinese Communist Party Central Committee and State Council on the last day of 2003. The formulation and drafting process kicked off in a Politburo meeting in September 2003, producing the first draft in mid-November and the main contents nailed down by mid-December. See a report in *Liaowang* (Beijing), 13 January 2004, at http://news.xinhuanet.com/fortune/2004-01/13/content_1273182.htm, accessed on 6 September 2004.

24 Total budgetary outlay from the central coffers to agriculture and rural areas was planned to increase by 20 per cent in 2004 over 2003, to a total of around 150 billion yuan, as stated in Finance Minister's Budget Speech 2004 to the National People's Congress, March 2004. This purportedly would include the 10 billion yuan of direct subsidies to grain growers, and the additional transfer payments to provinces compensating for lost revenue from stepped up reduction/suspension of Agriculture Tax. Ministry of Finance Notice No. 77 (2004), 'A notice on some issues on the further reduction of Agriculture Tax and suspension of Agriculture Tax collection in selected piloting provinces', 6 April 2004.

25 The direct impact of the lowering of Agriculture Tax rate and the suspension of tax collection in selected provinces is estimated to lower total extraction by 11.8 billion yuan. See Finance Minister's Budget Speech 2004 to the National People's Congress, March 2004.

26 Author's interviews, Beijing, April 2004.

27 Author's interviews, Beijing, April 2004.

28 For example, Li, L. (2004: 248–9) and the literature cited therein.

29 Other reliefs are (1) exempting peasants' turnover of sales of agricultural produce of less than 5000 yuan per month (or 200 yuan daily) from value-added tax and (2) exempting 'mobile' rural petty traders without a fixed trading venue from registration with the tax authorities. See National Taxation Bureau Document No. 13 (2004), 'A notice on further implementing the tax relief policy to enhance peasant income growth', 20 January 2004, full text at http://www.chinatax.gov.cn/view.jsp?code= 200402101421438335, accessed on 5 September 2004.

30 A second notice was issued in March to launch a nationwide examination to monitor the implementation, suggesting the complexities and difficulties in implementation. See http://www.chinatax.gov.cn/view.jsp?code=200404131640496998, accessed on 12 August 2004.

31 Author's interviews, Wuhan, 2004.

32 Chen proceeded on elaborating some of his ideas of the new system in the interview, as reported in *Zhongguo Paodao Zhoukan*, available at http://www.mlcool.com/html/ ns001679.htm, accessed on 14 August 2003.

33 One such proposal is in Li, Z. (2003: 35–40).

34 Author's interviews, Beijing, April 2004.

35 Taking Agriculture Tax and Special Product Tax together, tax revenues dropped from the high point of 4.23 per cent of total national budgetary revenue in 1996 (31.3 billion out of 740.8 billion yuan) to 2.57 per cent in 1999, 2.23 per cent in 2000, 1.75 per cent

in 2001 and 2.23 per cent in 2002. In absolute terms, total national budgetary revenue increased by 155 per cent between 1996–2002, to nearly 1900 billion yuan, while tax revenue from agricultural products stagnated, even decreasing by almost 9 per cent from 1996 to 2001 before seeing a rise in 2002, when many provinces started implementing the tax-for-fee reform and thus channelling formerly extrabudgetary fee revenue to tax revenues. See *China Finance Yearbook* 2003, 338, 344. For an example of an analysis of the 'affordability' of phasing out Agriculture Tax, see Chen's interview, note 32.

36 Central Document No. 7 (2000), Section 3, clause (1), gives a list of: (1) the five township 'coordination' (*tongchou*) fees, (2) the three village 'retention' (*tiliu*) fees, (3) education levies and surcharges and (4) all other kinds of administrative fees, charges and government funds that targeted specifically peasants. The first three categories had been introduced incrementally since the 1980s, with central endorsement, to supplement the inadequate budgetary funds at township and village levels. The fourth was a diverse group with origins at central/provincial/local levels.

37 Ministry of Finance Notice No. 10 (2000), 'On the subject of peasant-related fees in the regions piloting the rural fee-to-tax reform', 4 July 2000. In addition to administrative fees, the notice also elaborates guidelines on the imposition of user charges, which are supposedly market-regulated and do *not* form part of government revenue. In practice, the boundary is ambiguous and abuses abound.

38 The list was contained in a tiny pamphlet supposedly sent to villagers with the title, 'The Second Open Letter to Peasant Friends in Hubei', by Hubei Party Committee and the Provincial Government, dated 23 October 2002. The nine departments are: agriculture, forestry, public security, education, family planning, land, construction, civil affairs and water. The list was confirmed to be still up to date in 2004. Author's interviews, Wuhan, 2004.

39 For reports on the resurgence of rural fees after reform, see for instance http://www. ccrs.org.cn/newsgl/ReadNews.asp?NewsID=3986 and http://www/aweb.com.cn/2003/7/8/20037883858.htm, accessed on 14 September 2003.

40 The urgency of abolishing rural fees and stamping out abuses was a common theme in various central documents issued since 2000.

41 State Council Notice No. 50 (2003), 'On Approving a notice by the Ministry of Agriculture, etc. on the issue of reducing peasants' burden', 29 May 2003.

42 This is the observation obtained from an internet search of provincial responses. For a typical example, see a notice by the Beijing Municipal Government issued on 2 July 2003, available at http://www.china.org.cn, accessed on 22 August 2003.

43 All alteration of fee levels should be approved by the Provincial Fiscal Bureau and Price Bureau. Yet in practice, the departments often made their own decisions. Author's interviews, Wuhan, 2004.

44 The reference to decentralized decisions is found towards the end of the first major section of the Document, which addresses the 'significance' of the reform.

45 The Agriculture Tax Regulation 1958 specifies the tax rates for various provinces and a national average of 15.5 per cent and has remained in force nominally until fee-to-tax reform sets in. The effective tax rates have seen a continuous decline to some 2.9 per cent by the year 2000, due to a combination of factors. See He and Sun (2000:131–2).

46 The regime consisted of three components: (1) a rise of tax rate from a *de facto* national average of 3 per cent to a cap of 7 per cent; (2) provincial discretion on taxes on 'special products' and (3) up to 20 per cent of local surcharge on agricultural tax to compensate for the abolition of traditional village levies. See Central Document No. 7 (2000), Section 3.

47 State Council Document No. 143, 'A regulation on the imposition of Agriculture Tax on agricultural special products', 30 January 1994.

48 Ministry of Finance Notice No. 94, 'On the details of implementation of the Agricultural Special Products Tax', 24 March 1994, clause 8. The phrase 'where Agriculture Tax normally applies' implies the existence of areas where the Tax does not normally apply. This usually refers to newly formed land or peripheral pieces of land newly brought under cultivation, and have yet to be brought under the tax system, or areas that for various reasons are excluded from agricultural taxes. Agricultural produce from these lands goes untaxed.

49 Shunde City Government Notice No. 35 (2002), 'The implementation plan of rural tax for fee reform in Shunde', Section 2, clause (5). Fish and flowers were two major agricultural products in Shunde.

50 Aquatic products and flowers attracted a flat tax rate of 8 per cent under the Agricultural Special Products Tax, while the upper ceiling of Agriculture Tax (regular) was only 7 per cent. When 20 per cent local surcharge was added, the difference would be 9.6 per cent versus 8.4 per cent.

51 One exception is tobacco, the tax rate of which remains 20 per cent. Anhui Provincial Government Notice, 'On the pilot scheme of shifting the Special Products Tax to Agriculture Tax', 31 March 2003.

52 'Wen Jiabao emphasized to continue the rural "tax-for-fee" reform', 3 April 2003, Xinhua News, accessed on 5 August 2003 at http://big5.xinhuanet.com/gate/big5/news.xinhuanet.com/newscenter/2003-04/03/content_814822.htm.

53 Ministry of Finance and National Taxation Bureau Notice No. 136, 'On a few issues relating to the Agricultural Special Products Tax in rural "tax-for-fee" reform areas', 10 June 2003.

54 'The rural "tax-for-fee" reform plan in Guangdong', *Guangzhou Daily*, 7 July 2003.

55 Matland (1995: 145–74). For a similar, but weaker, attempt in the Chinese context, see O'Brien and Li (1999: 167–86).

56 Margaret Archer reviews the Individual account, the Collectivist account and the Structuration Theory, which conflate the structure–agency relation in different directions in *Realist Social Theory*. For a similar argument against conflation, without using the language, see Grafstein (1988).

57 Another attempt to meet the theoretical challenge is made in the context of the local political economy of Tianjin, in Li and Qiu (2004).

58 See Brehm and Gates (1997), for an example of implementation studies employing the principal–agent framework outside the China context.

59 For more on this point, see Li and Qiu (2004).

3 Embedded institutionalization

* This chapter was originally published in *The Pacific Review*, 19, 1 (2006): 63–84, reprinted here with slight revisions. References to 'author's interviews' in the chapter, except where the location of interviews is specified, refer to interviews conducted in Xian-an District, Hubei Province. An early version of the chapter was presented at the 2004 conference of Hong Kong Political Science Association, at City University of Hong Kong, 8 May 2004, and benefited from comments of John Burns, Hsin-chi Kuan and other participants, and from Jonathan Unger and Paul Wilding among others outside the conference.

1 In all three major types of institutional change (institutional formation, development and reinstitutionalization), the institutionalization of new additions is key to the process of institutional change. Reinstitutionalization sees those changes to the original institutions being institutionalized again, while adopting a different logic and structure from the previous institutions. It is an 'exit from one institutionalization, and entry into another institutional form'. In institutional development, the original institutionalization process extends to incorporate new elements and contents. It is a continuation,

and elaboration, of the same institutionalization process, 'a change within an institutional form'. Institutional formation refers to the process of exiting from one of the three situations: social entropy, non-reproductive behavioural patterns, or reproductive patterns based upon 'action' (Jepperson 1991: 152).

2 Indeed the power of path dependence in an institutionalized state is observed to be so strong that in the case of deinstitutionalization, there is a tendency for the changes to undergo a parallel process of reinstitutionalization simply to keep the momentum of exit from the original institutionalization process. An example is the deinstitutionalization of gender and family in Western societies, accompanied with the (partial) reinstitutionalization of single parenthood.

3 A reference to the recurrence of the problem of peasants' burden is the so-called 'Huang Zhongxi rule', first coined by Tsinghua University scholar Qin (1997). A scholar-official during the late Ming/early Qing period, Huang Zhongxi had commented on the futility of previous taxation reforms. He maintained that the combination of multiple fees into one tax had only created room for further fees to be added to the new, and enlarged, tax after some time, resulting in a *deepening* of peasants' burden. Qin wrote a second article on this theme (Qin 2000), which reportedly caught the attention of Premier Wen Jiabao. See a report in *Liaoning Daily*, 21 March 2003, accessed on 3 May 2004 at http://libwisesearch.wisers.net/print.php. The concern over sustainability of the reform was explicit in early central policy documents on the reform, including Central Document No. 7 (2000), 'A decision on launching pilot reforms to rural fee and tax system', 2 March 2000, and State Council Notice No. 5 (2001), 'On furthering the work of rural tax-for-fee pilot reform', 24 March 2001.

4 In 2002, some 20 provinces implemented the reform on a province-wide basis. All provinces adopted reform by the second half of 2003, with an average burden reduction rate of 30 per cent, surpassing the national requirement of 20 per cent. See http://www.mos.gov.cn/template/article/display0.jsp?mid=2004322001794, accessed on 15 April 2004. Guangdong topped the country at 84 per cent, see http://gzdaily.dayoo.com/gb/node/2004-02/09/node_282.htm, accessed on 8 April 2004. In 2004 the central government, *vide* Premier Wen Jiabao's government report at the second session of the 10th National People's Congress, 5 March, 2004, announced new plans to phase out Agriculture Tax in 5 years. By 2005, 26 provinces had abolished the tax, with the rest to do likewise in 2006 (http://www/mof.gov.cn/news/20050302_1862_4745.htm, accessed on 10 May 2005).

5 Chapter 2 of this volume discusses the high risk of the reform from an agency control framework. The concern over sustainability also featured prominently in central government inspection of Guangdong's implementation of rural tax-for-fee reform in February 2004 (http://www.gdczt.gov.cn/cz_news_nr.jsp?news_id=2070, accessed on 14 April 2004).

6 The literature has noted two parallel dimensions on the constitution of interests of the local officials. First, local officials are seen as predatory and corrupt. The second sees local officials' reliance on fees being embedded in an ill-developed national fiscal system, which overburdens local governments and left many mandates unfunded. Both dimensions have similarly made local officials resistant to cuts to the fees they could charge from peasants, though for different reasons and demanding different solutions.

7 Central Committee Secretariat Notice No. 30 (2000), 'On reducing the staff establishment at city, county and township levels', issued in December 2000, followed by a similar reference in State Council Notice No. 5 (2001).

8 Total amount of transfer payments from central coffers for the purpose of rural tax-for-fee reform was 3.3 billion yuan (2001), 24.5 billion yuan (2002), 30.5 billion yuan (2003) and 52 billion yuan (2004) (Budget Speeches of the Finance Minister at

National People's Congress annual sessions, various years). A lion's share of 3.3 billion yuan in 2001 was given to Anhui (1.7 billion yuan), the only province implementing the reform on a province-wide basis in 2001. In 2002, 20 provinces were conducting reform on a province-wide basis, and by 2003 all provinces were involved. Monies were limited as each province would have a notional average subsidy of 1 billion yuan, just over half of what Anhui secured in 2001 (Author's interviews, Beijing, 2002, 2004).

9 This theme was subject of a high-profile conference, 'Conference on the reform of the township/town level of government', held at the Center for Chinese Rural Studies, Central China Normal University, Wuhan, 27–29 February 2004.

10 The limits to downsizing included the difficulty to find alternative employment opportunities, in areas where economic development was still lacklustre, for the leaving government officials in downsizing exercises. There was also the observation that the major bottleneck to relieving peasants' burden rested in rural land reform and increasing agricultural, and rural, productivity; that is, on increasing the supply of revenue, rather than focusing on reducing expenses through cutting government staff. See discussion in http://ah.anhuinews.com/system/2005/01/26/001117840.shtml, accessed on 15 April 2007.

11 Xian-an District was Xianning City (county-level) until 1999, when it was renamed Xian-an and made a district of the new and enlarged Xianning City (Prefecture-level). It has a population of about half a million, of which 77 per cent are rural. The district is accessible by main national highways and rail routes, and is 1-hour drive from Wuhan, the provincial capital.

12 Local budgetary expenditures surged 56 per cent from 118 million yuan in 2001 to 184 million yuan a year after, while local budgetary revenue (based on the tax-sharing system formula) shrank 30 per cent from 104 million yuan to 71 million yuan, excluding transfers (Author's interviews 2004). The significant drop in local revenue in 2002 was attributable to a revision in 2002 by the provincial government to centralize more revenues to provincial coffers. See State Council Notice No. 37 (2001), 'On reforming the tax-sharing scheme for Enterprise Income Tax', 31 December 2001, and Hubei Provincial Government Notice No. 29 (2002), 'A decision to further adjust and improve the tax sharing fiscal system', 24 July 2002.

13 The years 1999 and 2001 were the years of reference Hubei's authorities adopted in assessing reform implementation. Peasant burden for all households after reform was required to be no higher than that in the year before reform, which is 2001 for most counties in Hubei, and at least 20 per cent lower than that in 1999 (http://www.cnhubei.com/aa/cal45760.htm, accessed on 6 January 2004, and http://www.cnhubei.com/aa/cal45718.htm, accessed on 19 July 2003).

14 As part of a package of additional measures intended to reduce further tax/fee extractions on peasants and to raise rural incomes, introduced by the central government in January 2004, peasants selling agricultural consumer products (e.g. grains, edible oils, cooked foods) of less than 5,000 yuan per month or 200 yuan per transaction were waived paying value-added tax (http://www.china.org.cn/chinese/2004/Jan/484675. htm, accessed on 11 May 2005). Agricultural 'productive' goods, for example, fertilizers, animal feed, agricultural equipments, have been exempted from value-added tax *vide* the 1996 Ministry of Finance, National Taxation Bureau notice, 'A notice on exempting value-added tax from certain agricultural productive goods'.

15 According to Central Document No. 16 (1990), 'A decision to prohibit firmly abuses in fees, charges and *tanpai*', 16 September, only central government may approve government funds, while central and provincial governments share the approval authority of 'administrative' fees (*xinzhengshiyexing shoufei*).

16 State Council No. 92 (1991), 'Regulation on the management of fees and corvee services shouldered by peasants', 7 December 1991.

17 Only the central government had, officially, the authority to impose *new* fees/charges that specifically targeted peasants after the rural tax-for-fee reform (Author's interviews, Wuhan, 2004).

18 While largely a nationwide phenomenon, abandoned land syndrome was rather serious in Xian-an. About a third of the rural population in Xian-an had left home for work in cities, leaving as many as 40 per cent of total agricultural land uncultivated as a result. Abandoned land was often reallocated to remaining households or migrant rural workers for cultivation, and they were taxed at a reduced rate, if at all (Author's interviews 2004).

19 See 'Chinese peasants' burden will be reduced by 20 per cent', *Wen Hui Pao* (Hong Kong), 13 June 2002, p. A2.

20 There were a total of 21 performance indicators, but the four most important ones were: (1) calculation of taxable land area in accordance with policy; (2) a cap of agriculture tax (and surtaxes, including Agriculture Special Products Tax) at 100 yuan per *mou*; (3) burdens per *mou* (about 670 square metres) not exceeding the level in 2001, the year before reform and (4) full rebates of excess burdens collected before reform to peasants. The other lesser indicators include, for instance, adequate publicity work on the reform, implementation of the individual burdens' cards scheme, delivery of agriculture tax notices to every rural household, abolition of all other kinds of local extractions and so on (Author's interviews 2004).

21 Computed from information in Table 3.1 and local budget expenditure figures.

22 Ministry of Finance Document No. 468 (2002), 'Temporary methods of central transfer payments under rural tax-for-fee reform', 26 July 2002; 'Operational details of sub-provincial transfer payments in rural tax-for-fee reform in Hubei Province', in Hubei Provincial Government Secretariat Notice No. 39 (2002); 'A notice on promulgating the documents on reforms related to the rural tax-for-fee reform', 8 August 2002.

23 In many cases, enhanced and early retirement arrangements were offered (Author's interviews, Beijing, 2002). The former Party Secretary of Xian-an noted that a neighbouring county (Jian-li) had a bill of over 100 million yuan for its downsizing exercise (http://ah. anhuinews.com/system/2005/01/26/001117840.shtml, accessed on 21 March, 2005).

24 Ministry of Finance (MoF) and the State Commission Office for Public Sector Reform No. 75 (2001), 'The method of the central coffers providing subsidy for payroll of *bianzhine* personnel during the period of *fenliu*', 2 November 2001.

25 The provincial report stated that central transfer payments under the rural tax reform comprised two parts: regular and transitional. But a few months back, a provincial document issued in August 2002 ('Operational details of sub-provincial transfer payments in rural tax-for-fee reform in Hubei Province'), still stated that transitional payments were provincial and municipal responsibility, with no mentioning of any central role.

26 There was no breakdown of the proportion of rural tax reform transfer payments coming from the central *vis-à-vis* provincial/municipal coffers which Xian-an received. Province wide, in 2003, the central government supplied a sum in the range of 1.3 or 1.7 billion yuan to Hubei, while provincial government supplied another 700 million yuan to the counties (Author's interviews, Wuhan, 2004).

27 In late 2003, it was announced that merit-based transfer payments were to become part of a revised and more elaborate province-wide mechanism in 2004. Hubei Provincial Bureau of Finance Notice No. 14 (2003), 'Temporary methods to manage provincial transfer payments', printed in *Finance and Development* (internal journal edited by Hubei Provincial Fiscal Research Institute), 1 (2004), 50–3.

28 These are, for 2003: (1) achievements in downsizing (4 million yuan); (2) overall performance in government reforms (0.5 million yuan); (3) compensation to the non-collection of Agricultural Special Products Tax in 2002 (0.4 million yuan); (4) award of a 'progressive unit' in rural tax reform (0.1 million yuan) and (5) others (1 million yuan) (Author's interviews 2004).

29 See note 27.
30 Another example of this kind of 'implementation-led' approach to policymaking was discussed in Li (1998: Ch 7), regarding Guangdong's influence on national policy on infrastructural investment.
31 The main changes introduced include: ownership reforms to state-owned enterprises, social insurance system for all state-salaried personnel, administrative restructuring and downsizing, job assignment reform, coastal experience exposure for cadres, education restructuring, streamlining fee-administration for enterprises and township government reforms (Xian-an District Party Committee Secretariat 2003).
32 Xian-an's government reforms were making a wider impact with the promotion of its party secretary Song Yaping to the Provincial Policy Research Office in November 2003. Hubei's provincial leadership in November 2003 promulgated a decree to promote reform experiments in Xian-an throughout localities in the province, with trial implementation in seven counties in 2004, and full implementation intended for all counties province wide by end of 2005 (http://news.sina.com.cn/c/2004-11-04/15534814599.shtml, accessed on 21 March 2005; Author's interviews, Wuhan, 2005).
33 One source reported a cost of 70 billion yuan for the central government downsizing initiative of 1998 (Author's interviews, Beijing, 2002, Hong Kong 2003).
34 The county-level budget sees the largest imbalance between these two categories of expenditure, with productive expenditures accounting for a mere 6–7 per cent of the total on average. Nationally, productive expenditure amounted to about 40 per cent of the total. See Ministry of Finance (ed.), *Fiscal Statistical Information of Prefectural and County Levels*, various years (Beijing: Zhongguo caizheng jingji chubanshe); *Zhongguo Caizheng Nianjian*, various years.
35 Computed from Ministry of Finance (2002: 296–7).
36 The shares in the years from 1998 to 2001 are, respectively, 54, 58, 61 and 60 per cent (Ministry of Finance 2002 and various years).
37 The figure on China was computed from *China Statistical Yearbook*, 2003, 123, 158. The share in Germany and Hungary was around 8 per cent, Portugal, Denmark and Finland around 14 per cent, Luxembourg around 5 per cent, Spain around 10 per cent and the Netherlands 3 per cent (Public Governance and Territorial Development Directorate Public Management Committee 2002).
38 Song Yaping, a doctorate in Economics of the Central China Normal University before he joined the Hubei Provincial Government in the mid-1980s, resigned from the government after a few years and worked in enterprises in Guangdong – Guangzhou and Shenzhen, and Hainan, as well as in Hong Kong as visiting scholar during 1988–9 – before he rejoined the rank of cadres in 1998. As District Party Secretary of Xian-an from 1999 to 2003, Song was instrumental in the initiation of government reforms there. He left Xian-an after a full 5-year term and joined the Policy Research Office of Hubei Provincial Government as vice-director in November 2003.
39 For those sent-off between 2001 and 2003, 646 cadres in total 20 per cent went to the southern Guangdong cities of Shenzhen, Guangzhou and Dongguan, 12 per cent to Wuhan, 11 per cent to three Zhejiang cities of Wenzhou, Taizhou and Hangzhou, with the rest in dispersed cities, and a small minority of ten went overseas, including two in the United Kingdom, and four each in Hong Kong and Singapore. Most worked in enterprises, with most earning a monthly pay ranging from 800 yuan to 8,000 yuan. Another 200 left in late February 2004 (Author's interviews, Xian-an, February 2004). Song Yaping confirmed with the author in spring 2005 that this programme continued to operate with a new batch of cadres sent-off in 2005 (Author's interviews, Wuhan, 2005).
40 Extracted transcripts of 'I am doing quite fine in the south', Central Television programme, '*Shihua Shishuo*' (Talking the Truth), 10 June 2001, in Xian-an District Party Committee Secretariat (2003: 148–63).

41 Xian-an District Party Committee Notice No. 3 (2001), 'Selecting and sending off cadres to economically developed areas for enhancement', in Xian-an District Party Committee Secretariat (2003: 37–40).
42 After the first batch, the benchmark was lowered to under 45 years of age and high-school qualification (Author's interviews 2004).
43 About 30 per cent of the first batch of returnees secured leadership positions in the government, or had promotions (Xian-an District Government 2003).
44 Eligible cadres were estimated to number about 2,000, out of a total of about 3,000 cadres in the administrative establishments (Author's interviews 2004).
45 Total fiscal expenditure in 2003 was 200 million yuan, including a net fiscal inflow of 35 million yuan (Author's interviews 2004).

4 State and market in public service provision

* This chapter was originally published in *The Pacific Review*, 21, 3 (2008): 257–78. Earlier versions were presented at the Provincial China Workshop organized by the University of Technology, Sydney and Uppsala University, Sweden, at Taiyuan, China in September 2006, and at the 'State Capacity' conference at the City University of Hong Kong in April 2007. Comments and suggestions by participants, in particular, Vivienne Shue, David Goodman, Christine Wong, Maria Heimer and Minglu Chen are much appreciated.
1 Two recently published studies on peasants' needs are Liu (2006) and Yuan *et al.* (2006). The situation is not much better in more democratic political systems, however, as noted by Chhibber and Sisson (2004) writing on India.
2 Unless otherwise stated, information in this chapter comes from author's interviews in Hubei during 2003–7.
3 See full text of budget available at http://news.xinhuanet.com/misc/2006-03/17/content_4313792.htm, accessed on 10 July 2006; and '2008 government report', available at http://www.xinhuanet.com/2008lh/gzbg/20080305.htm, accessed on 8 March 2008.
4 Hubei Province, while also home to traditional heavy industries including iron and steel and automobiles, is one of the agricultural 'heartlands' of China (like Hunan to its south and Sichuan in the south-west) and has shared similar problems including heavy peasant burdens.
5 Xian-an District was Xianning City (county level) until 1999, when it was renamed Xian-an and made a district of the new and enlarged Xianning City (prefecture level). It has a population of 570,000, of which 77 per cent are rural (available at http://www.xajw.com/Article/ShowArticle.asp?ArticleID=318, accessed on 15 July 2006). The 'district' in the Chinese hierarchy of governments occupies a near-equivalent ranking as the county. The only difference is that a district government is considered part of an urban municipality so that the municipal government often exercises more coordinating functions.
6 This account is based on the pilot reform experience in Henggouqiao Town, Xian-an District (Author's interviews; Song 2006; and 'Xian-an government report on the reform experience', available at http://www.xaxx.gov.cn/vallagechange/exprienceone.htm, accessed on 10 July 2006).
7 Jianli County is infamous for its high peasant burden and violent clashes between village and township cadres and peasants during tax-fee collection. Li Changping's famous book on the plight of peasants (Li 2002) is based on his observations as township party secretary in Jianli County.
8 A county official and formerly township party secretary admitted to the author in 2007 that most opinion-gathering exercises conducted in townships were at best loosely executed.

9 Temporary regulation on fund management of rural public services in Xian-an District, March 2006, available at http://www.hbcz.gov.cn/421202/lm3/lm340/2006-12-01-14443.shtml, accessed on 12 June 2007.

10 Song was reportedly the first senior cadre from Hubei to resign from the government to work as a 'private individual' in south China, when he left the government for Shenzhen/Guangzhou in 1988, after 2 years in the Provincial Policy Research Office. After a few years in the south, he returned to Wuhan to study and earned a doctorate in history in 1993. From 1993 to 1998, Song went to Hainan and participated in the 'Yangpu' project there. He rejoined the government ranks during a recruitment drive by the Hubei government in 1998, and was Party Secretary of Xian-an District from August 1999 to late 2003 (available at http://www.nanfangdaily.com.cn/rwzk/20040630/sz/200408030039.asp, accessed on 11 July 2006, and http://www.phoenixtv.com.cn/home/phoenixweekly/145/20page.html, accessed on 25 July 2006).

11 Hubei Provincial Government Document No. 17 (2003), 4 November 2003, 'Advice on implementing comprehensive township government reforms', promulgated provincial–wide reforms of township government and service agencies along the line of reforms in Xian-an. From January 2004, Song became vice-director of the Research Office at the Provincial Party Committee and vice-director of the Leading Group of the Hubei Township comprehensive reform.

12 *Hubei Daily*, 26 March 2004, available at http://www.chinarural.org/old/readnews.asp?newsid=%7B70BA71C6-3718-45E3-AF33-8D5B780D40A1%7D, accessed on 10 July 2006.

5 Path dependence, agency and implementation in local administrative reform

* This chapter was originally published in *Public Administration and Development*, 29 (January 2009): 79–87, slightly adapted here.

1 Bennett and Howlett (1992: 288) and Winter (2006: 158) observe that many scholars on policy analysis have dwelt on developing general framework and models with little applicability and argue for the need for more empirical-based work.

2 The township (rural; town for the urban equivalent) replaced the 'commune' in 1984 to become the lowest formal level of government in PRC, marking the end of the collectivization period that had started in the mid-1950s. The five-tiers of government are central, provincial, prefectural/municipal, county and township. In 2006, China had a total of 34,675 townships, down 20 per cent from 43,511 in 2000 due to mergers as a result of reform.

3 The 350–550 salaried workers include civil servants, rural service workers and teachers (teachers usually accounted for more than half of the total).

4 Since the 1990s, the main method of reducing the number of government employees who have not yet reached normal retirement age adopted since the 1990s has been so-called 'streamlining' [*fen-liu*], or literally diverting part of the water (the staff) into sub-streams (categories) so that the main stream has a reduced water flow volume. The diverted, or 'streamlined', employees are paid a portion (60–70 per cent) of their basic salary for 3 years, during which time they are expected to settle in another job in the 'market'. Their pay and employment relations with the government are to be terminated at the end of the 3-year transitional period.

5 This started from the promulgation of State Council Document No. 85 (2003) on 30 September 2003 (State Council, General Office 2003), which calls for adjustments to the township–county fiscal relations, an increase in downward transfer payments, and measures to secure the smooth operation of township and village-level agencies and service delivery.

6 This is from my field observations in Hubei Province (2003–6). See also Li and Yuan (2007).

7 Author's field observations. On one occasion, even the main architect of Hubei's PSU reform failed to give a response when being asked the responses of peasants to the reform (Author's interview, Hubei, 2006).

8 See He and Thøgersen (2006) for a local experiment of participatory budgeting at the upper, township level.

6 Working for the peasants

* This chapter was originally published in *The China Journal*, 57 (January 2007): 89–106, and is reprinted here with slight revisions. My stay at the University of California, Berkeley, as Fulbright Scholar in autumn of 2005 provided the perfect space for drafting the chapter, with supportive staff at the Center for Chinese Studies and receptive friends at my warm and tranquil Milvia home. An early version of the chapter was presented at the Research Seminar Series (2005) at the Center for Chinese Studies, University of California, Berkeley, and at the Conference on 'Continuing Transformation in Public Administration' (2006) City University of Hong Kong.

1 The 'Construct the New Socialist Countryside' (*jianshe shehui zhuyi xin nongcun*) campaign was first endorsed by the CCP central plenum in November 2005, and by the National People's Congress in March 2006 (http://news.qq.com/a/20060310/ 001383.htm, accessed on 14 March 2006). Borrowing the idea from a similarly named campaign in South Korea (in Chinese, *xin cun* [new village] *yundong*) in the 1970s and 1980s, this initiative aims at enhancing rural development and improving rural welfare in the Chinese countryside. Ten provinces and municipalities started piloting the 'green GDP' notion in their development in 2005 (see http://finance.sina.com.cn/ g/20050301/04291391079.shtml, accessed on 6 April 2006), and three (Guangdong, Zhejiang and Guizhou) had 'green GDP' formally written in provincial 5-year plans in 2006 (see http://www.gdepb.gov.cn/hjgl/lsgd/zxdt/t20051101_18812.htm, http:// www.gov.cn/test/2006-02/07/content_181020.htm, http://www.gov.cn/test/2006-02/ 08/content_181813.htm, accessed on 6 April 2006).

2 Two good examples of such rhetoric are in 'Chen Xiwen Elaborating on New Countryside Initiatives – 5 Reasons Why the Center Embarks on the Initiative', retrieved at http://finance.people.com.cn/GB/1037/4131151.html, 20 August 2006, and the 11th 5-year plan, especially Part 1, retrieved at http://news.xinhuanet.com/ misc/2006-03/16/content_4309517_1.htm, accessed on 1 September 2006.

3 See Chapter 2 of this volume for more on this specific development.

4 This was part of a speech that Wen gave during a work conference on rural tax reform in July 2004. See http://www.ccrs.org.cn, accessed on 20 August 2004.

5 See Chapter 2 for an extended analysis of the 2000 reform design.

6 See http://news.xinhuanet.com/zhengfu/2004-02/09/content_1304169.htm for the 2004 Document. Central outlay on the direct subsidy (the policy is 10 yuan per acre of crop-growing field) reached 11.6 billion yuan (2004) and 13.2 billion yuan (2005) (Budget speeches 2004–5).

7 The Chinese economy grew on average 9.7 per cent per year during the 1990s, whereas OECD and ASEAN countries grew by 2.6 and 6.1 per cent, respectively. National fiscal revenue has nearly doubled between 2000 (1,340 billion yuan) and 2004 (2,640 billion yuan), see OECD Factbook 2006: Economic, Environmental and Social Statistics, http://www.worldbank.org/data and http://www.stats.gov.cn/tjsj/ndsj/ 2005/indexch.htm. In the 2006 budget, a total of 340 billion yuan was pledged to rural sector expenses, a rise of 42 billion from 2005 (see http://news.xinhuanet.com/misc/ 2006-03/17/content_4313792.htm, accessed on 28 March 2006). These observations were matched in discussions in the Chinese literature. See He (2000: 12–14); Fu

(2001: 35–7); Chen (2002a, 2002b); He (2002: 2–5); J. Zhang (2002: 2–13); Xiang (2004b: 1–62) and Liu and Zhao (2004: 49–52).

8 Chapter 1 tells the story of how the reform started in Anhui and made its way to Beijing. Hubei was the background of the widely circulated book on the plight of peasants and the rural crisis by the former Party Secretary of Qipan Township, Li (2002), which had had considerable influence on official discourse on rural policy.

9 Li (2005a: 87–108). Yining District was formerly Yichang County until July 2001.

10 These include:

> stop all local fund-raising activities, ban all expenditures geared to raising 'standards' or reaching 'benchmarks', establish transparent tax-fee collection and monitoring mechanisms, adjust and improve fiscal relations between county and township levels, and promulgate laws to protect better the rights of peasants.
>
> (See Ren, 2002: 49–64)

11 The supplementary reform measures did include one item (adjust and improve fiscal relations between county and township levels) that addressed the broader fiscal institutional context, but was limited to the county–township interface only.

12 Also of relevance to the simplification process discussed here is James Scott's notion of 'state legibility project', in his *Seeing Like a State: How Certain Schemes to Improve the Human Condition Have Failed*, which refers to attempts by the state, through measures such as the imposition of permanent surnames on communities, to simplify social diversities and thus enhance its control capacity.

13 The status of the township as an independent level of government was the subject of a high-profile conference, 'Conference on the Reform of the Township/Town Level of Government', in Wuhan in February 2004.

14 Some scholars argue against blaming townships alone for the excessive burdens, pointing out that, despite some waste and misuse, fee incomes have supported important public goods provision including education and village roads. One example is Wu (2004a: 271–2).

15 For a collection of major views in the Chinese debate, see Li and Dong (2004). For an analytical review of the literature, see Wu (2004b: 307–23). In the English-language literature, John James Kennedy's 'Death of a Township' offers a brief account of two strands of opinions, featuring Xu Yong, Director of Center for Chinese Rural Studies (CCRS) at Central Normal University, Wuhan, in favour of making townships a branch of county government, and Wu Licai, also of CCRS, advocating a form of democratic governance. For their views, see Xu (2004) and Wu (2004c: 33–65). In a symposium at the City University of Hong Kong, October 2004, Anhui reform activist He Kaiyin explicitly advocated a three-tiered government structure, without townships and prefectures (He and Zhang 2004).

16 Like other tax reform measures, the practice of xiangcai xianguan (county governments managing township budgets) started in Anhui Province in 2003. The major objective was to tighten up oversight and improve efficiency in fiscal management. See Anhui Provincial Government Directive No. 13 (2004), 'On fully implementing the Township Fiscal Management System', 12 July 2004. Earlier on, accounting at the subtownship agencies had been centralized at the township fiscal bureau in a pioneering reform in Yichang County, Hubei Province, in 1998. A crucial control measure was prohibiting agencies from holding independent bank accounts, hence the name of the reform, 'zero-bank-account initiative'. On this last point, see Li (2005a).

17 Fu (2001) argues that tax extraction was always the main activity undertaken in subcounty administrative units throughout Chinese history. To contain their growth and save costs, these units had been kept from developing into full-fledged administration units until 1984.

18 Li, L. (2004: 228–58). At the same time, one should also say that while malpractice can be common at each level of government, local officials' malpractice is easier to spot. So this 'perception' is not entirely the result of 'active' scapegoating.
19 This respondent is a provincial level official in Anhui and has played a critical role in the gestation stage of the reform leading to its adoption as national policy. For the story of this stage of the reform process, and the role of the network of actors, see Chapter 1 of this volume.
20 See http://www.china.org.cn/chinese/2001/Feb/20993.htm, accessed on 20 August 2006, and Chen and Chun (2004: 395).
21 See http://www.lzagri.gov.cn/02/sfgg_004.htm for a news report on the meeting (accessed on 13 October 2005) and Chen and Chun (2004: 396).
22 See http://www.people.com.cn/GB/shizheng/16/20010316/418508.html, accessed on 14 October 2005. The 'sloppiness' in Zhu's answer on the rural tax reform was also noticed by many respondents in field interviews.
23 State Council Document No. 5, 'On further improving the pilot work of the rural tax-for-fee reform', 24 March 2001.
24 Interviews with central fiscal officials, Beijing, 2002, 2004.
25 See also Ren (2002), which notes central policymakers' intention to use the revenue 'deficit' to force township governments to downsize.
26 Rural affairs, including those of a fiscal nature, fell under the jurisdiction of the Ministry of Agriculture, while the Ministry of Civil Affairs was in charge of developing grassroots-level rural administration. Agricultural taxes and fees, until the onset of rural tax reforms, were collected by a township agency under the leadership of the Ministry of Agriculture. Township fiscal departments, which come under the Ministry of Finance, have remained underdeveloped despite townships nominally having their own budget.
27 The tension between Jiang and Zhu was well documented in a book reportedly by a former aide of Zhu (Zong 2001).
28 Liangshi shougou tiaoli (Regulation on the State Purchase of Grains) passed in June 1998. The new law prohibited the deduction of tax and fees from the prices paid to peasants at the time of state procurement, which ran against the practice of tax collection in the tax-for-fee reform localities. All pilot localities, except those in Anhui, stopped the reform as a result. See Chen and Chun (2004: 340–7, 350–3). On Jiang's speech in Hefei, see *Ta Kung Pao* (Impartial Daily) (Hong Kong), 5 October 1998, p. A6.
29 Contributing to Zhu's quick change of stance was the controversy that the circulation reform aroused soon after implementation. An influential CCTV public affairs programme, 'Jiaodian Fangtan' (Focus), featured a sensational report in November 1998 on county leaders fabricating evidence and lying to Zhu regarding the 'success' of the reform during an inspection tour (see a CCTV report on the background of the programme at http://www.cctv.com/news/special/C12572/20040706/101527.shtml, accessed on 19 October 2005). Guangdong Provincial Fiscal Bureau's official journal, *Guangdong Caizheng*, ran a collection of chapters in the October 2002 issue criticizing the reform design and, implicitly, Zhu.
30 The three members were Finance Minister, Agriculture Minister and the head of the central leading group on economics and finance.
31 Interviews in Anhui, 2004.
32 Although the Chinese securities market was relatively cushioned during the Asian Financial Crisis as a result of the non-convertibility of renminbi (yuan) internationally, the crisis indirectly triggered the collapse of major investment corporations such as Guangdong International Trust and Investment Corporation, exposing the huge fiscal risk that local governments across the country had taken when underwriting loans of state-owned banks and enterprises. The central government eventually lent Guangdong Provincial Government several hundreds of billions of yuan to help it through the crisis (Interviews, Guangzhou 2003; see also Wu (2002).

33 State Council General Office Document, 'A notice on some issues on the pilot work on rural tax-for-fee reform in 2001', 25 April 2001. For international coverage on the 'abortion' of the reform, see a report in *Wall Street Journal* (2001, p. 3). See also Ren (2002), which quotes a deputy bureau chief of State Council Rural Tax Reform Work Leading Group, Yang Suizhou, citing these same two reasons for the suspension decision in April 2001: (1) inaccurate initial calculation of reform costs and (2) the perceived need to conserve for the financial crisis.

34 See budget speeches by Finance Minister delivered to the National People's Congress during 2003–5.

35 Taxing of transfers by intermediate layers appears to be an endemic practice. In both Hubei counties (Yichang and Xian-an), for instance, county officials complained of 'taxes' by superiors at the prefectural level when provincial and central funds earmarked for the localities passed through prefectural hands.

36 See 'Executive Vice-Provincial Governor and Deputy Party Secretary of Hubei Province Deng Daoquan Speaking to the Press, 28 June 2002', in http://ncxb.cnhubei.com, accessed on 6 January 2004. Hubei Province started to 'trial-run' the reform in spring 2002 with a small number of townships in preparation for the formulation of reform plan for the entire province. I was at the site of such a trial run in a field trip during spring 2002 (Interviews, 2002).

37 These were the themes raised in a Provincial Tele-conference on Rural Tax-for-Fee Reform Pilot-runs, as reported in *Hubei Daily*, 25 June 2002, accessed at http://ncxb.cnhubei.com on 6 January 2004.

38 Heimer (Edin) (2004). The chapter identifies three 'must-not-happen' situations of social unrest arising from peasant burdens that township officials are subjected to: (1) tensions leading to major use of force, with serious injury or death of peasants; (2) clashes with peasants resulting in major roads/train lines being blocked or government properties being attacked and (3) situations in which force is used to collect taxes, or where peasants commit suicide.

39 In Hubei as of 2003, the main benchmarks were: (1) burden per acre of farmland had to go below 100 yuan; (2) the level of burden for any household after reform must not exceed the level of burden before reform (Interviews, Guangzhou and Wuhan, 2004). Anhui Province in a 2002 directive ('On penalizing administrative behavior contravening the rural tax-for-fee reform policy', 30 November 2002, accessed at http://www.ah.gov.cn on 10 March 2005) lists 12 circumstances that may lead to the firing of officials, and more for demotions.

40 Both Anhui and Hubei, where I conducted fieldwork, set up inspection teams. In Hubei, each team was headed by a senior official of deputy-bureau-chief level with members temporarily seconded from other provincial bureaus. A special inspection office was established inside the Provincial Fiscal Bureau to provide secretarial and logistical support (Interviews, 2004). See 'The Speech by Zhang Ping at the Provincial Tax-for-Fee Reform Inspection Work Meeting, 20 June 2002', accessed at http://www.ah.gov.cn on 5 March 2005, for announcement of inspection teams in Anhui.

41 I had interviews, during 2003 and 2004, with members in these inspection teams as well as county officials receiving the teams.

42 Interviews, 2003 and 2004.

43 The highest reduction rate in 2003 was achieved by Guangdong (74 per cent), while all provinces exceeded the 20 per cent required by the central government. See Chapter 2 of this volume.

44 A provincial source once commented that the most difficult part in reform implementation was to know exactly how much had been taken from peasants pre-reform, since 'illegal', or 'extra-system', items were rarely carefully recorded. Nevertheless, he also agreed that, due to the stepped up post-reform monitoring, by and large the peasant

burden had been brought under control. This view was widely shared by our interviewees across provinces.

45   This town had an average annual rural income of 2,249 yuan (2002), slightly lower than the national average of 2,476 yuan (Interviews, 2002; *China Statistical Yearbook* 2003). It has industries in bamboo handicraft, building and construction materials, and food processing, and a robust wholesale market in bamboo products, generating a total profit and tax income of some 40 million yuan in 2004. The foreign joint venture, with a Hong Kong partner, is in the food-processing industry. The town was merged with another well-off town in the county in a consolidation exercise in late 2004.

46   Information from interviews with town officials, May 2004. This was less than half of the fiscal revenue in 2002 (3.9 million yuan), when the burden-reduction reforms had yet to have an impact. The basic social security payments refer to those paid to the most vulnerable groups of rural residents, for example, orphans, the elderly without children and disabled people, in accordance with the 'Regulation on providing for the 5-guarantees for the needy'. Before the reform, these payments were financed by a fee collected by the town government. The fee was abolished along with others as a result of the tax reform, and the payments had to come from the town budget coffers.

47   This town is in Qianshan County, southwest Anhui. It had an average annual rural income of 1,486 yuan in 2002, 40 per cent below the national average. Annual local fiscal income in 2001, a year after rural tax-for-fee reform was implemented, was around 1.3 million yuan, while expenditure was 2.7 million yuan, the balance financed by fiscal subsidies from above. The town was mostly dependent on agriculture and remittance income from outgoing migrant workers, though there was also some revenue from local trade, being in the middle of a 'catchment' of neighbouring towns (Interviews 2002). See also Wu and Li (2003: 15–24).

48   This town is in Feixi County, with annual rural per capita income of 2,950 yuan as of 2005, compared to a national average of 3,255 yuan (Interviews 2005; http://www.stats.gov.cn/tjfx/ztfx/tjgbjd/t20060302_402308142.htm, accessed on 10 August 2006).

49   Anhui piloted the management of township finance at the county level in nine selected counties in 2003, ahead of most of the country, and extended the centralization province wide in 2004.

50   The other two objectives are reducing peasants' burden (and sustaining the reduction), and maintaining the smooth functioning of rural schools and guaranteeing the pay of schoolteachers (Document No. 7, 2000).

51   Provincial governments, rather than counties, are made responsible for making sure that school education is properly funded under the newly amended *Law on Compulsory Education*. The amendments were put to the NPCSC in February 2006 and passed in late June 2006. See *South China Morning Post*, February 26, 2006, p. A6, and http://www.qgbzb.cee.edu.cn/article_show.asp?articleid=259, retrieved on 15 November 2006.

Conclusion

1   Greenwood *et al.* (2002) suggests a six-stage process, progressing from precipitating jolts, deinstitutionalization, preinstitutionalization, theorization, diffusion to reinstitutionalization. The first two are substages in my stage (1) deinstitutionalization; preinstitutionalization is equivalent to my (2) emergence of new actions; and the last three refined processes in (3) reinstitutionalization.

2   In an elegant reinterpretation of the Chinese economic reform as 'reform without theory', Zhu (2007: 1513) also stresses structural pluralities rather than contradictions between the differential logics, and points out the possibilities of complementarities between the different institutional fields or domains, as well as conflicts.

Bibliography

Adcock, R., Bevir, M. and Stimson, S. (2007) 'Historicizing the new institutionalisms', in R. Adcock, M. Bevir and S. Stimson (eds.) *Modern Political Science*, Princeton, NJ: Princeton University Press: 259–89.

Ai, J. (2005) 'Nongmin yu nongmin wenti de tantao yu sisuo' (Discussion on nongmin and related issues), available at http://www.chinaelections.org/newsinfo.asp?newsid=45537, accessed on 19 March 2011.

Ai, Q. and Zhou, X. (2007) 'Hubei jingjian jigoubianzhi quansheng caizheng gongyang renyuan jian 10 wan yuren' (Hubei Province institutional reform to reduce civil servants by 100,000), available at http://news.sohu.com/20071229/n254381309.shtml, accessed on 20 July 2008.

Archer, M. (1995) *Realist Social Theory: The Morphogenetic Approach*, Cambridge: Cambridge University Press.

Arthur, W.B. (1989) 'Competing technologies, increasing returns, and lock-in by historical events', *The Economic Journal*, 99 (March): 116–31.

Barnett, D. and Vogel, E. (1967) *Cadre, Bureaucracy and Political Power in Communist China*, New York: Columbia University Press.

Bennett, A. and Elman, C. (2006) 'Qualitative research: recent developments in case study methods', *Annual Review of Political Science*, 9: 455–76.

Bennett, C.J. and Howlett, M. (1992) 'The lessons of learning: reconciling theories of policy learning and policy change', *Policy Sciences*, 25: 275–94.

Berger, P.L. and Luckmann, T. (1967) *The Social Construction of Reality*. New York: Doubleday.

Bernstein, T.P. and Lü, X. (2003) *Taxation without Representation in Contemporary Rural China*, Cambridge: Cambridge University Press.

Bhaskar, R. and Lawson, T. (1998) 'Introduction', in M. Archer, R. Bhaskar, A. Collier, T. Lawson and A. Norrie (eds.) *Critical Realism: Essential Readings*, London and New York: Routledge.

Bogason, P. and Zolner, M. (eds.) (2007) *Methods in Democratic Network Governance*, Basingstoke and New York: Palgrave Macmillan.

Brehm, J. and Gates, S. (1997) *Working, Shirking, Sabotage: Bureaucratic Response to a Democratic Public*, Ann Arbor, MI: The University of Michigan Press.

Bremer, J. (1984) 'Building institutional capacity for policy analysis: an alternative approach to sustainability', *Public Administration and Development*, 4: 1–13.

Brodsgaard, K.E. (2002) 'Institutional reform and the *Bianzhi* system in China', *The China Quarterly*, 170 (June): 361–86.

Burns, J. (2003) '"Downsizing" the Chinese state: government retrenchment in the 1990s', *The China Quarterly*, 175: 775–802.

Cao, J. (2000) *Huang He Bian di Zhongguo* (Along the Border of the Yellow River), Shanghai: Shanghai Wenyi Chubanshe.

CCP Central Committee, State Council. (1996) 'Guanyu qieshi zuohao jianqing nongmin fudan gongzuo de jueding' (Decision of Party Central Committee and State Council on alleviating peasants' burden), No. 13, available at http://cpc.people.com.cn/GB/64162/71380/71382/71481/4854241.html, accessed on 30 December 1996.

CCP Central Committee, State Council. (2000) 'Guanyu jinxing nongcun shuifei gaige shidian de tongzhi' (A notice on piloting the rural tax reform), Central Document (2000) No. 7, 24 June 2000, available at http://www.yfzs.gov.cn/gb/info/ZFFZ/CZFZ/SFGG/2005-05/26/1131083368.html, accessed on 20 July 2011.

CCP Central Committee Secretariat, State Council Secretariat. (1993) 'Guanyu qieshi jianqing nongmin fudan de jinji tongzhi' (An urgent notice on genuinely alleviating the burden of the peasants), 19 March 1993, available at http://www.law-lib.com/law/law_view.asp?id=55897, accessed on 20 July 2011.

Chen, G. and Chun, T. (2004) *Zhongguo Nongmin Diaocha* (A Survey of the Chinese Peasants), Beijing: Renmin Wenxue Chubanshe.

Chen, J. and Duan, Y. (2010) '1978–2006 nian zhongguo nongmin fudan wenti yanjiu' (A study of the peasants' burden issues in China, 1978–2006), *Jianghan Luntan*, 1 (January), available at http://www.21ccom.net/articles/lsjd/lsjj/article_201005139399.html, accessed on 4 April 2011.

Chen, W. (2007) *Xiangcun Zhaiwu de Weiji Guanli* (Managing the Debt Crisis in Townships and Villages), Changsha: Hunan renmin chubanshe.

Chen, X. (ed.) (2002a) *Zhongguo Xianxiang Caizheng Yu Nongmin Zengshou Wenti Yanjiu* (A Study of County and Township Finance and Issues Around Increasing Peasants' Income), Taiyuan: Shanxi Jingji Chubanshe.

Chen, X. (2002b) 'Nongcun shuifei gaige buzhishi nongmin jianfu wenti' (The rural tax reforms are not about reducing peasant burden only), *Caijing*, 8 (6 August): 68, Beijing, available at http://caijing.hexun.com/text.aspx?ID=1137888, accessed on 20 October 2005.

Chen, X. (2003) 'Nongcun shuifei gaige ruhe yingxiang nongmin de mingyun?' (How does the rural tax-fee reform change the life of peasants?), available at http://www.zhinong.cn/data/detail.php?id=3996, accessed on 30 July 2008.

Chen, X. (2009) 'Nongcun gaige fazhan de xingshi he zongti silu' (Situation and general concepts of rural reform and development), *Zhongguo Dangzheng Ganbu Luntan* (Chinese Cadres Tribune), 8: 4–9.

Chen, X., Han, J. and Zhao, Y. (2005) 'Woguo nongcun gonggong caizheng zhidu yanjiu' (Research on rural fiscal system), *Hongguan Jingji Yanjiu* (Macroeconomics), 5: 8–10.

Chen, Y. (2004) 'Lun Zhongguo xiangji caizheng' (On the finance of township governments in China), *Zhongguo Nongcun Guancha* (China Rural Survey), 5: 60–8.

Cheng, G. (2006) 'Jinnian woguo nongcun shuifei gaige de zhuanyi zhifufei jiang chao 1000 yi' (Total transfer payments on rural tax reform this year will exceed 100 billion yuan), available at http://www.sccs.gov.cn/html/csyw/2007-2/8/14_47_35_137.htm, accessed on 30 July 2008.

Chhibber, S. and Sisson, R. (2004) 'Federal arrangements and the provision of public goods in India', *Asian Survey*, XLIV (3): 339–52.

Chinese Public Administration Society Project Group. (2002) 'A study on social clashes in transitional China: main features, causes and policy recommendations', *Chinese Public Administration*, 203 (5): 6–9.

Clarke, D. (2007) 'Legislating for a market economy in China', *The China Quarterly*, 191: 567–85.

Clemens, E.S. and Cook, J.M. (1999) 'Politics and institutionalism: Explaining durability and change', *Annual Review of Sociology*, 25: 441–66.

Cohen, M.D., March, J.G. and Olsen, J.P. (1972) 'A garbage can model of organizational choice', *Administrative Science Quarterly*, 17 (1, March): 1–25.

Cooper, T.L. (1996) 'The paradox of responsibility: an enigma', in *'Spirited Dialogue' forum on Michael Harmon's Responsibility as Paradox, Public Administration Review*, 56 (November/December, no. 6).

Cooper, T.L. (1998) *The Responsible Administrator: An Approach to Ethics for the Administrative Role*, 2nd ed., San Francisco, CA: Jossey-Bass.

Cui, R. (2004) 'Chen Xiwen: xiangzhen caizheng weihe nan?' (Chen Xiwen: Why is the finance of town governments so tough?), *Caijing Jie* (Financial and Economical Issue), 4: 35–5.

Dacin, M.T. and Dacin, P.A. (2008) 'Tradition as institutionalized practice: implications for deinstitutionalization', in R. Greenwood, C. Oliver, K. Sahlin and R. Suddaby (eds.) *The Sage Handbook of Organizational Institutionalism*, London: Sage: 327–51.

David, P. (1985) 'Clio and the economics of QWERTY', *The American Economic Review*, 75 (2): 332–7.

David, P. (1986) 'Understanding the economics of QWERTY: the necessity of history', in W. Parker (ed.) *Economic History and the Modern Historian*, London: Blackwell: 30–49.

deLeon, L. (2003) 'On acting responsibly in a disorderly world: individual ethics and administrative responsibility', in G. Peters and J. Pierre (eds.) *Handbook of Public Administration*, London: Sage: 569–80.

Deleon, P. and Martell, C.R. (2006) 'The policy sciences: past, present, and future', in G. Peters and J. Pierre (eds.) *Handbook of Public Policy*, London: Sage.

Diamond, L. (2003) 'The rule of law as transition to democracy to China', *Journal of Contemporary China*, 12 (35): 319–31.

Ding, C.W. (2007) 'San nong tupo: Nongmin quanyi baohufa wunian changpao' (A breakthrough in rural issues: The five-year long march of the Law on the protection of peasants' rights and interests), available at http://finance.sina.com.cn/g/20040305/1447658426.shtml, accessed on 25 March 2011.

Ding, Q. (2004) 'Sannong tupo: Nongmin quanyi baohufa wunian changpao' (Breakthrough of rural reform: Five years progress of Rural Peasants Protection Law), available at http://finance.sina.com.cn/g/20040305/1447658426.shtml, accessed on 28 March 2011.

Donnithorne, A. (1967) *China's Economic Systems*, London: George Allen and Unwin.

Edwards, L. (2009) 'Diversity and evolution in the state-in-society: international influences in combating violence against women', in L.C. Li (ed.) *The Chinese State in Transition*, London: Routledge, 108–26.

Fagaiwei. (2006) 'Fagaiwei: shi buzai guan xian, jiang jian zhongyang sheng shi/xian sanji caizheng' (National development and reform commission: The city will no longer supervise the county level; three level fiscal systems (central–provincial–city/county) are to be established), available at http://cz.tyjcp.gov.cn/DetailServlet?siteID=45&infoID=207, accessed on 28 July 2008.

Fan, L. and Shi, S. (2005) 'Nongcun shuifei gaige hou de xianxiang caizheng yuxing fenxi— yi lingyi shi weili' (An analysis of rural fiscal operation after rural taxes and fees reform: The case of Lingyi City), available at http://tgs.ndrc.gov.cn/dfgg/t20051231_55484.htm, accessed on 28 July 2008.

Feinerman, J. (2007) 'New hope for corporate governance in China?' *The China Quarterly*, 191: 590–612.

Feng, G. (2008) 'Guanyu xin nongcun jianshe zhong "yishi yiyi" de qingkuang diaocha yu sikao' (Thoughts from an investigation on the 'Deliberation on Each and Every Item' measure during the construction of the new countryside), available at http://www.pccz.gov.cn/E_ReadNews.asp?NewsID=650, accessed on 28 July 2008.

Fitzgerald, J. (ed.) (2002) *Rethinking China's Provinces*, London: Routledge.

Friedland, R. and Alford, R.R. (1991) 'Bringing society back in: symbols, practices, and institutional contradictions', in W.W. Powell and P.J. DiMaggio (eds.) *The New Institutionalism in Organizational Analysis*, Chicago: The University of Chicago Press, 232–66.

Fu, G. (2001) 'Chexiao xiangzhen: gaige xianxing xiangzhen zuzhi he caizheng tizhi yunxing moshi de tantao' (Abolish the township level: exploring the reform of the mode of operation of township administration and fiscal system), *Juece yu Zixun* (Decision-making and Consulting) (Anhui, China), 10: 35–7.

Fu, G. (2007) '*Xin Nongcun Jianshe touru jizhi yanjiu*' (A study on the financing channels of the New Village Initiative), paper submitted to the '*International Conference on Villager's Self-Governance and the Building of a New Socialist Countryside*', organized by the Centre for Chinese Rural Studies, Central Normal University, Wuhan, 16–17 June 2007.

Gao, C. *et al.* (2003) 'Jianren, jianshi, jianzhi de lilun fenxi yu yige shijian yangben' (Trimming staff size, responsibilities and expenditures: theory and implementation), in Wang Huaxin (ed.) *Nian Zhongguo Difang Caizheng Yanjiu Baogao: Hubeisheng Nongcui Shuifei Gaige Shijian Yu Tansuo* (Local Finance Research Report, 2003: Practice and Research on the Tax Reform in the Rural Area of Hubei Province), Beijing: Jingji Kexue Chubanshe, 37–63.

Garud, R. and Karnoe, P. (eds.) (2001a) *Path Dependence and Creation*, Mahwah, NJ: Lawrence Erlbaum Associates.

Garud, R. and Karnoe, P. (2001b) 'Path creation as mindful deviation', in R. Garud and P. Karnoe (eds.) *Path Dependence and Creation*, Mahwah, NJ: Lawrence Erlbaum Associates.

Garud, R., Hardy, C. and Maguire, S. (2007) 'Institutional entrepreneurship as embedded agency: An introduction to the special issue', *Organization Studies*, 28 (7): 957–69.

Giddens, A. (1984) *The Constitution of Society*, Berkeley: University of California Press.

Göbel, C. (2010) *The Politics of Rural Reform in China: State Policy and Village Predicament in the Early 2000s*, London: Routledge.

Goodman, D.S.G. (ed.) (1984) *Groups and Politics in the People's Republic of China*, Armonk, NY: M.E. Sharpe.

Goodman, D.S.G. (1989) 'Power, policy and process', *British Journal of Political Science*, 19 (July): 425–44.

Goodman, D.S.G. (ed.) (1997) *China's Provinces in Reform*, London: Routledge.

Goodman, D.S.G. (2000) 'Centre and periphery after twenty years of reform: redefining the Chinese polity', *China Perspectives*, 31: 4–18.

Goodman, D.S.G. and Segal, G. (eds.) (1994) *China Deconstructs: Politics, Trade and Regionalism*, London: Routledge.

Grafstein, R. (1988) 'The problem of institutional constraint', *Journal of Politics*, 50 (3, August): 577–99.

Granovettor, M. (1985) 'Economic action and social structure: the problem of embeddedness', *American Journal of Sociology*, 91 (3): 481–510.

Greenwood, R. and Suddaby, R. (2006) 'Institutional entrepreneurship in mature fields: The big five accounting firms', *Academy of Management Journal*, 49: 27–48.

Greenwood, R., Suddaby, R. and Hinings, C.R. (2002) 'Theorizing change: The role of professional associations in the transformation of institutionalized fields', *Academy of Management Journal*, 45 (1): 58–80.

Greenwood, R., Oliver, C., Sahlin, K. and Suddaby, R. (2008) 'Introduction', in R. Greenwood, C. Oliver, K. Sahlin and R. Suddaby (eds.) *The Sage Handbook of Organizational Institutionalism*, London: Sage, 1–46.

Gregory, R. (2003) 'Accountability in modern government', in G. Peters and J. Pierre (eds.) *Handbook of Public Administration*, London: Sage, 557–68.

Grin, J. and Loeber, A. (2007) 'Theories of policy learning: agency, structure, and change', in F. Fischer, G.J. Miller and M.S. Sidney (eds.) *Handbook of Public Policy Analysis*, London: Taylor & Francis.

Guo, X. (1990) 'Zhongguo nongye: gaigezhong di wenti yu xin di tupo' (Agriculture in China: problems amidst reform and new breakthroughs), in H. Kang and W. Yuzhao (eds.) *Zhongguo Nongcun Gaige Shi Nian*, Beijing: People's University of China Press.

Guo, W. (2006) 'Xin Nongcun Jianshe xuyao zhengque renshi he bawo de jige wenti' (A few issues to grasp on the 'New Socialist Countryside' program), available at http://theory.people.com.cn/GB/49154/49369/4283005.html, accessed on 10 July 2006.

Gupta, A. (1995) 'Blurred boundaries: The discourse of corruption, the culture of politics, and the imagined state', *American Ethnologist*, 22 (2): 375–402.

Hardy, C. and Maguire, S. (2008) 'Institutional entrepreneurship', in R. Greenwood, C. Oliver, K. Sahlin and R. Suddaby (eds.) *The Sage Handbook of Organizational Institutionalism*, London: Sage, 199–217.

Harmon, M. (1995) *Responsibility as Paradox: A Critique of Rational Discourse on Government*, Thousand Oaks, CA: Sage.

He, B. and Thøgersen, S. (2006) '*Recent experiments with political participation in rural China: deliberative forums and consultative township elections*', paper for *Workshop on local governance in China*, Taiyuan, China, 19–21 September.

He, K. (2000) 'Nongmin jianfu: luzai hefang' (Looking for a way to reduce peasants burden: thoughts on township administrative reform in association with rural tax-for-fee reforms), *Diaoyan Shijie* (Explorations), 2: 12–14.

He, K. and Wang, Y. (eds.) (1990) *Zhongguo Nongcun Gaige Shi Nian* (Ten Years of Rural Reform), Beijing: People's University of China Press.

He, K. and Sun, L. (eds.) (2000) *Zhongguo Nongcun Shuifei Gaige Chutan* (The Early Probes into the Rural Tax-For-Fee Reform in China), Beijing: Zhi Gong Chubanshe.

He, K. and Zhang, D. (2004) '*Zhongguo nongcun wenti ji zhengfu zhengce fazhan di huigu*' (A review of Chinese rural issues and the development of related government policies), paper presented at *Symposium on 'China's Rural Governance: The Role of Government and NGOs'*, City University of Hong Kong, 25 October 2004.

He, X. and Wang, X. (2002) 'Lun xiaoji xingzhen – jianlun jianqing nongmin fudan de jiben zhice' (On negative implementation: fundamental measures on alleviating peasants' burden), *Zhejiang Xuekan* (Zhejiang Academic Journal), (6): 22–7.

He, X. and Wang, X. (2003) 'Nongmin fudan de xianzhuang yu zhengjie – Hubei J shi diaocha' (Current situations and crux of peasants' burden – a case in city J, Hubei), *Zhongguo Nongshi* (Agricultural History of China), (2): 99–108.

He, Z. (2002) 'Shenhua nongcui shuifei gaige xinfanglui di tansuo' (Exploring new strategies of deepening the rural 'tax-for-fee' reform), *Shuiwu Yanjiu* (Taxation Affairs Research), 204 (5): 2–5.

Heilmann, S. (2008a) 'Policy experimentation in China's economic rise', *Studies in Comparative International Development*, 43: 1–26.

Heilmann, S. (2008b) 'From local experiments to national policy: The origins of China's distinctive policy process', *The China Journal*, 59 (January): 1–30.

Heimer (Edin), M. (2000) '*Market Forces and Communist Power: Local Political Institutions and Economic Development in China*', doctoral dissertation at Uppsala University, Department of Government.

Heimer (Edin), M. (2003) 'State capacity and local agent control in China: CCP cadre management from a township perspective', *The China Quarterly*, 173 (March): 35–49.

Heimer (Edin), M. (2004) '*Taking an aspirin: implementing tax and fee reform at the grassroots*', paper presented at the *Grassroots Political Reform in Contemporary China Conference*, Fairbank Center, Harvard University, 29–31 October.

Hendrischke, H. and Feng, C. (eds.) (1999) *The Political Economy of China's Provinces*, London: Routledge.

Hill, M. and Hupe, P. (2002) *Implementing Public Policy: Governance in Theory and in Practice*, London: Sage Publications.

Hirsch, P. and Gillespie, J. (2001) 'Unpacking path dependence: differential valuations accorded history across disciplines', in R. Garud and P. Karnoe (eds.) *Path Dependence and Creation*, Mahwah, NJ: Lawrence Erlbaum Associates.

Holbig, H. (2004) 'The emergence of the campaign to open up the west: ideological formation, central decision-making and the role of the provinces', *The China Quarterly*, 178 (June): 335–57.

Huges, E.C. (1936) 'The ecological aspect of institutions', *American Sociological Review*, 1: 180–9.

Hupe, P.L. and Hill, M.J. (2006) 'The three action levels of governance: re-framing the policy process beyond the stages model', in G. Peters and J. Pierre (eds.) *Handbook of Public Policy*, London: Sage, 13–30.

Jeffreys, E. (ed.) (2009) *China's Governmentalities: Governing Change, Changing Government*, London: Routledge.

Jepperson, R.L. (1991) 'Institutions, institutional effects, and institutionalism', in Wa.W. Powell and P.J. DiMaggio (eds.) *The New Institutionalism in Organizational Analysis*, Chicago: The University of Chicago Press, 143–63.

Jiang, Z. (1996) 'Jiajiang nongye jichu, shenhua nongcun gaige, tuijin nongcun jingji he shehui quanmin fazhan' (Strengthen the basis of agriculture, deepen the rural reforms, advance the full scale socio-economic development of the countryside), speech made during a field visit in Henan Province, 4 June 1996, available at http://news.xinhuanet.com/ziliao/2005-03/14/content_2696290.htm, accessed on 20 July 2011.

Jin, H., Qian, Y. and Weingast, B.R. (2005) 'Regional decentralization and fiscal incentives: federalism, Chinese style', *Journal of Public Economics*, 89: 1719–42.

'Jinnian' (2007) 'Jinnian woguo nongcun shuifei gaige de chuanyi zhifufei jiang chao 1000 yi' (Total transfer payments on rural tax reform this year will exceed 100 billion yuan), available at http://www.sccs.gov.cn/html/csyw/2007-2/8/14_47_35_137.htm, accessed on 30 July 2008.

Kelliher, D.R. (1992) *Peasant Power in China: The Era of Rural Reform, 1979–1989*, New Haven, CT: Yale University Press.

Kennedy, J.J. (2005) '*Death of a township: impact of the 2002 tax-for-fee reform in Northwest China*', paper presented at the *Association of Chinese Political Science 18th Annual Conference* in San Francisco, California, 30–31 July 2005.

Kennedy, J.J. (2007) 'From the tax-for-fee reform to the abolition of agricultural taxes: the impact on township governments in north-west China', *The China Quarterly*, 189 (March): 43–59.

Knight, J. and Song, L. (1995) 'Towards a labour market in China', *Oxford Review of Economic Policy*, 11 (4): 97–117.

Kong, X.Z. and He, A.H. (2009) 'Xin zhongguo chengli 60 nian lai nongmin dui guojia jianshe de gongxian fenxi' (An analysis of the contributions of peasants during the 60 years of the New China), *Jiaoxue yu Yanjiu* (Teaching and Research), 9: 5–13.

Lampel, J. (2001) 'Show and tell: product demonstrations and path creation of technological change', in R. Garud and P. Karnoe (eds.) *Path Dependence and Creation*, Mahwah, NJ: Lawrence Erlbaum Associates.

Lampton, D. (ed.) (1987) *Policy Implementation in Post-Mao China*, Berkeley: University of California Press.

Lasswell, H.D. (1956) *The Decision Process: Seven Categories of Functional Analysis*, College Park: University of Maryland Press.

Latour, B. (1987) *Science in Action: How to Follow Engineers and Scientists through Society*, Cambridge, MA: Harvard University Press.

Latour, B. (2005) *Reassembling the Social: An Introduction to Actor-Network-Theory*, Oxford: Clarendon.

Law, J. (1992) 'Notes on actor-network theory', *Systems Practice*, 5 (4): 379–93, available at http://www.lancs.ac.uk/fss/sociology/papers/law-notes-on-ant.pdf.

Li, C. (2002) *Wo Xiang Zongli Shuo Shihua* (Telling the Truth to the Premier), Beijing: Guangming Chubanshe.

Li, C. (2006a) 'Xin Nongcun Jianshe de zuida zuli zai Beijing' (The largest source of resistance to the 'New Countryside' plans comes from Beijing), available at http://www.snzg.com.cn/ReadNews.asp?NewsID=1271, accessed on 25 July 2006.

Li, C. (2006b) 'Jiedu Hu-Wen xinzheng xia de sannong zhengce: dui weilai wunian sannong xingshi de jiben panduan' (Rural policies under the Hu-Wen new administration: some fundamental assessments of rural issues in the next five years), available at http://www.zhinong.cn/data/detail.php?id=5395, accessed on 10 July 2006.

Li, C. and Dong, L. (2004) *Shuifei Gaige Beijingxia de Xiangzhen Tizhi Yanjiu* (Studies of the Township Government System in the Context of Rural Tax-for-fee Reforms), Wuhan, Hubei: Hubei Renmin Chubanshe.

Li, L. (2004) 'Political trust in rural China', *Modern China*, 30 (2, April): 228–58.

Li, L. and O'Brien, K. (1996) 'Villagers and popular resistance in contemporary China', *Modern China*, 22 (January): 28–61.

Li, L.C. (1997) 'Towards a non-zero-sum interactive framework of spatial politics: The case of centre-province in contemporary China', *Political Studies*, 45 (1, March): 49–65.

Li, L.C. (1998) *Centre and Provinces: China, 1978–1993. Power as Non-Zero-Sum*, Oxford: Clarendon Press.

Li, L.C. (2000) 'The "rule of law" policy in Guangdong: continuity or departure? Meaning, significance and process', *The China Quarterly*, 161 (March): 199–220.

Li, L.C. (2004) 'Prelude to government reform? – The big sale in Shunde', *China Information*, XVIII (1, March): 29–66.

Li, L.C. (2005a) 'Understanding institutional change: fiscal management in local China', *Journal of Contemporary Asia*, 35 (1): 87–108.

Li, L.C. (2005b) '*Shirking and shouldering responsibility: strategic interactions and unintended consequences in the Chinese rural tax reforms*', paper presented at *Center for Chinese Studies Seminar*, University of California, Berkeley, 26 October 2005.

Li, L.C. (ed.) (2009) *The Chinese State in Transition: Processes and Contests in Local China*, London: Routledge.

Li, L.C. and Qiu, H. (2004) '*Sorting out the details: structure, agency and interactions in China's local political economy*', paper presented at the *2004 Annual Conference of the British International Association*, 20–22 December 2004, Warwick, UK.

Li, L.C. and Wu, L. (2005) 'Daobi haishi fandaobi? Nongcun shuifei gaige qianhou zhongyang yu defang zijian di hudong' (Pressure for changes: central–local interactions in rural tax-for-fee reform), *Sociological Research* (4): 44–63.

Li, L.C. and Yue, F. (2005) 'Guangdong Shunde nongcun shuifei gaige jizhi xiaoying' (Township fiscal institutional change? A case study of rural tax-for-fee reform in Shunde, Guangdong), *South China Economy*, 195 (December): 86–8.

Li, L.C. and Yuan, F. (2007) 'Ruhe chaoyue gaige "gudao"? jiankan gaige de chengben yu xiaoyi: Hubei Xian-an xiangzhen zhansuo gaige de qishi' (Transcending the 'isolation' effect of reform pilots: importance of 'cost and benefit' analysis – observations from township agency reform in Xian-an, Hubei), in X. Yong (ed.) *Zhongguo Nongcun Yanjiu 2006* (Chinese Rural Studies 2006), Beijing: Zhongguo Shehui Kexue Chubanshe, 101–16.

Li, L.C. and Wu, L. (2008) 'Lishi jiyi yingxiang ze xiangzhen gaige juece' (How history and memory impacts on decision-making on township government reforms), *China Social Sciences* (Internal Version), 1 (February): 146–54.

Li, R. (1996) *Dayuejin Qin Li Ji* (Personal Experience of 'Great Leap Forward'), Shanghai: Shanghai Yuandong Chubanshe.

Li, Z. (2003) 'Tiaozheng guomin jingji shuoru fengpei guanxi, zhuanjian xindi nongmin shuifei fudan jidu' (Adjust redistributive relations in national income, Create a new tax system for peasants), *China Rural Economy*, 2: 35–40.

Lieberthal, K. and Oksenberg, M. (1988) *Policy Making in China: Leaders, Structures and Processes*, Princeton, NJ: Princeton University Press.

Lieberthal, K. and Lampton, D. (eds.) (1992) *Bureaucracy, Politics and Decision-Making in Post-Mao China*, Berkeley: University of California Press.

Liu, H. (2000) 'Gonggong caizheng yu "chifan caizheng" bianxi' (An analysis of public finance and 'subsistence finance'), *Sichuan Caizheng*, 2: 16–18.

Liu, W. and Zhao, P. (2004) 'Nongmin fudan fantan dongyin fenxi ji huajie celue' (Why peasant burden rebounces? Causes and resolving strategies), *Journal of Guangxi Financial College*, 17 (2, April): 49–52.

Liu, Y. (2006) 'Jiangou nongmin xuqiu daoxiang de gonggong chanpin gongji zhidu' (Constructing a client-need-oriented system of public goods provision), *Huazhong Shifan Daxue Xuebao: Renwen ShehuiKexue Ban* (Journal of Central China Normal University, Humanities and Social Sciences) (Hubei, China), 45 (2): 15–23.

Luo, Z. (2007) 'Guanyu jinyibu jiejue xianxiang caizheng kunnan de jianyi' (Suggestions on further resolving fiscal difficulties), available at http://www.lianghui.org.cn/2007lianghui/2007-03/13/content_7954626.htm, accessed on 4 April 2008.

Mah, D.N. and Hills, P. (2008) 'Central–local relations and pricing policies for wind energy in China', *The China Review*, 8 (2, Fall): 262–93.

Martinez-Vazquez, Qiao, B. and Li, Z. (2008) 'The role of provincial policies in fiscal equalization outcomes in China', *The China Review*, 8 (2, Fall): 135–68.

Matland, R.E. (1995) 'Synthesizing the implementation literature: the ambiguity-conflict model of policy implementation', *Journal of Public Administration Research and Policy*, 5 (April): 145–74.

May, P.J. (2003) 'Policy design and implementation', in G. Peters and J. Pierre (eds.) *Handbook of Public Administration*, London: Sage, 223–33.

Ministry of Agriculture, Office of the Rural Reform Experimental Zones. (1995) 'Shiguan nongcun fazhan he wendi di yixiang zhongyao gaige jucuo' (An important reform initiative with impacts for rural development and stability: a report on local rural tax reform pilots), in K. He and L. Sun (eds.) *Zhongguo Nongcun Shuifei Gaige Chutan* (The Early Probes into the Rural Tax-For-Fee Reform in China), Beijing: Zhi Gong Chubanshe, 391–404.

Ministry of Agriculture. (2000) 'Guanyu yinfa "Cunji Fanweinei Chouzi Choulau Guanli Zhanxin Guiding" di tongzhi' (A notice on the temporary regulations on raising funds and labor in villages), *Caijing Luncong* (Discussion of Fiscal and Economic Affairs), 5: 1–8.

Ministry of Finance. (ed.) (2002) *Difang Caizheng Tongji Jilu, 2001* (Statistical Information of Local Finance, 2001), Beijing: Zhongguo CaiZheng Jingji Chubanshe.

Ministry of Finance, Fiscal Research Institute (2004) 'Xiangcun zhengfu zaiwu huajie duice yanjiu' (A study to resolve the rural local governments' debts), *Caijing Luncong* (Discussion of Fiscal and Economic Affairs), 4: 1–8.

Mok, K.H. (2000) 'Marketizing higher education in post-Mao China', *International Journal of Educational Development*, 20 (2, March): 109–26.

Mosher, F.C. (1968) *Democracy and the Public Service*, New York: Oxford University Press.

National Bureau of Statistics of China. (2003) *China Statistical Yearbook, 2003*, Beijing: China Statistics Press.

Nayak, P.R. and Ketteringham, J.M. (1986) *Breakthroughs!* New York: Rawson.

O'Brien, K. (1996) 'Rightful resistance', *World Politics*, 45 (1): 31–55.

O'Brien, K. (2002) 'Collective action in the Chinese countryside', *China Journal*, 48 (July): 139–54.

O'Brien, K. and Li, L. (1995) 'The politics of lodging complaints in rural China', *China Quarterly*, 143 (September): 757–83.

O'Brien, K. and Li, L. (1999) 'Selective policy implementation in rural China', *Comparative Politics*, 31, (2, January): 167–86.

Office of the State Council Rural Tax-for-fee Reform Working Group. (2004) 'Nongmin shuifei fudan zhuan kuang ji shenhua nongcun shuifei zhidu gaige' (The situation of the peasants' burden and deepening the rural tax reform: a background report for the legislation of the Peasants' Right Protection Law), available at http://zgb.mof.gov.cn/zhengwuxinxi/diaochayanjiu/200806/t20080619_47035.html, accessed on 2 August 2010.

Oliver, C. (1992) 'The antecedents of deinstitutionalization', *Organization Studies*, 13: 563–88.

Ou, C. (2008) 'Zhengfu zhijian zhuanyi zhifu jidai lifa' (There is a necessity to legislate on intergovernmental transfers), available at http://www.gov.cn/2008lh/zb/0308b/content_913537.htm, accessed on 28 July 2008.

Pan, C. (2008) 'Contractual thinking and responsible government in China: a constructivist framework for analysis', *The China Review*, 8 (2, Fall): 49–76.

Pan, C. (2009) 'Peaceful rise and China's new international contract', in L.C. Li (ed.) *The Chinese State in Transition*, London: Routledge, 127–44.

Pan, W. (2003) 'Towards a consultative rule of law regime in China', *Journal of Contemporary China*, 12 (34): 3–43.

Pierre, J. (2006) 'Disciplinary perspectives', in G. Peters and J. Pierre (eds.) *Handbook of Public Policy*, London: Sage.

Pou, W. (2003) 'What can a representative of peasants' interests achieve in China?', *Zhongguo Gaige* (China Reform) (the rural version), 3: 42–3.

Public Governance and Territorial Development Directorate Public Management Committee. (2002) *Highlights of Public Sector Pay and Employment Trends: 2002 Update*, Paris: OCED Headquarters.

Qiao, X. (2004) 'Zhongguo di "mingxing cun" yu nongcun zhili jiegou' ('Star villages' and rural governance structures in China), *Shijiao* (Perspectives), 4 (2) 30 April, available at http://www.oycf.org/Perspectives/Chinese/Chinese_14_04302004/2b_Qiao_final.pdf, accessed on 24 November 2005.

Qin, H. (1997) 'Nongmin fudan wenti de fanzhan chushi: Qinghua daxue xuesheng nongcui diaocha baogao zi fenxi' (How the issue of 'peasants' burden' is developing? – An analysis of rural survey from Tsinghua University students), Reform No. 2, available at http://wwwguoxue.com/economics/ReadNews.asp?NewsID=426&BigclassName, accessed on 3 May 2004.

Qin, H. (2000) 'Binshuishi gaige yu "Huangzhongxi" dinglu' (Merging fees-into-tax reform and the 'Huangzhongxi' rule), *China Economic Times*, available at http://www.guxiang.com/xueshu/others/jingji/200209/200209210023.htm, accessed on 3 May 2004.

Ren, B. (2002) 'Nongcun shuifei zi bian' (How the (reform on) rural taxes and fees have evolved), *Caijing* (Beijing), 8 (6 August): 49–64.

Rural Tax-for-fee Reform Research Group (2003) 'Quxiao nongyeshui, gaizheng zengzhishui: guanyu jinyibu shenhua nongcun shuifei gaige de sikou' (Abolish the agricultural taxes, impose instead the value-added tax: some thoughts to further deepen the rural tax reform), *Hongguan jingji yanjiu* (Macro economic studies), 7: 3–10.

Sahlin, K. and Wedlin, L. (2008) 'Circulating ideas: imitation, translation and editing', in R. Greenwood, C. Oliver, K. Sahlin and R. Suddaby (eds.) *The Sage Handbook of Organizational Institutionalism*, London: Sage, 218–42.

Schurmann, F. (1968) *Ideology and Organization in Communist China*, Berkeley: University of California Press.

Scott, J.C. (1998) *Seeing Like a State: How Certain Schemes to Improve the Human Condition Have Failed*, New Haven, CT: Yale University Press.

Seo, M. and Creed, W.E.D. (2002) 'Institutional contradictions, praxis, and institutional change: a dialectical perspective', *Academy of Management Review*, 27 (2): 222–47.

Shi, X. (2008) *Nong Cun Gaige de Fansi* (Reflecting the Rural Reforms), Beijing: Central Compilation and Translation Press.

Sinha, A. (2005) 'Political foundations of market-enhancing federalism', *Comparative Politics*, April: 337–56.

So, A.Y. (2007) 'Peasant conflict and the local predatory state in the Chinese countryside', *Journal of Peasant Studies*, 34 (3): 560–81.

Solinger, D.J. (1999) *Contesting Citizenship in Urban China: Peasant Migrants, the State, and the Logic of the Market*, Berkeley: University of California Press.

Song, Y. (2006) 'Xiangzhen guanli tizhi gaige yu zhengfu gonggong fuwu' (Reform of township management system and public service provision), available at http://www.china.org.cn/chinese/OP-c/698137.htm, accessed on 10 July 2006.

State Council, General Office. (1998) 'A notice on formulating reform packages for the rural "tax-for-fee" reform', 20 November 1998, in Office of State Council Rural 'Tax-for-Fee' Reform Working Group (ed.) *Nongcun Shuifei Gaige Gongzuo Shouce* (A Manual of Rural 'Tax-for-Fee' Reform), Beijing: Jingji Kexue Chubanshe.

State Council, General Office. (2003) 'Guanyu jinyibu jiaqiang nongcun shuifei gaige shidian gongzuo de tongzhi' (A notice on how to strengthen further the piloting of rural tax reforms), State Council Document 85, 30 September 2003, available at http://www.gov.cn/zwgk/2005-08/14/content_22500.htm, accessed on 20 July 2011.

State Council. (2006) Document No. 34, 'Guanyu zuohao nongcun zhonghe gaige gongzuo youguan wenti de tongzhi' (A notice on how to address well several issues on comprehensive rural reforms), 8 October, available at http://www.gov.cn/zwgk/2006-10/13/content412168.htm, accessed on 19 March 2007.

State Council Rural Development Research Center Experimental Zone Office. (1990) '1988: Zhongguo Nongcun Gaige Shiyanqu' (The rural reform experimental zones in China: 1988), in H. Kang and W. Yuzhao (eds.) *Zhongguo Nongcun Gaige Shi Nian*, Beijing: People's University of China Press.

Su, F. (2002) 'Agency, Incentive, and Institutional Design: Bureaucracy Control and Evolution of Governance in Contemporary China', doctoral dissertation, University of Chicago.

Tanner, M.S. and Green, E. (2007) 'Principals and secret agents: central versus local control over policing and obstacles to "rule of law" in China', *The China Quarterly*, 191 (September): 644–70.

Tao, R. and Liu, M. (2004) 'Government regulations and rural taxation in China', *Perspectives*, 5, (2), (30 June), available at http://www.oycf.org/Perspectives/25_0603004/6.pdf.

Tao, T., Liu, M. and Zhang, Q. (2004) 'Nongmin fudan, zhengfu guanzhi yu caizheng tizhi gaige' (Peasants' burden, governmental regulation and fiscal institution reform), *Perspectives*, 2 (4): 1–12.

Tian, X., Zhao, F. and Zhao, Y. (2003) 'Cong nongcun shuifei gaige kan xiangzhen caizheng de kunjing he chulu' (Difficulties and opportunities in township finance: an analysis of the impact of the rural tax-for-fee reform), *Hongguan Jingji Yanjiu* (Macro-Economic Analysis), 9: 33–6.

The State Council. (1991) Nongmin Chengdan Feiyong he Laowu Guanli Tiaoli' (Regulation on peasants' burden and labour services), State Council Resolution No. 92, available at http://www.law110.com/law/guowuyuan/2112.htm, accessed on 7 December 1991.

The State Council, General Office. (2006) 'Guowuyuan bangongting guanyu jianqing nongmin fudan de gongzuo de yijian' (Document of General Office of National State Council on alleviating peasants' burden), Document No. 48 (2006), available at http://

news.xinhuanet.com/politics/2006-06/27/content_4757139.htm, accessed on 20 July 2011.

Tsai, L.L. (2007) *Accountability without Democracy: Solidary Groups and Public Goods Provision in Rural China*, New York: Cambridge University Press.

Tsui, K.Y. and Wang, Y. (2004) 'Between separate stoves and a single menu: fiscal decentralization in China', *The China Quarterly*, 177 (March): 71–90.

Unger, J. (2002) *The Transformation of Rural China*, Armonk, NY: M.E. Sharpe.

Wan, Z. (2003) 'Shidi nongmin quanyi liushi' (Cutting into the interests and rights of the landless peasants), *Jingji Tizhi Yanjiu* (The Study of Economic Systems), 6: 73–6.

Wang, H. (ed.) (2003) 'Jingchu dadi jinxin "sange daibiao" de weida shijin: Hubeisheng nongcui shuife gaige de jiben zuofa yu chengxiao' (Implementing the spirit of 'the Three Representations': practice and results of the rural tax reforms in Hubei), in W. Huaxin (ed.) *2003 Nian Zhongguo Difang Caizheng Yanjiu Baogao: Hubeisheng Nongcui Shuifei Gaige Shijian Yu Tansuo* (Local Finance Research Report, 2003: Practice and Research on the Tax Reform in the Rural Area of Hubei Province), Beijing: Jingji Kexue Chubanshe, Preface: 1–12.

Wang, H. (2004) 'Hubeisheng fazhan xianji jingji caizheng zhengce yanjiu' (A study of the fiscal policy on developing the county-level economy of Hubei Province), *Caizheng Yu Fazhan*, 1: 21–30.

Wang, H.W. (2007) 'Nongmin quanyi baohufa: hushengfu? zhexiubu?' (Is the law on protection of peasants' powers offering protection for peasants or facilitating exit of the authorities?), available at http://www.efaw.cn/html/sdbd/20071128/8IBI8873.html, accessed on 25 March 2011.

Wang, L. (2006) '2008 niandi qian woguo jiang quanmian shixian "xiangcaixianguan"' (The system of 'county oversight of township finances' will be in place nationwide by the end of 2008), available at http://finance.people.com.cn/GB/1037/4574982.html, accessed on 28 July 2008.

Wang, T. (1998) 'Lun guojia caizheng de shencenci maodun' (On the deeper contradictions of government finance), *Southern Economy*, 6: 7–9.

Wedeman, A. (1997) 'Stealing from China's farmers: institutional corruption and the 1992 IOU crisis', *China Quarterly*, 152 (December): 805–931.

Wen, J. (2000) 'A speech at the rural "tax-for-fee" reform mobilization meeting in Anhui', in Zhang Ping (ed.) *A Practical Manual*, 211.

'Wen Jiabao zhuchi zhaokai guowuyuan changwuhuiyi bushu nongcun gongzuo' (Wen Jiabao holding the State Council Standing Committee meeting to make arrangements on rural work), 30 June 2006, available at http://politics.people.com.cn/GB/1024/4551377.html, accessed on 28 July 2008.

Wen, T. (2000) *Zhongguo Nongcun Jinben Jingji Zhidu Yanjiu* (A Study of the Fundamental Economic Institutions of the Chinese Agriculture), Beijing: Zhongguo Jingji chubanshe.

Wen, T. (2001) 'Zhouqixing jingji weiji yu duiying zhengce fenxi' (An analysis of economic crisis cycles and possible strategies), available at http://www.macrochina.com.cn/zhtg/20010608007807.shtml, accessed on 12 November 2005.

West, L. (1997) 'Provision of public services in rural PRC', in C.P.W. Wong (ed.) *Financing Local Government*, Hong Kong: Oxford University Press.

Winter, G. (1966) *Elements for a Social Ethic: Scientific and Ethical Perspectives on Social Process*, London: Macmillan.

Winter, S. (2006) 'Implementation', in G. Peters and J. Pierre (eds.) *Handbook of Public Policy*, London: Sage.

Wong, C.P.W. (ed.) (1997) *Financing Local Government*, Hong Kong: Oxford University Press.

World Bank. (1990) *China: Between Plan and the Market*, Washington, DC: World Bank.

World Bank. (2002) *China: National Development and Sub-National Finance: A Review of Provincial Expenditures*, Washington, DC: World Bank Report No. 22951-CHA.

World Bank. (2003) *Making Services Work for Poor People, World Development Report 2004*, Washington, DC: World Bank and Oxford University Press.

World Bank. (2005a) *East Asia Decentralizes: Making Local Governments Work*, Washington DC.: World Bank.

World Bank. (2005b) *China: Deepening Public Service Unit Reform to Improve Service Delivery*, Washington, DC: World Bank and Oxford University Press.

Wu, J. (2002) *Yue Hai Cong Zu Shi Lu* (A Record of the Restructuring of Guangdong International Trust and Investment Corporation), Hong Kong: Hong Kong Commercial Press.

Wu, L. (2004a) 'Nongcun shuifei gaige dui xiangzhen caizheng di yingxiang ji qi houguo: yi Anhui weili' (Impacts and consequences of the rural tax reforms on township fiscal finance: the case of Anhui Province), in *Xiang Jiquan Zouchu 'Huang Zhongxi dinglun' di guaiquan: Zhongguo nongcun shuifei gaige di diaocha yu yanjiu* (Investigation and Research on China's Fee-For-Tax Reform), Xian: Northwest University Press, 258–78.

Wu, L. (2004b) 'Shuifei gaigezhong "xiangzhen" gaige di lujing xuanche' (Options for township government system reforms in the context of rural tax-for-fee reform), in *Xiang Jiquan Zouchu 'Huang Zhongxi dinglun' di guaiquan: Zhongguo nongcun shuifei gaige di diaocha yu yanjiu* (Investigation and Research on China's Fee-For-Tax Reform), Xian: Northwest University Press, 307–23.

Wu, L. (2004c) 'Guanmin hejiu tizhi: xiangzhen zizhi', in *Li Changping and Dong Liuming Shuifei Gaige Beijingxia de Xiangzhen Tizhi Yanjiu* (Studies on Township Government System in the Context of Rural Tax-For-Fee Reforms), Wuhan: Hubei Renmin Chubanshe, 33–65.

Wu, L. (2006) 'Zhili zhuanxing zhong de xiangzhenzhengfu–xiangzhen gaige yanjiu' (Township government under transforming governance: a positive study on the reform of township government), PhD thesis, Central China Normal University, Wuhan, China.

Wu, L. and Li, L.C. (2003) 'Xiangzhen caizheng ji qi gaige chutan' (A preliminary analysis of township public finance and reforms), *China Rural Survey*, Beijing: Rural Economy Journal Press, 4: 15–24.

Xia, Z. (1990) 'Nongcun gaige shinian huigu yu qianzhan' (Ten years of rural reform: appraisal and prospects), in H. Kang and W. Yuzhao (eds.) *Zhongguo Nongcun Gaige Shi Nian*, Beijing: People's University of China Press.

Xian-an District Government. (2003) '*A progress report on the work of sending off cadres*', unpublished document.

Xian-an District Party Committee Secretariat. (ed.) (2003) '*Compendium of Materials on Xian-an's Reform*', internal document.

Xiang, J. (1999) 'Xiangcun jitihua yu minzuhua: ruogan xiangcun de shizheng fenxi' (Collectivization and democratization in villages: an empirical analysis of several villages), *China Rural Survey 2*. Available at http://www.chinaelections.org/readnews. asp?newsid=%7B85EE0340-6C8D-4B15-BA79-A630784EDCA5, accessed on 18 November 2005.

Xiang, J. (2004a) 'Introduction: the rural tax-for-fee reform – a yet-to-complete revolution', in *Xiang Jiquan Zouchu 'Huang Zhongxi dinglun' di guaiquan: Zhongguo nongcun shuifei gaige di diaocha yu yanjiu* (Investigation and research on China's fee-for-tax reform), Xian: Northwest University Press, 1–62.

Xiang, J. (2004b) *Zouchu 'Huang Zhongxi Dinglun' di Guaiquan: Zhongguo Nongcun Shuifei Gaige di Diaocha yu Yanjiu* (Investigation and Research on China's fee-for-tax Reform), Xian: Northwest University Press.

Xiang, J. and Chang, J. (2007) '*Guanyu Nongmin Baohufa de Xiugai Jianyi* (Proposed revisions to the law on the protection of peasants' rights and interests), unpublished report submitted to the *National People's Congress, Agriculture and Villages Standing Committee.*

'Xianxiang caizheng' (2005) 'Xianxiang caizheng xianshing zeiwu da 4000 yi' (The county–township fiscal debts exceed 400 billion yuan), available at http://www.gxcz. gov.cn/newsinfo.asp?id¼519&CataID¼36, accessed on 30 July 2008.

Xu, Y. (2004) 'Xianzheng, xiangbai, cunzhi: xiangcun zhilide jiegouxing zhuanhuan' (Country government, township branch and village self-rule: the structural transformation of rural governance), *Zhongguo Shiji* (China Century), No. 771, available at http:// www.cc.org.cn/newcc/browwenzhang.php?articleid=1470, accessed on 27 September 2005.

Xue, M.B. (2006) 'Tuzaishui: Lishi huigu' (The slaughter tax: A historical review), *Zhongguo Shuiwu* (China Taxation), 5: 26–7.

Yan, R.Z. *et al.* (1990) 'Zhongguo gongnongye chanpin jiage zhandaucha de xianzhuang, fazhan qushi ji duice' (Price scissors of industrial and agricultural goods in China: Current situation, future trends and policy measures), *Jingji Yanjiu* (Economic Research), 2: 64–70.

Yang, D.L. (2001) 'Rationalizing the Chinese state: the political economy of government reform', in B.J. Dickson and Chien-Min Chao (eds.) *Remaking the Chinese State*, London: Routledge, 19–45.

Yang, M. (2003) 'Xiangzhen caizheng zaiwu wenti diaocha' (An investigation into township debts), available at http://finance.sina.com.cn/roll/20030309/1235318457.shtml, accessed on 28 July 2008.

Yang, W. (2001) 'An interview of Wang Wenliang: why "public grain system" was implemented in Hebei', *China Economic Times*, 2 March 2001, available at http:// finance.sina.com.cn, accessed on 25 November 2005.

Yang, Y., Wang, M. and Wang, T. (2005) 'Qiantan yishi yiyi' (On 'deliberation on each and every item'), available at http://www.myagri.gov.cn/new/view.asp?id=6344&;typeid=60, accessed on 28 July 2008.

Yao, R. and Dong, J. (2006) 'Chen Xiwen: sanda jucuo ezhi nongmin fudan juantu chonglai' (Chen Xiwen: three measures to prevent peasants' burden being aggravated), available at http://news.xinhuanet.com/politics/2006-02/22/content_4213248.htm, accessed on 2 April 2008.

Yeo, Y. and Pearson, M. (2008) 'Regulating decentralized state industries: China's auto industry', *The China Review*, 8, (2 Fall): 231–60.

Yep, R. (2004) 'Can "tax-for-fee" reform reduce rural tension in China? The process, progress and limitations', *The China Quarterly*, 177 (March): 43–70.

Yuan, F. (2008) *Shi Fuwu YunZhuan Qilai: Jiceng Zhili Zhuanxing Zhong de Xiangzhen Shiye Zhansuo Gaige Yanjiu* (Making Services Work: The Transformation of Government Function and the Innovation of Grassroots Governance. A Case Study of Township Public Service Unit Reform in Xian-an, Hubei), Xian: Northwest University Press.

Yuan, F. (2009) *Kuayue: Zhongguo Nongcun Jiceng Zhili de Gaige he Zhuanxing* (Leaping forward: Reforms and Institutional Changes in Grassroots-level Governance in China. A Report of Reforms in Xian-an), Wuhan: Central Normal University Press.

Yuan, F. *et al.* (2006) 'Nongmin de gonggong xuqiu yu xiangzhen shiye danwei gaige: dui Hubei Xian'an nongmin gonggong xuqiu de diaocha yu fenxi' (Peasants' needs for public goods and township agency reform: a survey on Xian-an, Hubei), *Journal of Central China Normal University: Humanities and Social Sciences*, 45 (5): 12–19.

Zhang, J. (2002) 'Xiangzhen caizheng jidu cuixian yu nongmin fudan' (Institutional defects of the township public finance and peasants' burden), *China Rural Survey*, 4: 2–13.

Zhang, S. (2002) 'Nongcun wenti de genyuan: geren chanping he gonggong wuping guanxi hunxiao' (Root cause of rural problems: confused relations between public and private goods), available at http://www.dajun.com.cn/nongcunw.htm, accessed on 4 April 2008.

Zhou, T. (2007) 'Xiandaihua yao duideqi wei fazhan zuochu juda gongxian de nongmin' (Modernization needs to pay back the sacrifices of the peasants), *Zhongguo Jingji Shibao* (China Economic Daily), 12 July.

Zhu, G. (2002) 'Nongcun shuifei gaige yu xiangzhen caizheng quekou' (Rural tax-for-fee reform and township budget deficits), *China Rural Survey*, 2: 13–20.

Zhu, X. and Xue, L. (2007) 'Think tanks in transitional China', *Public Administration and Development*, 27: 452–64.

Zhu, Z. (2007) 'Reform without a theory: Why does it work in China?', *Organization Studies*, 28: 1503–22.

Zong, H. (2001) *Zhu Rongji Zai 1999* (Zhu Rongji in 1999), Hong Kong: Mirror Books.

Index

functions 83; embracing demise of 99,
100; failures of reform 80–2; fiscal
pressures 71–2; future challenges 77;
intentional weakening of 93; lack of
new initiatives 82–4; local proposal for
reform 84–7; public service funding
provision 69–70; size of 92
township leaders: need for reform vision
and strategic decisions 76; networking
with 28–31; reactions to reform 96–100
townships, status of 48
training programme, cadres 55–9
transitional payments, Xian-an 51–2
transparency 34, 36, 37, 40
Tsai, L.L. 61

uncertainties, embracing and transcending
109–11
Unger, J. 37, 92
unintended consequences 18, 31, 91–102,
109
urban–rural divide, public awareness of 85
user charges 39–40, 70
user feedback, public services 87
user surveys 68

Value-Added Tax 37, 50
veterinary services, income sources 70
village and township levies 5–9: abolition
of 36; reform measures 10
village-level elections, introduction of 34,
37
voluntarity principle, 'sending off'
programme 56, 57

Wang, H. 52, 54
Wang, L. 83
Wang, T. 54
Wang, X. 8, 12
Wang, Y. 22
Wang, Yuzhao 23, 24
Wang, Zhaoyao 27–9, 30
water works and irrigation services 67–8

Wedeman, A. 48
Wen, Jiabao 36, 83, 91
Wen, T. 7, 35
West, L. 92
Winter, G. 2, 79
Wong, C.P.W. 12
World Bank 2, 12, 61, 62, 63, 64, 68
Woyang County, support for reform 30
Wu, L. 2, 80, 82, 93

Xian-an District: cadre reforms 53–9;
compensation 50–3; fieldwork in 92;
fiscal crisis 71; peasants' burden 49–53;
peasants' burden reduction 49–50;
public service funding 69–70; PSU
reform 64–6, 71, 70–5
Xiang, Huaizheng 95
Xiang, J. 93
Xinhua news agency 24–5, 94–5
Xinxing Town, support for reform 29–30, 31
Xue, L. 88

Yan, R.Z. 7
Yang, D.L. 30, 48
Yang, M. 81
Yang, Wenliang 29–30
Yang, Y. 87
Yao, R. 13
Yeo, Y. 2
Yep, R. 13, 35, 48, 92
Yining District, fieldwork in 92
Yongshang County People's Congress 29
Yu, Zhengsheng 72
Yuan, F. 64, 70, 71, 73, 88
Yue, Qifeng 30

Zhang, S. 12
Zhou, Enlai 24
Zhou, T. 7
Zhou, X. 81
Zhu, G. 93
Zhu, Rongji 91, 94, 95–6, 104
Zhu, X. 88